GLOBAL UNIONS

Frank W. Pierce Memorial Lectureship and Conference Series
Number 13

GLOBAL UNIONS

Challenging Transnational Capital through Cross-Border Campaigns

EDITED BY

KATE BRONFENBRENNER

ILR Press
AN IMPRINT OF
Cornell University Press
Ithaca and London

First published 2007 by Cornell University Press
First printing, Cornell Paperbacks, 2007

Printed in the United States of America

Library of Congress Cataloging-in-Publication Data
Global unions : challenging transnational capital through cross-border campaigns / edited by Kate Bronfenbrenner.
    p. cm. — (Frank W. Pierce memorial lectureship and conference series ; no. 13)
    Papers originally presented at a conference held Feb. 9, 2006 in New York, N. Y.
    Includes bibliographical references and index.
    ISBN 978–0–8014–4616–0 (cloth : alk. paper) — ISBN 978–0–8014–7391–3 (pbk. : alk. paper)
    1. International labor activities—Congresses.   2. Labor unions—Congresses.   3. International business enterprises—Congresses.   4. Globalization—Congresses.   I. Bronfenbrenner, Kate, 1954–   II. Title.   III. Series.

    HD6475.A1G57 2007
    331.88091—dc22

                                                    2007018957

Cornell University Press strives to use environmentally responsible suppliers and materials to the fullest extent possible in the publishing of its books. Such materials include vegetable-based, low-VOC inks and acid-free papers that are recycled, totally chlorine-free, or partly composed of nonwood fibers. For further information, visit our website at www.cornellpress.cornell.edu.

Cloth printing   10 9 8 7 6 5 4 3 2 1
Paperback printing   10 9 8 7 6 5 4 3 2

This volume is dedicated to former United Steelworkers of America president George Becker (1929–2007), who set the standard for comprehensive cross-border campaigns, and to all those striving to build global unions in their quest to bring economic and social justice to workers, their families, and their communities around the world.

CONTENTS

ACKNOWLEDGMENTS

This book and the conference that was its genesis represent many years of dedication and assistance from countless individuals in the labor movement and academia from around the globe. In a project of this scope there were too many hands involved for me to individually thank each person who contributed. Thus I will focus on those who were most central to making this book a success, recognizing that the success of the conference and the book depended on the full participation and support of everyone involved.

First and foremost I thank three individuals: Ron Blackwell and Richard Trumka from the AFL-CIO and Bruce Raynor from UNITE HERE. Without their initial inspiration and ongoing support the conference and this book would never have come to fruition. I especially thank Ron Blackwell, who offered a steady voice of encouragement, sound advice, and a port in the storm, even when the going got roughest and the odds seemed most insurmountable throughout the entire process. Second, I thank the nearly forty unions, universities, and NGOs who sponsored the conference and in doing so made this book possible by paying for the travel for participants from the Global South and the research costs associated with compiling this book. In particular I want to thank the individuals on the paper proposal review committee who helped solicit, review, and select the papers that were presented at the conference, from which I ultimately selected the ten chapters that make up this book. These individuals include the following: Tim Beaty, Teamsters; Ron Blackwell, AFL-CIO; Meg Casey, Change to Win; Bill Cooke, Wayne State; Ginny Coughlin, UNITE HERE; Joe Drexler, USW; Peter Fairbrother, Cardiff University; Paula Finn, Joseph F. Murphy Institute; Paul Garver, IUF;

Robert Hickey, Cornell (now at Queens University); John Hogan, University of Hertfordshire; Jane Holgate, London Metropolitan University; Andrew Jackson, Canadian Labor Congress; Tom Juravich, UMass Amherst; Jose La Luz, AFSCME; Robert Masciola, AFL-CIO; Doug Meyer, UFCW; Ruth Milkman, UCLA; Gregor Murray, University of Montreal; Peter Olney, ILWU; Darryn Snell, Monash University; Erin Young, AFSCME; and Ken Zinn, AFL-CIO.

The much more critical support in helping me shape this book came from a small group of friends and colleagues in academia and the labor movement, who have offered me advice, criticism, encouragement, and support over the last eight months, constantly challenging me to push the authors, and myself, to a higher standard, and to express in my own voice my views about global unions and cross-border campaigns. These include Peter Fairbrother, Dorian Warren, Darryn Snell, Robert Hickey, Joe Drexler, David Van Arsdale, Ruth Needleman, and Ken Zinn. Without question it is their criticism and insights that helped make this book the best that it could be.

Of course, the person who did the most to support me in this project is my assistant, Tamara Lovell. From the very beginning of the conference coordination to finishing up the references on her last day of work as she went out the door, Tamara made this book her highest priority. Her professionalism and attention to detail and her unwavering enthusiasm for the project ensured that somehow we would be able to get it done and done right despite all the hurdles in our path. It has been a privilege to work with her. In addition to Tamara I also thank other Cornell staff, including Laurie Konwinski for helping to coordinate the paper proposal process, Anitha Vermury for her work on the references, Sara VanLooy and Martha Stettinius for an excellent job on copy editing, and Wes Hannah, Meryl Bursic, and Nischit Hegde for their overall support work in the last weeks of the editing.

I also want to express my thanks and appreciation to Fran Benson and her staff at ILR/Cornell University Press for believing in this book from the very beginning and doing everything possible to make a challenging task under a tight deadline as painless as possible.

Finally, I would like to thank the authors. This is a unique collection of original research that reaches across different disciplines, methodologies, countries, and, in several cases, languages of origin. It was not easy to combine this varied material into a common format, idiom, and style, particularly under the short time frame in which we had to operate. Yet the authors responded to each step of the editing process with grace and flexibility and were always willing to push themselves to the highest standard in their writing and analysis. Special recognition must be made of Terry Boswell, one of the coauthors of the chapter on international framework agreements (chapter 9), who passed away in the summer of 2006 after the original draft of the chapter had been submitted for publication. His contribution to the field and the labor movement was significant, and he will be sorely missed.

It has been an honor and privilege to work with all the authors, and I am proud of the work we have been able to create together. My fervent hope is that it will lay the groundwork for more original research and more effective cross-border comprehensive campaigns around the world.

GLOBAL UNIONS

INTRODUCTION

KATE BRONFENBRENNER

On February 9, 2006, more than 560 representatives from unions, union federations, academia, and nongovernmental organizations (NGOs) from around the world gathered at the Crowne Plaza Hotel in New York City for the "Global Companies–Global Unions–Global Research–Global Campaigns" conference. The overall goal of the conference was to strengthen labor's capacity to conduct more effective strategic corporate research and run more effective comprehensive cross-border campaigns against the world's largest transnational firms. Yet perhaps the theme of the conference was best summed up by AFL-CIO secretary treasurer Richard Trumka in his remarks in the opening plenary:

> Brothers and Sisters, I like the theme of this conference because it lays out the challenges before us in almost biblical terms—global companies begat global problems for workers—global problems begat the need for global unions—and if global unions want to truly match the might and power of global corporations we have to undertake global research and global campaigns. (Trumka 2006)

Unions around the world continue to operate in an ever-more complex and rapidly changing corporate environment. Increasingly the employers they face across the bargaining table or in organizing campaigns are part of diffuse transnational companies that have minimal loyalty to any single industry, product, or country. At the same time, never before have the ties between governments and supragovernmental institutions such as the World Trade Organization (WTO), the European Union (EU), or the World Bank been more closely integrated with the interests of the world's largest transnational corporations than they are now. In today's environment, large sectors of the public have come to believe that Wal-Mart is unstoppable in leading the pursuit of a worldwide race to the bottom. On this issue there is little difference between workers in North Carolina who watch their jobs move to Mexico and those in Ireland who watch their jobs go to India or in China who lose their jobs to Vietnam (Bronfenbrenner and Luce 2004). They only need look at Oscar-nominated films such as *Syriana* or *The Constant Gardener* to find out what happens to those who dare to challenge capital when it is in cahoots with the highest levels of government.

However, this is just one piece of the story. In the real world not every effort to fight back against the forces of global capital ends in devastating defeat. The more than 560 people gathered in New York in February demonstrated that there is a strategic front uniting against the combined power of the neoliberal state and transnational corporations. The labor movement and its allies have done battle with some of the most powerful transnational firms and governments and won. They can do it again, but only if they understand the power structure and vulnerabilities of these new kinds of corporations, the extent of their operations, and the relationships they have with their stakeholders. Equally important, they will succeed only if they build a global labor movement based on equality and respect through cross-border campaigns. It will be critical to involve unions and NGOs locally, nationally, and internationally. The Global Unions Conference and this book, which came out of the conference, address these challenges.

A Historic Perspective

In 1986, the United Mine Workers of America (UMWA), under the leadership of its new young president, Richard Trumka, joined with the National Union of Mineworkers (NUM), other South African unions, the Free South Africa Movement (FSAM), and the rest of the U.S. labor movement to unleash a worldwide campaign against oil companies operating in South Africa, with Royal Dutch/Shell as the first target of a global boycott (Walker 1986; Multinational Monitor 1986).

Shell was not chosen randomly as the target by either the South African or the U.S. unions. Oil companies were the focus of the boycott because oil was critical to the South African economy; the military and the police, for example, depended on oil to break strikes and crush demonstrations. Having no indigenous supplies of oil to rely on, the South African regime was wholly dependent on the big oil companies for its very survival. Royal Dutch/ Shell in particular stood out as a target because it had continued to ignore pressure from the United Nations' voluntary oil embargo to stop supplying oil to South Africa, but also because it had a long history of serious health and safety violations and antiunion actions in its mines and refineries in South Africa (Multinational Monitor 1986; Knight 2001). The fact that two of its coal subsidiaries, Shell SA's Reitspruit and Shell USA's A.T. Massey, had just been involved in two brutal strikes involving the UMWA and NUM provided additional grounds for making Shell a key target (Walker 1986).

The global campaign against Shell was perhaps the most comprehensive and most effective example of cross-border solidarity of labor and its allies in history. Unions, antiapartheid groups, churches, civil rights organizations, and social justice NGOs from around the world came together in common cause not out of their own self-interest but to make clear to the world's largest transnational firms that they were going to make the cost of doing business with South Africa prohibitive and the costs to the South African apartheid government even greater. Profits were cut and businesses withdrew. Some corporations, such as Mobil Oil, pulled out quickly; others, such as Shell, endured great costs but never left. But eventually the apartheid government could no longer withstand the combination of external pressure and escalating action by the black majority inside South Africa. What made the story even more remarkable was that it occurred during the period when much of the world's labor movement was still bitterly divided along cold-war lines. Despite the close ties between the Congress of South African Trade Unions (COSATU), the African National Congress (ANC), and the Communist Party, not only unions such as the UMWA, the United Auto Workers (UAW), and the American Federation of State, County, and Municipal Employees (AFSCME)—allied with TransAfrica and FSAM from early on—but the American Federation of Labor and Congress of Industrial Organizations (AFL-CIO) endorsed the Shell boycott as well (Knight 2001; Walker 1986).

The boycott was active in more than a dozen countries, particularly in Royal Dutch/Shell's home countries of Britain and the Netherlands. While unions in Europe were not enthusiastic about the boycott tactic, most supported antiapartheid sanctions, including the oil embargo, and South Africa's nascent trade union movement in other ways. Seafarers' unions from several countries, for example, provided critical support for the oil embargo by helping to track and to expose the global oil trade with South Africa. The Danish and Norwegian labor movements successfully convinced their governments to impose bans on oil transports and exports to South Africa (Hengeveld and Rodenburg 1995).

There were unionized workers at oil companies in all countries affected, particularly in South Africa, who actively questioned the risks and benefits of the oil boycott (Baskin 1991). These were particularly important lessons to learn: global alliances and the long-term battle against transnational firms have short-term costs that affect workers and unions differently in different countries. How to balance interests and identify common goals in this context can be the most difficult challenge for global campaigns.

Without question, workers and their representatives around the world would be living and working in a very different environment if similar stories of coordinated struggles had occurred during the last twenty years. Stopping the collusion of governments and transnational corporations in depriving workers of fundamental political, social, and economic rights has become harder today because, unfortunately, labor did not learn this lesson from its involvement in the South Africa divestment campaign. Instead of being emboldened to challenge global capital and construct a more united, progressive, and internationalist vision, in most cases organizations returned to their own struggles. Periodically one or another group asked for support in their individual contract or organizing struggles with employers, and different organizations stepped forward. The support, however, was sporadic and temporary. Some of those battles reached a truly global scale, such as the Steelworkers' struggle against Bridgestone Firestone to keep their union and hold on to pattern bargaining in the rubber industry, which ultimately involved solidarity actions in eighty-three countries (Juravich and Bronfenbrenner 2003). Another example was the successful campaign to organize 1,200 workers at Gina Bra Form Company in Thailand, which won support from the National Human Rights Commission of Thailand and from more than a dozen international union organizations, labor NGOs, and consumer and student solidarity organizations from around the globe (Robertson and Plaiyoowong 2004).

Yet twenty years after the global labor movement launched its boycott against Royal Dutch/Shell, the world's largest corporations wield more power and are more globally connected and less fettered by global union solidarity than they were in 1986. Now the challenges are greater. Where before transnational corporations seemed at least somewhat bounded by loyalty to product, firm, industry, or country, today the largest of these firms increasingly supersede most government authority and are constrained only by the interests of their biggest investors, lenders, and shareholders.

For too long most union members and their leaders tended to see their collective bargaining environment as truly limited by the national boundaries of their own labor laws and the interests of their dues-paying members. Even as more of the employers they dealt with became foreign-owned or had foreign operations, and as nearly every industry in every part of the world was faced with having jobs outsourced from higher-wage countries to lower-wage countries, unions continued to think of themselves as part of a national, not international, labor movement. There were noteworthy exceptions. In some cases, such as Ravenswood Aluminum Corporation or Chunghwa Telecom, these were defensive actions, in which local unions, with the help of national unions, global union federations (GUFs), and local, national, and international NGOs, mounted global campaigns to save the members' jobs and in many cases the union itself (Juravich and Bronfenbrenner 1999; Chang 2006).

In contrast, other organizations have moved aggressively to build alliances as part of organizing campaigns. These include the AFL-CIO, Teamsters, and Union Network International (UNI), which supported a global campaign to organize workers at Quebecor in the United States, Europe, and Latin America (Trumka 2006; Brecher, Costello, and Smith 2006); the global organizing campaigns at Nestlé and Coca-Cola by the International Union of Food, Agricultural, Hotel, Restaurant, Catering, Tobacco and Allied Workers' Associations (IUF) (Garver et al. 2006); and UNITE HERE's campaign to organize Pinault-Printemps-Redoute (PPR) subsidiary Brylane (Clean Clothes Campaign 2002). But these campaigns have been few and far between. The greater capital's capacity to increase the power and speed with which it restructured its organization, the more difficult it was for labor to find its bearings. In the words of Hassan Yussuff from the Canadian Labor Congress, labor struggled to "match the other side's speed and mobility and capacity to change" (Yussuff 2006).

Global Unions Conference

In recent years there have been many in both the labor movement and academia who have been thinking and strategizing on just how labor can best meet the challenge it faces in organizing and bargaining with the world's largest and most powerful transnational corporations. Starting in the fall of 2002 a group of union leaders, union researchers and strategic campaigners, and labor scholars, led by Richard Trumka, now secretary treasurer of the AFL-CIO; Bruce Raynor, president of UNITE HERE; Ron Blackwell, director of corporate affairs, AFL-CIO; and Kate Bronfenbrenner, Cornell ILR, came together to begin discussing these issues. This collaboration led to the Global Unions Conference in 2006. From the beginning its primary mission focused on improving labor's capacity to take on the world's largest transnational corporations and shift global economic and political power back into the hands of workers and communities. The framework for our initial discussions grew from the following assumptions.

First, there continued to be a severe shortage of individuals in the United States and around the world who were trained in strategic corporate research. Even those who were conducting research tended to use a simplistic model that failed to capture the complex and diffuse nature of corporate structure and ownership among the world's largest transnational employers. We now have developed a model for teaching strategic corporate research that better captures the complex and changing character of these firms. The challenge, however, was how we could best disseminate our model to the widest audience possible.

Second, most unions were not researching the employer they were dealing with in organizing or bargaining campaigns. While some industrial unions had run noteworthy cross-border campaigns when confronted with aggressive employer opposition at the bargaining table, such campaigns were rare in the organizing context and infrequent in the bargaining context, and were almost always defensive in nature.

Third, even those campaigns that did exist were too often unilateral in nature, with the expectation that unions in other countries would come to the rescue of U.S. unions faced with tough foreign-owned transnational firms. U.S.-initiated campaigns to support organizing and bargaining by unions and workers in other countries were much less common. This problem was not limited to the United States. Unions engaged in struggles with employers in the United Kingdom, Canada, Australia, and, to a lesser degree, western Europe, sought help from workers in the Global South or eastern Europe but did not reciprocate.

Another critical tension developed among some unions in Europe over whether the comprehensive campaign model interfered with their own positive relationships with employers. At the same time, others in Europe wanted to link more with unions in North America and the Global South in these campaigns as they watched the same employers that had been battling unions in North America begin to move toward privatization and shifting of union work out of western Europe toward eastern Europe and the Global South. Unions in the Global South continued to raise the question of how much workers in the Global North understood that their lifestyle and living standards depended on the continued degradation of living standards and environmental conditions in the South.

Finally, there was an extreme shortage of quality academic research relating to all aspects of these questions, from the changing nature of corporate ownership structure and practices of the world's largest transnational firms to the extent and effectiveness of union responses to these changes in the structure and power of global capital.

With these concerns in mind, the initial planning group reached out to the larger labor and academic community around the world in order to move forward with the planning process. In February 2006 this collaboration bore fruit, when the conference opened to a standing-room-only crowd, with registrants from fifty-three countries and six continents. The majority of the participants were from outside the United States, and more than seventy came from the Global South, including fifty-seven whose travel was funded by contributions from unions, universities, and NGOs supporting the conference.

Representatives from every GUF and many national trade union federations were in attendance.

The conference also featured strategic research on ten key transnational corporations from diverse sectors and industries such as Wal-Mart, Alcoa, Starwood, Exxon Mobil, Kraft, and Sanofi-Aventis. These companies were the focus for discussions of both a strategic analysis of the structure and flow of corporate power within each company and how best to build and strengthen lasting cross-border networks among unions, scholars, and NGOs working with these target multinationals.

One of the most important aspects of the conference was the effort made to ensure representation from the Global South for all ten target firms and the connections that resulted from that effort between trade unionists from Europe and North America and trade unionists from Asia, Africa, and Latin America from the same company. However, this coming together of participants from the Global North and Global South was not limited to the target company sessions alone. It was a common thread in every part of the conference, from the plenary sessions to the workshops and panel presentations. In fact, this may have been the single most significant accomplishment of the conference and part of what made it such a historic event. In a time when global outsourcing has led too many workers and their unions to complain that seemingly undeserving workers in the Global South are stealing jobs that "rightfully" belong in North America or western Europe, this was one space where the framework for that debate had shifted to a common understanding that this was not a U.S. problem or a European problem but a global labor problem that could be solved only through a united effort.

The large number of participants from unions from Europe and the full support from the GUFs also represented a significant change in the perception of where the European labor movement and GUFs stood on the issue of comprehensive cross-border campaigns. In fact, the sessions were filled with stories of unions in Europe beginning to link with one another and with unions in other countries, as employers with whom they had heretofore had a stable labor relationship were now engaging in large-scale cutbacks in jobs and demands for concessions in wages and social benefits.

Representatives from every country denounced the growing power of neoliberal governments in the economic, political, environmental, and military arena and their oppressive impacts on workers, sacrificing their economic and democratic rights in the name of global capital. As Bertha Lujan, former national coordinator of Mexico's Authentic Labor Front (FAT), argued in her plenary speech, political struggles against neoliberal governments, such as the recent victory in Bolivia, are of equal importance in challenging capital.

> We need an ideological campaign so that we can be victorious over those
> who have power over us, and we can then become organized only in so far as

our organizations are strengthened, and each one of us needs to contribute our grain of sand so that we can have a new world at home, at our workplace, in our country, in the world. (Lujan 2006)

Organizing the conference involved surmounting enormous hurdles—financial, geographic, and political. In fact from planning to fruition it would take four years. It was a historic event, not just because 560 trade unionists and academics came together to talk about how to take on global capital but specifically because of who was in the room. From around the world the people gathered there were representatives from unions, academia, and NGOs who were actively involved in either researching or conducting cross-border campaigns with the world's largest transnational firms, a group that had never gathered in one place before. The conference, both inside and outside the formal sessions, focused on a chance to share strategies, make connections, learn from one another, and build lasting networks for the future. For the three days of the conference the divisions that fell by the wayside were the split in the U.S. labor movement, the tensions over GUF protocols, and old cold-war legacies about which unions should be invited to the table. It felt as if a global labor movement was indeed possible.

Compiling This Book

The conference planners believed that one of the ways that trade unionists and academics were going to gain an objective understanding of how to best strengthen labor's capacity to mount more strategic, comprehensive, and effective cross-border campaigns was to generate more high-quality research on labor's efforts to date—both successful and unsuccessful—at running cross-border campaigns with transnational firms. Thus part of the conference-organizing process was a call for papers, sent out in English, French, and Spanish to scholars and trade unionists all over the world. The best papers would be published by Cornell University Press as part of an edited book.

More than ninety-six paper proposals were submitted, and of those, fifty-one were accepted for the conference. The subjects ranged from critical debates on the role of IFAs to tactical questions on the use of the Internet in cross-border campaigns, as well as analyses of cross-border campaigns in specific industries such as logistics, auto, bananas, or the retail sector or in specific countries such as Thailand, India, or China. Prior to the conference, the literature on global unions consisted of a handful of books and articles. By the end of the conference, for the first time, there was a body of original research relating to global comprehensive cross-border campaigns.

As editor, my challenge was to put together a book that would do the best job of moving forward the goals and themes upon which the conference was based. That meant, first of all, presenting the model of strategic corporate research and comprehensive campaigns that had provided the theoretical framework for the entire conference. Second, the collection would need to capture the challenges of running comprehensive cross-border campaigns in the current global environment as well as the range of innovative strategies that unions have attempted to use to adapt to different circumstances, industries, countries, and corporations. Finally the chapters had to communicate the global character of comprehensive cross-border organizing and bargaining campaigns. My goal was a book that included original research from scholars around the world on cross-border campaigns involving different companies, industries, regions, and sectors that took place, for the most part, outside the United States.

The book starts with a chapter by Tom Juravich that describes the evolution of the theoretical framework and model for strategic corporate research and comprehensive campaigns upon which the conference was based (and the model that was used to prepare the research reports on the ten target companies for the conference). Juravich not only provides a detailed road map for understanding how power flows in the more diffuse and complex structures that dominate the transnational landscape today but also lays out a framework for moving from research to a critique of the company and identifying profit centers, growth strategies, decision makers, and the key relationships that then become the multiple points of leverage upon which comprehensive campaigns are built.

The nine chapters that follow provide a cross section of examples of comprehensive cross-border campaigns in different kinds of industries, corporations, regions, and circumstances. Each is distinct because each campaign was entirely different from all the others, with no overlap in either company or union characteristics or in industry. Yet in combination they provide a full picture of the range of strategic responses that unions are using in trying to develop a more global response to a complex world economy. The common thread for each of the campaigns is that in each case the unions involved had to tailor their campaign to adjust to the unique environment in which they were operating.

The first three chapters cover three very different campaigns in Asia—workers in a medical supply company in Malaysia, Unilever workers in India, and women apparel workers in Sri Lanka. In chapter 2, Peter Wad tells the story of how the workers at a Malaysia medical supply company were able to organize a union in their factory through an alliance with a Danish NGO that was dominated by the Danish labor movement rather than through the expected route of using pressure from the unionized workers at the heavily unionized company headquarters of APM-Maersk in Denmark. This example not only captures the largely untold story of links between unions organizing in the Global South and unions in Europe but also demonstrates how the model presented in chapter 1 will require the development of a unique strategy depending on the differing vulnerabilities of the company, and how alliances with other stakeholders can best be utilized in exerting pressure on the firm.

The challenge of alliance building between unions in the Global South and those in the Global North is given some historical context by Ashwini Sukthankar and Kevin Kolben in chapter 3. They remind us that even in the earliest days of colonial India, labor struggles had a cross-border consciousness. Workers in India protested issues such as the establishment of a subcontracting employment system because it led to absent and unaccountable employers. More currently, as they argue in their two case studies of Unilever subsidiaries, cross-border campaigns are most effective when the strategies are largely shaped by the issues and interests of Indian unions and consumers rather than decided top down by northern unions and NGOs. Only then can they overcome the negative legacy of job protectionism from Europe and North America and the sense among many Indian trade unionists that the emphasis of northern unions and NGOs on corporate social responsibility often ends up being offered as an alternative to unionization.

Using data collected through participant observation research while she worked as an apparel worker in an export processing zone (EPZ) apparel factory in Sri Lanka for eleven months in 2003, Samanthi Gunawardana tells, in the voices of the workers themselves, how even in the most hostile of environments, workers can and do organize through cross-border comprehensive campaigns (chapter 4). Victory did not come easily but in stages. First, women-to-women networks grew out of the women's common identity as EPZ workers and the multiple problems they faced in the workplace and in their living situation. Then the women began coalition building with local NGOs, which was then followed step by step by national and international labor and NGOs from around the world. Gunawardana argues that in this kind of environment these worker-to-worker networks, nationally and internationally, are necessary for success. Given that between 2003 and 2006 the number of unionized workers in the Sri Lankan EPZs grew from six thousand to fourteen thousand, this appears to be a strategy worth heeding.

The book then switches gears by moving to a campaign on a very different scale in the banana sector in Latin America and the Caribbean. Here Henry Frundt presents union comprehensive campaigns at a much more advanced level. He explains how the banana unions used a combination of cross-border strategies to increase or rebuild union density and strengthen bargaining power, not just in one company in one country but in multiple transnational firms throughout the banana sector in Latin America and the Caribbean (chapter 5). As Frundt describes, not only did the banana unions utilize multiple coalitions with small farmer associations, European and North American NGOs, and the IUF, but they also employed a diversity of strategies. These ranged from directly negotiating with transnational banana firms for both local contracts and IFAs to challenging international trade policies that adversely impact banana workers. The banana unions have also worked to establish independent certification programs and Fair Trade Labeling programs that recognize organizing and collective bargaining rights as well as social and environmental standards.

The next three chapters focus on three campaigns in Europe involving dockworkers and General Motors workers Europe-wide, and the Service Employees International Union (SEIU)-Transport and General Workers Union(T&G) campaign with school bus drivers in the United Kingdom. The dockworkers, or dockers, the focus of Peter Turnbull's research in chapter 6, may have one of the longest traditions of cross-border solidarity of any industry, since international linkages are a natural outgrowth of the work process in marine shipping. However, Turnbull's research focuses on cross-border campaigns strictly within the EU context—namely, the response of European dockers to directives issued by the European Commission in 2001 and 2006, both of which seriously threatened job security, social benefits, and union power on the docks across Europe. In what would be called the "war on Europe's waterfront," docker unions and the International Transport Federation (ITF) launched a campaign of demonstrations, strikes, and coordinated workplace education and action across Europe to get the first directive voted down in an unexpected victory for the dockers in 2003. This was followed by a more nuanced but equally successful campaign of lobbying and legislative action in 2004–6 backed up by the threat of the capacity to strike. As Turnbull explains, the European dockers' story is a lesson in how unions can adapt to the changing political and economic environment, in this case the EU, by developing new "repertoires of contention" to tilt the balance of power away from transnational capital.

Valeria Pulignano provides a critical analysis of how the European Metal Workers' Federation, absent any historical tradition of cross-border bargaining or organizing, worked to coordinate workplace and community actions across borders throughout Europe in response to the recent wave of corporate restructuring and threats of plant closings, job loss, and cutbacks in wages and benefits at GM and its subsidiaries (chapter 7). She describes how unions were able to coordinate activity across borders to restrain, but not prevent, GM from forcing locals and regions to compete against each other to save jobs in their communities. Pulignano argues that the GM case suggests that union bargaining power in a restructured Europe depends on moving from national to European bargaining structures and coupling this process with constant communication and linkages across borders at every level of the trade union movement.

Amanda Tattersall explores the challenges and possibilities of attempting cross-border alliances in the service sector through her analysis of SEIU's global partnerships unit and the Driving Up Standards campaign between SEIU and the T&G in the United Kingdom from 2004 to 2006. Chapter 8 explores the structural innovation of the global partnerships unit and draws out the possibilities and difficulties for this form of global union collaboration. Tattersall notes the strengths of the campaign—its success in global coalition building to stop employers in the United Kingdom and Europe from treating their U.S. employees and unions differently than they treat those in their headquarters countries. She also points out that there are some significant limitations in the current practice of the Driving Up Standards campaign that provide important lessons for effective global partnerships. Using criteria developed for evaluating the effectiveness of labor-community coalitions, Tattersall found that obstacles to global union collaboration can arise where there is a lack of clear-cut mutual interests, distinct differences in practice and organizing style between the two unions, and uneven partnership in decision making. Still, given the lack of cross-border organizing in the service sector, the global partnerships unit offers significant opportunities for future endeavors, where SEIU and other unions can build on this initiative to create more mutual partnerships and effective campaigns in the future.

In chapter 9 Dimitris Stevis and Terry Boswell address the opportunities and limitations that International Framework Agreements (IFAs) and other IFA-like global agreements provide unions when taking on large transnational corporations. As Stevis and Boswell explain, these global agreements are a fairly recent and primarily European phenomenon that many GUFs and European national unions see as their most significant accomplishments. Some even consider them to be the closest the labor movement has gotten to truly global negotiations with the world's largest transnational corporations. Those with a more critical view of IFAs, including many national union federations and national unions outside Europe, emphasize IFAs as unenforceable agreements that are almost entirely concentrated in European countries. At best IFAs can be one element in a multifaceted comprehensive cross-border campaign, but at worst they can be used by employers to co-opt or undermine the union campaign. Stevis and Boswell contend that the answer is to address the limitations of IFAs by making them truly global and enforceable and by also empowering GUFs to act more like real global unions, suggestions that are also emerging from the IUF's review of the effectiveness of IFAs.

Finally the last chapter, by Darryn Snell, looks at the true outlaws among the world's largest transnational corporations. These include firms that have been charged with direct involvement in a wide range of human rights violations in the Global South, such as mass executions, rape, torture, forced labor, forced relocation of indigenous populations, and active involvement in or direct support for military operations ranging from toppling governments to crushing rebellions. This group also encompasses those who are charged with more indirect involvement with human rights abuses because of their failure to do anything to correct or prevent the conflicts and human rights violations that are occurring around them. Snell looks first at how NGOs and trade unions have worked together to investigate and prove the extent of human rights abuses taking place and then at how they have held corporations accountable through lawsuits, shareholder actions, boycotts and divestment campaigns, and developing codes of conduct. As Snell points out, none of these are simple, because many companies that NGOs may target for a financially damaging lawsuit, a boycott, or divestment, may have large numbers of unionized facilities in Europe or North America or in other countries in the Global South that could suffer severe hardship if these campaigns were successful. But as Snell concludes, partnering with NGOs to stop these abuses cannot be optional for the global labor movement. As in the fight against apartheid, if unions do not put everything they have into a global challenge of these firms, then they have lost their moral standing.

Building a Sustainable Global Network

The third and final goal of the conference was to "lay the groundwork for building a sustainable global network of unions and academics to continue to work together to effectively engage transnational corporations worldwide." Certainly just holding the conference and allowing the connections to be made accomplished a big part of this goal, as does the conference website, which includes all the company research reports, video streaming of all the conference speeches, and copies of all the papers presented at the conference (see http://www.ilr.cornell.edu/globalunionsconference/). Yet in the end it is this edited book that the conference planners hope to have as the most lasting legacy of the conference. We hope that it will be read by researchers and strategic campaigners from unions and NGOs around the world to help them critically analyze how their organizations could more effectively work together to take on transnational corporations in their industry or regions. We hope that it will also be read by labor scholars across many disciplines to encourage more and better research in both cross-border campaigns and the changing nature, structure, and practice of transnational corporations. We also hope that it will be read by young people in the labor movement and in universities and colleges around the world and will inspire them to work with unions and NGOs as part of the global effort to stop the race to the bottom.

The lessons that can be learned from this book are the lessons that we hoped were learned from the conference itself. As Hassan Yussuff said in his closing speech, the simplest lesson of all is that "[w]e need to meet like this more often. This kind of critical, collective reflection among researchers, activists, union staff and leaders produces formal and informal exchanges that are valuable for action" (Yussuff 2006). Unions and academics wrestling with these same core issues must find ways to come together on a much more frequent basis and must make the effort to raise the funds so that the north-south connections that were initiated at the conference are no longer the exception but the norm.

We also desperately need more and better research from a much wider range of scholars, but even more important, we need more scholars to actively engage with the research issues raised by the themes of this conference. This includes more in-depth research focusing on every aspect of large transnational firms, as well as both quantitative and qualitative cross-cultural research on employer and union strategies in organizing and bargaining in the global environment. I issue this challenge knowing full well the risks that are entailed in conducting research on powerful transnational corporations. But these are risks that we as scholars must take if there is to be an informed challenge to the neoliberal agenda.

This book demonstrates how much further the labor movement needs to go in truly building a global labor movement. As Valeria Pugliano points out, unions in Europe are still in the nascent stages of understanding that they have more to gain as a united European labor movement than by putting their local interests first. Unions from the Global North, particularly the GUFs, also must understand that IFAs and cross-border campaigns that do not take into consideration the interests and concerns of workers in the Global South are doomed to failure.

Finally, unions can no longer afford to limit their cross-border activity to defensive actions. Strategies such as strategic corporate research, worker-to-worker exchanges, global coalition building, and comprehensive campaigns need to become a constant in the organizing and bargaining relationship with these large transnational firms. Labor has an even greater capacity than capital to be globally connected because it can connect with workers at every level. Whether apparel workers in EPZ zones in Sri Lanka, dockworkers in Europe, or banana workers in Latin America, in the end, all the workers whose stories are told in this book took on capital and won by uniting, first with one another, then with other unions and NGOs, and then with the world. As Hassan Yussuff reminded us, "we need to make it an automatic reflex to appreciate that global capital has its weaknesses. Too often ... the strengths have been emphasized. The weaknesses and failings are real. The focus on them reminds us hope should always be more convincing than despair" (2006).

The chapters in this book make clear that unions have the capability to build the cross-border coalitions necessary to take on transnational corporations.

The question is whether they are willing to make the fundamental ideological and cultural changes necessary to make this happen on a global scale. If they are, then maybe it will be five, not twenty years before Wal-Mart is no longer driving the global race to the bottom; before firms such as Exxon Mobil, Coca-Cola, Talisman, Caterpillar, and any number of large pharmaceutical companies will no longer be able to profess to be good corporate citizens in some countries and operate entirely outside the law in others. All of us who put so much work into the conference and into this volume did so because we believe that unions and their allies do have the capacity to change and become a global movement. But most important of all, we believe that with these changes, the balance of power, like the arc of history, will finally be tilting away from capital toward workers, their unions, and communities in both the Global North and Global South.

1. BEATING GLOBAL CAPITAL

A Framework and Method for Union Strategic Corporate Research and Campaigns

TOM JURAVICH

As unions in the United States struggle to survive in the face of the globalization of firms combined with unprecedented employer opposition to unions, it is clear that new approaches, strategies, and tactics are imperative. The ways of organizing and bargaining forged during the labor-management accord in the 1950s and 1960s—approaches that relied heavily on the law and administrative proceduralism—simply have no place in this new reality, given the withdrawal of corporations from the accord and growing employer intransigence, as workers in the United States now find themselves on a world stage. If labor in the United States has any hope of remaining a source of power for working people on the job and in their communities, it must find a way to pick up the gauntlet thrown down by global capital in this new environment.

One of the fundamental ways the labor movement in the United States is rising to this challenge is through strategic corporate research and the development of comprehensive strategic campaigns in both organizing and collective bargaining. Sometimes referred to as simply strategic or coordinated campaigns, or by the older nomenclature of corporate campaigns, this approach recognizes that to be successful, unions need to gain a comprehensive understanding of the firm and the industry in which it is situated. Only as a product of this kind of research and analysis can unions design the appropriate strategies and tactics to be successful, taking into account both how power flows through the firm and how vulnerabilities can be exploited. The comprehensive strategic campaigns

The author would like to thank Kate Bronfenbrenner, Darryn Snell, Teresa Healy, and two anonymous reviewers for their comments and suggestions, and Beth Berry for copyediting.

that result go far beyond traditional organizing and bargaining and develop creative and complex processes that pressure firms in a multitude of ways.

Over the past two decades we have watched the maturation of strategic research and campaigns by unions in the United States. Indeed, it is difficult to identify a major union victory during the past decade that did not in some significant way employ strategic research and a comprehensive campaign. Ranging from the Service Employees International Union (SEIU)'s successful Justice for Janitors campaign in Los Angeles (Waldinger et al. 1998) to the International Brotherhood of Teamsters' victory at UPS (Witt and Wilson 1998) and the victory at Bridgestone/Firestone by the Steelworkers (Juravich and Bronfenbrenner 2003), unions in the United States have shown how they can win, and win big, using these approaches.

While this chapter is written from a U.S. perspective, it is important to note here that the use of strategic research and campaigns is not just a story about unions in the United States. Unions in the United States took a frontal attack by global employers; over the last three decades they have watched as entire industries were moved offshore and outsourced and an industrial relations system gutted. As we will see, over a decade of experimentation, U.S. unions began relying on strategic research and comprehensive campaigns to gain traction against the emerging global giants. Workers and their unions in the United States were not the only ones to feel the ravages of globalization, however, and these types of comprehensive campaigns are relevant responses not just for U.S.-based unions.

In fact, in many ways workers in the Global South have always been on the front lines in the struggles against global firms. Rooted in the legacy of colonialism, early transnational enterprises continued this oppression, spawning campaigns for workers' rights in the banana industry in the 1950s in Central America (see Frundt chapter 5) and for women textile workers in the "peace market" in Korea in the 1970s (Soonok 2003) and leading to the more recent struggles by Bolivian citizens to reclaim their water system (Schultz 2005). While rooted in social movements, a number of campaigns in the Global South are increasingly using sophisticated strategic research. For example, research by the Social Observatory, a nongovernmental organization (NGO) in Brazil, funded in part by the Brazilian labor movement, documented that children working in Brazilian mines produced materials for the British-based ICI (Goodwin 2006), and clandestine shops supplied apparel for a Dutch transnational (Social Observatory 2006). And while the social, political, and economic contexts are indeed quite different, there is a growing synergy between strategic research and comprehensive campaigns in the United States and throughout the Global South.

The situation in western Europe has historically been quite different. While their specific industrial relations systems differ, many countries provide institutional voice for unions on works council or similar structures, provisions shored up in European Union (EU) law. Historically, this has meant that labor-management relations have been considerably less adversarial than those in the United States. Given the presence of these institutions and European tradition, some have questioned the relevance of American-style strategic research and comprehensive campaigns for unions in the EU. Several factors, however, suggest that trade union practice in the EU may be changing.

The first is the very integration of the EU. While unions had national-based institutions in place, the question is how they dovetail with larger EU structures (Hyman 2005). As Valeria Pulignano writes in chapter 7 of this book, "[O]ne of the factors limiting the capacity of the labor movement to coordinate across borders is the difficulty in creating links between the European, the national, and the local levels of union structures." Her case study illustrates how this lack of coordination empowered General Motors' pitting of workers against one another across national boundaries. In contrast, Peter Turnbull (chapter 6) documents how dockworkers, in a sector with a long tradition of global solidarity, including in Europe, were much more effective in overcoming national barriers and mounting a successful European-wide cross-border campaign. Thus it remains to be seen how well traditional structures, now in flux as a result of EU integration, will constrain the behavior of global capital in Europe. It is in this context that European unionists are exploring the possibilities of strategic research and comprehensive campaigns.

Despite these successful campaigns and the growing reliance by unions in the United States and around the world on these methods, there is a surprising lack of information on strategic research and its use in the development of strategic campaigns.[1] One of the pioneers in training corporate researchers, the former Food and Allied Service Trades (FAST) Department of the AFL-CIO, for many years published its *Manual of Corporate Investigation* (FAST 2006). More recently a number of unions, such as SEIU and American Federation of State, County and Municipal Employees (AFSCME), have provided basic guides to finding corporate information on the Internet. While these resources provide important sources of information, what is lacking is an overall research framework or primer for conducting strategic corporate research and applying it to strategic campaigns.

---

[1]   To some degree this lack of instructional materials by unions may be purposeful. As soon as these strategic campaigns started becoming successful, employers retaliated by filing lawsuits against unions for using them. For example, during the Ravenswood campaign by the Steelworkers, the employer filed charges under the Racketeer Influenced and Corrupt Organizations Act (RICO) against individual activists in the local union (Juravich and Bronfenbrenner 1999). The Steelworkers, along with several other unions, have been sued a number of times subsequently, with several suits hanging over the union for years at a time and employers using the deposition process to try to gain access to a wide range of union documents and information. Given this situation, unions have been reticent about preparing materials that could help them educationally but could be used against them in a court of law.

Similarly, the scholarly community has focused little attention on strategic research and campaigns. While there is some research about specific strategic campaigns (Brisbin 2002; Franklin 2002; Juravich and Bronfenbrenner 1999; Waldinger et al. 1998; Hickey 2004; Quan 2006; Witt and Wilson 1998), there have been few efforts to examine the theory or methods of strategic corporate research. The last issue of a journal dedicated to strategic research and campaigns was the 1993 issue of the *Labor Research Review* (1993).

This chapter aims to fill this gap by providing a basic framework for conducting strategic corporate research, as well as describing how this research can be applied to the development of comprehensive campaigns in organizing and bargaining. The model is designed to be applicable to a wide variety of employers and can be used by trade unionists and their allies at a number of different levels. Before we begin exploring this model, it is important to step back and place comprehensive campaigns in a larger historical framework. As important as the techniques of corporate research are, we cannot understand them thoroughly without also exploring the evolution of comprehensive strategic campaigns.

Corporate Power and Union Forms of Resistance

While it is tempting to look at comprehensive campaigns as something entirely new, in many ways they are the latest adaptation by labor to the changes in corporate structure and practice. If we look back at the history of the labor movement around the world, I would argue that labor has been successful when it develops forms of resistance that take into account how employers are structured and how they operate in the context of the state. While the recent development of comprehensive strategic campaigns is indeed innovative, these campaigns belong to a long line of strategic thinking by the labor movement.

While we could trace the evolution of forms of resistance in a number of different countries, table 1.1 outlines the development of union strategies and tactics and their relationship to corporate structure in the United States by examining four employers over four different time periods. We begin in 1912 in Lawrence, Massachusetts, with the American Woolen Company. American Woolen owned four of the major textile mills along the canals in Lawrence, a planned New England city on the banks of the Merrimack River. As was common in the textile industry in the later part of the nineteenth century and the early part of the twentieth century, the mills were single operations that served regional markets. Run by William Wood, American Woolen was what we would think of today as a limited partnership (Watson 2005, 23).

In this first part of the twentieth century, the financial community had yet to establish the kinds of credit systems that would allow firms to borrow funds. This led to boom-and-bust cycles in the New England textile mills, as well as in

TABLE 1.1.
A historical analysis of corporate structure and successful forms of union resistance in the United States

	American Woolen, Lawrence (1912)	GM Flint (1937)	U.S. Steel (1965)	Bridgestone/ Firestone (1996)
Corporate Stucture				
Production	Single plant	Multiple plants	Multiple plants	Global plants
Distribution	Regional	National	Some international	Fully inter-national
Financing	Partnership	Early U.S.-based corporation	Mature U.S.-based corporation	Global corpor-ation
Role of the state	No institutional involvement in labor issues	Increasing militancy Pressure on state	Heavily in tripartite IR system	Undermining of extant IR system
Union form of resistance	Simple strike	Selective strike	Pattern bargaining	Comprehensive campaign

the larger economy. This meant that American Woolen, like every other firm, depended on a rapid turnover of its inventory to generate the cash to keep the company operating.

In January 1912, the largely immigrant workforce of women, organized by the Industrial Workers of the World (IWW), walked out of the Lawrence mills. In what many consider the first modern strike in the United States, the women marched and paraded through the streets of Lawrence, keeping workers from returning to work and effectively shutting down production (Juravich, Hartford, and Green 1996). By late March, the company, near economic ruin, capitulated to the strikers' demands.

While there is a great deal more to the story of what has been called the "Bread and Roses" strike, what is important to our discussion here is that American Woolen's structure meant that the company could be brought to its knees by the withdrawal of labor in a simple strike—a strategy used throughout the United States and around the world in the later part of the nineteenth and the early part of the twentieth century. This was a local strategy, one often based in craft unionism or unions at the local level. Without the ability of the company to shift production or to borrow funds, a simple work stoppage was an incredibly powerful weapon for labor. While there was no institutional role for the state in labor industrial relations, local law enforcement would often play a pivotal role in these disputes.

Corporate structure changed, however, and along with it labor's form of resistance had to change, too. In the opening chapters of John Steinbeck's *The Grapes of Wrath*, Tom Joad, the main character of the novel, returns to his home to find that his family's farm has been bought out by a large corporation and the family is moving west. As he goes out to the old place, he sees a large tractor tearing down the family's farm and barns. He threatens to kill the tractor driver to stop the destruction. The driver responds, "Joad, they'll just hang you, but before you're hung, there'll be another guy on the tractor, and he'll bump the house down. You're not killing the right guy" (Steinbeck 1939, 52).

Over the next several paragraphs, Joad suggests that he should instead kill the guy giving the orders or the bank president and so on. But with each suggestion the driver responds that it won't stop the destruction of the farms, valiantly trying to help Joad understand the nature of a modern corporation. This was not an operation controlled by one man, such as those run by mill owners of an earlier era, that could be stopped by the shooting of one man. Firms had changed, and union tactics would have to change as well if they were to be successful in this new milieu.

General Motors was one of the early corporations that emerged in the 1930s. Unlike American Woolen, it had a number of plants, many performing the same function, and serving not a regional but a national market. And, while financing was not as sophisticated as it is today, the corporate structure did allow for more cash flow to weather short-term downturns. Given these changes in corporate structure, the simple strikes used by the IWW in Lawrence were no longer appropriate. If the United Auto Workers (UAW) struck an individual plant during its organizational drive, the work would have simply been shifted to another plant, the workers fired, and the union's drive set back on its heels. This happened throughout the 1930s and 1940s as workers and their unions still clung to the strategies of the earlier era, struggling futilely against different kinds of firms.

In their campaign against General Motors, the UAW developed a strategy that anticipated this new corporate structure. From their research they knew that Fisher Body Plants 1 and 2 were the major suppliers of body parts for Chevrolets and Buicks (Lichtenstein 1995, 76). The union targeted these key plants and was planning a strike for January, after newly elected Michigan governor Frank Murphy's inauguration. However, when rumors spread that crucial dies were soon to be moved, local activists jumped the gun and initiated the famous sit-down strike that was fundamental to the UAW's wresting union recognition from General Motors (Zieger 1995, 50).

While the sit-down feature of this strike was crucial, what is also significant about the Flint strike is that it was not a simple strike like the one at Lawrence but a selective or tactical strike that took into account the new corporate form. By targeting the Fisher plants, the UAW understood the vulnerabilities of GM and was able to take full advantage of them. At the same time, the role of the state in industrial relations was changing. Under pressure from growing labor militancy President Roosevelt had provided union recognition in section 7 of the National Industrial Recovery Act of 1933 (NIRA). By the time of the strike in Flint, the more comprehensive Wagner Act was still in the courts, but the government was beginning a much deeper involvement in labor-management relations.

Corporations in the United States continued to mature, and in the wake of the involvement of the U.S. labor movement in tripartite agreements during World War II, an industrial relations system arose (Kaufman 1992). For the first and only time in U.S. history, an accord emerged between labor and management, and a complex set of state-supported procedures was put in place in an effort to level the playing field between the two parties. At this point there was an explosion in the length of union contracts, far beyond the single page that marked the initial agreement between GM and the UAW, and the institution of complex, multistage grievance and arbitration processes.

United States Steel emerged as one of the leading U.S. firms during this period, and it represented a further evolution of the corporation. Like GM it had a number of plants across the United States, distributing not only to the entire country but internationally as well (Hoerr 1988). United States Steel, along with the United Steelworkers of America (USWA), developed a complex set of rules governing the workplace, including a private arbitration system. The firm experienced rapid growth during the 1950s and 1960s and, with a command of the U.S. market, was hugely profitable. The evolution of both corporate law and banking further strengthened its economic security.

Against such a stable firm, the labor movement was losing the power of selective strikes. Given the labor-management accord and the legal and regulatory framework in place, the Steelworkers, and much of the labor movement in the United States, moved instead in a different direction. In the steel, auto, and many other basic industries, the labor movement moved to pattern bargaining, negotiating not with just one firm but with the major firms in an entire industry.

Until the mid- to late 1970s unions were able to use pattern bargaining to deliver increasingly stronger contracts to union members in these core industries. It is, however, important to note here that these adaptations marked a significant departure for labor, constituting forms of acquiescence to the new industrial relations system rather than the forms of resistance of earlier eras. As long as the accord held, the system delivered, but by the late 1970s, when the U.S. economy came to a standstill, the accord began to unravel as employers such as International Paper and Phelps-Dodge took off their gloves. The legal and procedural framework that had once brought a measure of justice and security to workers in the United States was now an empty shell, openly ignored by the U.S. government. It became clear that labor would need to return to its past and once again develop new forms of resistance that made sense, given the new corporate order.

Confronted with these new realities—plant closings, outsourcing, a new corporate adversarialism, and the failure of the postwar industrial relations system—the late 1970s and early 1980s were a time of great loss of membership in the labor movement in the United States. But it was also a time of great experimentation, as labor began to explore new approaches.

One important innovation was the work of Ray Rogers in the late 1970s, with his development of the first corporate campaign at J.P. Stevens, a notorious antiunion firm located largely in the south. The textile workers' union had been unsuccessful for years in trying to break into Stevens, in what were essentially company towns. Rogers, a young union staffer, came up with an important alternative. Instead of going head to head against the company in its strongholds, the union would bring pressure on the firm indirectly by pressuring members of the board of directors. By targeting key board members, Rogers brought Stevens to the bargaining table, doing in a matter of months what on-the-ground organizing had been unable to accomplish for years (Pauly and Walcott 1978, 58).

During the 1980s, unions also reached back to their roots in the communities where they had been born and began experimenting with building community coalitions and community campaigns. One of the best examples was the campaign run by the United Electrical Workers (UE) at Morse Cutting Tool in New Bedford, Massachusetts (Swinney 1982). Morse had been bought by the behemoth Gulf and Western, which was threatening to shutter the facility. The UE worked tirelessly with the community in this small fishing and industrial city on the Massachusetts coast. The campaign culminated with the mayor of New Bedford threatening to seize the plant through the power of eminent domain. Gulf and Western capitulated, the facility sold, and the jobs remained in New Bedford.

In addition to these early corporate and community campaigns, labor innovated in a number of areas, including running what were called inside campaigns. At Moog Automotive, under the leadership of UAW staff representative Jerry Tucker, workers stayed on the job and worked without a contract and were able to exert tremendous pressure on the production process, forcing a settlement (Metzgar 1985). This was part of a return to local militancy by trade unionists wanting to play more of a role in their future through direct action rather than waiting for the wheels of a largely dysfunctional industrial relations system to slowly turn.

While each of these tactics held tremendous promise, the wreckage of the 1980s demonstrated that none of these approaches was the silver bullet labor was hoping for. Not all companies had boards that were as highly leveragable as the Stevens board, not all companies were located in places where community pressure could be generated, and, in areas where community pressure could be counted on, firms were not as vulnerable to that kind of pressure as Gulf and Western was in New Bedford. In-plant strategies also required tremendous worker discipline and solidarity and also depended on corporate commitment to that specific site or facility. If either the work site or the workers themselves were expendable, then even the most militant and united inside action would be rendered entirely ineffective.

By the beginning of the 1990s, the lessons were clear. There would be no single route to labor's revival, and, in fact, campaigns that focused on only one issue or approach were doomed to fail. Instead, what began to emerge was that, given the changes taking place in corporate structure with the emergence of global firms, only multifaceted campaigns—campaigns that brought leverage on employers in multiple areas—would succeed. Perhaps the best example was the Steelworkers campaign against Japanese-owned tire giant Bridgestone/Firestone (BSFS).

Table 1.1 shows that production at BSFS was truly global, with plants located around the world. Distribution was global as well, and the Steelworkers were up against a firm that looked very different from U.S. Steel. Given these facts, the older approaches of selective strikes and pattern bargaining were no longer applicable.

The Steelworkers used lessons learned from their seminal victory in the twenty-two month lockout at Ravenswood Aluminum (Juravich and Bronfenbrenner 1999) and built a comprehensive strategic campaign at Bridgestone/Firestone that was anything but one-dimensional. It focused on major stockholders and lenders, mounted an ambitious end-user campaign pressuring consumers not to buy BSFS tires, built broad alliances with religious and civil rights leaders, and, as part of an ambitious international campaign, sent worker delegations to Japan (Juravich and Bronfenbrenner 2003).

As in the Ravenswood campaign, the basic modus operandi was to constantly escalate the campaign, starting new fronts against the company as other fronts were waning. In the words of former USWA president George Becker,

> The last thing I wanted the company … to think of before [they] went to bed at night, Monday, Tuesday, Wednesday, Thursday, Friday, Saturday and Sunday night … is all the problems and difficulties we caused them that day. And the first thing I wanted them to think of when they wake up is, "Oh Christ, I've got to go out and face them sons of bitches again." … We had to get them thinking about the Steelworkers continually, every day … if we let an hour go by that our name didn't cross their minds for some reason or another, then we were failing. (Juravich and Bronfenbrenner 1999, 132)

Using this approach, the Steelworkers were able to win at BSFS, demonstrating the power of strategic research and comprehensive campaigns against even global giants. This kind of multifaceted strategic campaign was precisely the form of resistance needed in this new corporate environment. Key to the victory here, as well as the one in Ravenswood, was the involvement of rank-and-file workers. Early corporate campaigns tended to marginalize rank-and-file workers, which was problematic. In fact, neither of these campaigns could have been won without the rank-and-file militancy that kept scabs out of the plants and kept the heat on the employer locally (Juravich and Bronfenbrenner 1999; Bronfenbrenner and Juravich 2001). Yet it is also important to note that, against global giants like BSFS, local militancy alone was not enough. We saw this in a number of battles that unions lost in the 1980s and 1990s. Workers stood tall, kept scabs out, and engaged in courageous actions, but without some larger strategic campaign to leverage the firm, the local militancy alone, which might have been enough at Lawrence, was no longer sufficient.

A Model for Strategic Corporate Research

Tracing the evolution of strategic campaigns provides an important foundation to lay out a model and framework for conducting strategic corporate research.[2] Several things have become clear. First, strategic corporate research is not just random information gathering on employers. This is not just research for its own sake but research directed both at understanding how power flows in firms and at identifying vulnerabilities and potential points of leverage. Second, strategic corporate research is not simply about "digging up dirt" on employers to use in more traditional bargaining and organizing campaigns. As we have seen from our analysis of the evolution of corporate structure, gathering dirt to use in old-style campaigns has little chance for success against today's global giants. Strategic research needs to be the first step in developing the kinds of multifaceted strategic campaigns that are necessary to win today.

In reviewing the small amount of material on corporate research, the only common analytical tool is what has been called a power analysis or web analysis. It typically involves placing the target firm in the center of a page and then brainstorming any and all connections to top management, board members, customers, community groups, and the like, and placing them in a large circle around the firm linked by arrows.

While it is a powerful brainstorming tool for initial thinking about a corporation, the web analysis has a number of limitations. First, it does not distinguish between what is inside the firm and what is outside. Management is inside the firm, while environmental groups are outside. This is important be-

---

[2]   This framework and materials were developed with the consultation of Kate Bronfenbrenner of Cornell University and Keith Mestrich, formerly of the AFL-CIO and now with UNITE HERE. I was fortunate to have worked with them for several years in helping to develop the curriculum for and teach in the Cornell University/AFL-CIO Strategic Corporate Research Summer School.

cause very different approaches are used in applying pressure on the firm itself than when using outside organizations to leverage firms. Second, this power or web analysis makes no effort to distinguish between the different kinds of activities of an employer. For example, operational issues, such as identifying suppliers or customers, are quite distinct from management issues, such as deciding new areas for corporate expansion. Third, this power analysis, as it has largely been used for corporate research, starts each campaign with a blank page. While this may encourage brainstorming, it also makes it likely that key elements are left out. For although each employer has a unique structure and environment, there are elements one will always want to investigate.

With these deficiencies in mind, we can turn to figure 1, which provides a basic model for strategic corporate research. It begins by first distinguishing what is inside and outside the target employer. It also distinguishes among three different levels: command and control, operational, and outside stake- holders. Finally, rather than just providing a blank slate, we made an effort to make an exhaustive list of the basic areas for strategic corporate research. Fig- ure 1 contains twenty-four boxes representing twenty-four areas that should be explored regardless of the particulars of the target company. For any spe- cific firm, information for all twenty-four may not be available or relevant, but the listing provides an important baseline and a series of checks and balances to ensure a comprehensive corporate profile.

While space does not allow us to include them here, we have developed a series of research questions for each of the twenty-four boxes. They are available online at the following websites: http://www.ilr.cornell.edu/globalunionsconference/ or http://www.umass.edu/lrrc/research/. In addition to the basic questions, we have also created a comprehensive listing of Internet sites where the information can be obtained.[3]

Note that the boxes are also numbered, suggesting an order for conducting research, which is especially helpful for first-time researchers. I have watched beginners start researching safety and health or environmental issues using the older power-analysis models before they really understand what a firm makes or its history or strategies. It makes the most sense to begin the research by locating basic information about the target employer.

Basic information (box 1) includes whether the firm is privately held, pub- licly held, or nonprofit. This is crucial, as the primary sources of informa- tion are very different for these different types of firms. Equally important are the kinds of products or services the company makes or provides (box 2). While we may know a firm because of a certain high-profile product it makes,

[3]   In addition to free Internet websites, universities, colleges, and public libraries frequently provide excellent databases that make conducting this research much easier. Many provide ways for the general public to use their services at no cost.

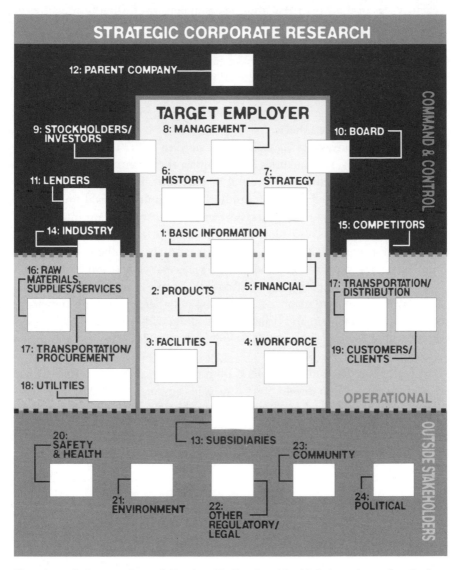

Fig. 1 Strategic Corporate Research. Developed by Tom Juravich with design assistance from Fred Zinn and Art Torres.

this may end up being a small part, or an unprofitable part, of the business. Here it is important to gather as much information as possible about various business segments and both the income and profit generated by each segment. For example, during the Offshore Mariners' United Union (OMU) campaign at TRICO Marine, although the union was organizing workers in the Gulf Coast, researchers discovered that the company's most profitable business segment was in the North Sea, and the campaign was shifted to pressure the firm there (War on Want 2006).

As suggested by box 3, it is essential to develop a comprehensive list of company facilities. Again, we may be most familiar with one facility or a certain subset of facilities, but it is fundamental to map out all the facilities. Are they owned? Leased? How old are they? Facilities built with industrial development bonds or other public monies provide opportunities to broaden a dispute and bring it into the public sphere.

In addition to inventorying facilities, we need to gather information on the workforce (box 4). This includes how many workers are unionized, their demographics, and whether they are full or part-time. For global firms, where is the workforce located and what kinds of opportunities does it provide and what kinds of linkages can be made? For example, during the Communications Workers of America (CWA) 1989 campaign with Nortel, research revealed that Nortel had a number of Canadian facilities, and because these were heavily unionized, they were instrumental in CWA's success (Cohen and Early 2000).

As suggested by box 5, we also need to gather some basic financial information. You need not have advanced accounting skills here. A working knowledge of the income statement and balance sheet, along with using the key financial ratios used by the analyst community, will both provide a baseline and suggest questions for further research.

It is also important to understand both the company history (box 6) and its strategy (box 7). In developing a strategic campaign, it is crucial to know where a company is heading because intervening here cuts to the heart of the firm's operations, as well as its promises to shareholders and investors. For example, in the global campaign to organize workers at Coca-Cola, the International Union of Food, Agricultural, Hotel, Restaurant, Catering, Tobacco and Allied Workers' Associations (IUF), which has been coordinating the effort, is well aware of Coca-Cola's strategy to move into emerging markets and has exploited this during its campaign (Garver et al. 2006). Sometimes this strategy is clearly articulated in company documents, while in other cases it must be gleaned from press releases, quarterly conference calls, or other materials.

It goes without saying that we need to have a thorough understanding of management (box 8). Do they serve on other boards? Are they involved in philanthropic activities? Do they have associations with governmental bodies? Here we must be cautious not to fall into the Tom Joad trap of thinking that only the CEO is important and should be the entire focus of the campaign. Indeed, knowing as much as possible about the CEO is important, yet there may be other top managers who may be both powerful and vulnerable.

Finishing up the information about the target employer is information on stockholders/investors (box 9) and the board of directors (box 10). Note that they straddle the line, since to some extent they indeed hold positions in the firm, yet they are fundamentally outsiders. For publicly held firms in the United States, stockholder information is readily available, and it is important to identify the largest shareholders. While major stockholders are often mutual fund and financial institutions, the unexpected does happen. For example, researchers looking at Republic Services, a major trash firm, as part of a Teamsters campaign were surprised to discover that one of the major stockholders was the Bill and Melinda Gates Foundation. Special attention should be given to retirement funds that hold stock, especially those connected to unions, as they may provide important leverage.

Unions have also become increasingly involved in shareholder actions. In the United Mine Workers of America (UMWA) battle against Peabody Coal they were able to get 230 million shares to vote against an important resolution by Lord Hanson of Hanson PLC, a British firm that controlled Peabody (Zinn 2000). An international shareholder campaign was brought against Rio Tinto in 2000, led by the Trades Union Congress (TUC) in the United Kingdom, the International Federation of Chemical, Energy, Mine and General Workers' Union (ICEM), the Australian Congress of Trade Unions (ACTU), and the AFL-CIO (see chapter 10).

Finally, we know from the early work of Ray Rogers that the other corporate identities of the directors may provide leverage against the board, as may their participation in civic and political activities. It is important to examine the profiles of board members carefully, yet, as we can see from figure 1, this is only one of twenty-four possible areas of leverage.

Outside the firm there are still two important areas at the command and control level. Lenders, in box 11, although outside the firm, may have a very strong influence on its direction. Particularly in the case of leveraged buyouts, or where the company is highly indebted, lenders may play a stronger role in the firm than upper management does. For example, one of the components of the Steelworkers campaign against Ravenswood Aluminum was pressure on the NMB Postbank in the Netherlands, one of the firm's major lenders (Juravich and Bronfenbrenner 1999).

Similarly, it is important to determine whether there is a larger parent company (box 12) or, in some cases, a series of parent companies and the role that the immediate and/or ultimate parent company plays in company operations, decision making, and control. In some instances the parent plays little or no role; in others the parent may actually place a majority of individuals on the board. In the same way, it is important to identify any subsidiaries (box 13) and their relationships to the target company.

For publicly held companies, finding the parent company or subsidiaries is fairly straightforward. For private companies, however, this can be an extremely challenging task, where the individual or company holding controlling interest in the firm may have gone to great lengths to keep its connection to the company hidden.

Once we have this basic working knowledge of the firm and what is happening at the command and control level, gaining a larger understanding of the industry (box 14) and the major competitors (box 15) is crucial. Companies do not exist as islands; they rise and fall with industry trends. Here industry publications can be very helpful. In addition to understanding the industry as a whole, it is important to first identify the major competitors that define the competitive context in which the firm operates. While time and resources may not allow for a complete corporate profile on competitors, it is important to gather as much comparative information as possible.

The operational level of a firm can provide numerous opportunities for leverage. On the input side, it is important to identify suppliers of goods or services (box 16). Is there only one? Are there many? Is there more than one source for the same supplies? Following the supply chain has been instrumental in the work of United Students Against Sweatshops (USAS), who discovered that the high-priced collegiate logo clothing they were buying was typically produced in sweatshop conditions in the Global South. They not only forced a number of universities to sign codes of conduct and designated supplier agreements, but in campaigns such as the struggles against Kudong in Mexico, also played a role in jump-starting organizing at the source facility (Hermanson 2004).

At the same time, how those goods or services are transported (box 17) and the utilities (box 18) used may provide important sources of leverage. On the output side, identifying customers (box 19) is vital. Are there only a few customers, or is the product or service available to the general public? While general consumer boycotts are difficult to build and sustain, in many situations firms supply a limited number of industrial consumers, making end-user campaigns very feasible. For example, during the struggle of the workers at the Gina Form Bra Company in Thailand, they were able to identify The Limited and Victoria's Secret as the major customers, and pressure on these firms was an important part of their campaign (Robertson and Plaiyoowong 2004).

It should also be noted here that information at the operational level is the most difficult to find online. However, this is precisely the kind of information that rank-and-file workers often know, particularly those working in the shipping and receiving department, and obtaining this operational information provides an excellent opportunity to involve rank-and-file members in the research process.

Finally, there is important information to be gathered about outside stakeholders. First we look at stakeholders who are part of the regulatory framework. Researching safety and health (box 20) is always crucial in building a strategic campaign. In the United States, general information can be gathered on the Occupational Safety and Health Administration (OSHA) website, while more specific details are available from the OSHA 200 logs that employers are required to keep. One major component of the comprehensive campaign at Bridgestone/

Firestone was a massive safety and health campaign, focusing on the deterioration of working conditions in the plants (Bronfenbrenner and Juravich 2001).

It is also important to gather information on the environmental (box 21) or possible environmental impact of the operation of the target firm. Environmental issues can be incredibly powerful in developing a critique of the company and in building community campaigns. An environmental campaign was central in efforts by the U.S. Paper, Allied-Industrial, Chemical and Energy Workers Union (PACE) in the battle with Crown Petroleum, once researchers had discovered that emissions from the plants increased significantly after the lockout began (Hickey 2004).

Depending on the industry and its location, there can be other regulatory or legal agencies (box 22) that have jurisdiction over the target firm. For example, a nuclear power plant is governed by the Nuclear Regulatory Commission (NRC), while health care in many states is governed by state-based boards. Here it is also important to investigate any pending litigation against the firm. While suits about falling in the parking lot may be routine, a discovery of racial discrimination claims or price fixing could be crucial in building a comprehensive campaign.

Researching community issues (box 23) is also a crucial means of discovering what kinds of leverage can be developed at the stakeholder level. These community issues include not only the official community relations of the company but also how community members view the firm and its operations. Not to be ignored here are community connections the union and rank-and-file members have made locally, nationally, and internationally. The local community campaign that organized families, shopkeepers, and the wives of strikers in the "daughters of Mother Jones" was pivotal during the Pittston strike by the UMWA (Brisbin 2002). But in this struggle, as in so many others, these were not simply connections the union made with the local community but made with the larger labor community around the world as well. Some of these may be institutional connections, such as employees of the same firm or members of a company or industry council. During the struggle by U.S. miners against Peabody Coal, miners in both Australia and Colombia struck in support of their brothers and sisters in the United States (Zinn 2002). As globalization continues, the creation of global labor communities will be fundamental in winning against global capital.

Amanda Tattersall has provided us with an excellent typology of labor-community coalitions in chapter 8. Through her examination of the SEIU's global partnership campaign in the United Kingdom, she reminds us that global coalitions depend on true mutuality of interest and are doomed to failure if one side always expects to direct coalition activities and is always asking other unions for support without giving anything in return.

Finally we need to examine the political connections (box 24) of the firm. Does the firm, its management, or its board donate regularly to the political process? To which political party or leader? Do they play at the local, regional, state, or federal level? Particularly when connected to other issues, this may be an important way of leveraging firms. Unions around the globe often have very different relationships to the political process, and international bodies can also play significant roles in campaigns. In the campaign by Jakalanka workers in Sri Lanka, petitions were filled with both the EU and the United States under the generalized system of preferences. As Gunawardana suggests (see chapter 4), it was the threat of trade talks that had a powerful impact on management at Jakalanka. We must be careful here not to overly rely on political processes alone, yet they can be incredibly powerful as part of a larger strategic campaign.

From Research to Campaigns

While it is important to be comprehensive in the collection of information about the target company, it is often easy at the end of the process to get lost in the details and not see the forest for the trees. It is sometimes not possible to gather information to fill all twenty-four boxes, and obviously some of the information gathered will not be pertinent or useful in building a campaign. Figure 2 is a blank research chart, which researchers have used successfully to summarize the key findings at each of the three levels. This begins the process of summarization and assists in the move toward developing a campaign.

However, moving to a campaign is not just about summarizing information—it requires reconceptualizing it. Figure 3 provides a method to create a strategic corporate summary and begin to shape the contours of a strategic campaign.[4] It focuses on four key concepts—profit centers, the growth plan, decision makers, and key relationships.

First, from our research we need to be able to identify the profit center of the firm. This is where a company makes its money and where it is most vulnerable. Several years ago, UNITE was organizing a Brylane distribution center that handled Lane Bryant stores, among others. Their research, however, indicated that this clothing distribution was not a major source of revenue for the firm but that major profits were made at its Gucci division. So, rather than focusing its energies on Lane Bryant facilities, UNITE organized activities in a small number of Gucci stores that brought the company to the table (Clean Clothes Campaign 2002).

In addition to the profit centers, it is crucial to understand the firm's growth plan. Growth is where companies put their energy, and it is often their growth plans that they use to generate investor and stockholder confidence. While in some cases these growth areas may constitute only a very small portion of corporate activity, they are places where firms are very vulnerable. Intervening

---

[4] This framework was initially developed by Keith Mestrich.

Fig. 2 Chart for key findings. Developed by Tom Juravich with design assistance from Fred Zinn and Art Torres.

in a firm's growth plans has become a hallmark of the new organization of hotel workers, now UNITE HERE. They discovered that because of all of the regulatory, legal, and governmental aspects of building a major hotel, they have the most power to intervene before and during the construction process

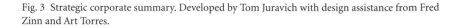

STRATEGIC CORPORATE SUMMARY

PROFIT CENTER

GROWTH PLAN

DECISION MAKERS

KEY RELATIONSHIPS

Fig. 3 Strategic corporate summary. Developed by Tom Juravich with design assistance from Fred Zinn and Art Torres.

rather than once the facility is built. This is true even with major hotel chains, which are vulnerable in their growth plans.

Third, we need to identify the decision makers in the company—those who are deciding how to keep the profit centers strong and in which areas to grow. It is very tempting again to fall into the Tom Joad trap—to simply identify the man on the tractor, the CEO of the firm. In the Ravenswood Aluminum lockout, for example, rank-and-file workers were convinced that local CEO Emmett Boyle was the main decisionmaker of the firm, and they spent tremendous energy putting direct pressure on him. When the Steelworkers broadened the campaign, they discovered through their research that Boyle was little more than a puppet and that the firm was controlled by Switzerland-based financier Marc Rich. Given the complexity of global firms, parent companies and subsidiaries, and the role of lenders and stockholders, it is extremely important to look beyond the company CEO.

Finally, in this process of developing a strategic corporate summary it is necessary to identify the key relationships that the firm needs to maintain its growth plan and profit center. These could range from relationships with key suppliers or customers to those with key lenders, board members, or regulatory organizations. This widens Ray Rogers's initial insight about pressuring board members and identifies a larger set of relationships that could be used in a strategic campaign. For example, during the Crown Petroleum Lockout, the company had developed a joint operating agreement with Statoli, a Norwegian state-owned oil company. This was a key relationship that the company needed to maintain to remain profitable, and consequently it became a major focus of the union's campaign (Hickey 2004).

Figures 4 and 5 use these four concepts to contrast a traditional bargaining campaign with a more comprehensive or strategic bargaining campaign. In a traditional bargaining campaign, as we can see from figure 4, the major activity of the union is on direct decision makers, either through the bargaining process or by picketing if in fact talks break down. In terms of the operations of the firm, there may be some effort to work –to rule while the contract is in effect, but once the union strikes or is locked out, the union will work to keep scabs out or perhaps launch a boycott of products or services.

As we can see from figure 5, a strategic comprehensive campaign looks very different and represents a much more sophisticated and nuanced way of leveraging firms. It begins by conceptualizing decision makers more broadly, as in-depth research allows unions to extend their focus beyond direct decision makers to those that might be located either inside or outside the company. As is also clear from figure 5, by identifying key relationships, strategic campaigns add an additional level between decision makers and the operations of the firm. This level provides an entirely new area where unions can exert pressure indirectly on the company.

Finally, as we can see from the bottom of figure 5, one of the important advances of strategic campaigns is that they do not make a generalized effort to pressure the entire operation of a firm. While this tactic may have made sense in relatively small, locally based firms, it is a very blunt instrument, particularly with large global firms. Instead, based on detailed research, comprehensive

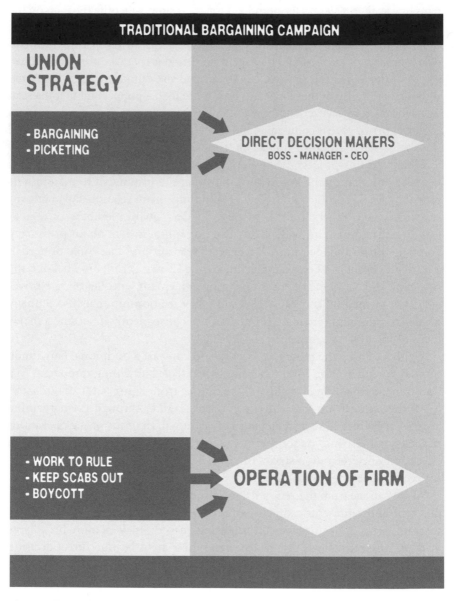

Fig. 4 Traditional bargaining campaign. Developed by Tom Juravich with design assistance from Art Torres.

strategic campaigns aim to pinpoint their pressure on profit centers and/or on the areas where the company is growing.

The four strategic concepts—profit center, growth plan, decision makers, and key relationships—can also be applied directly to a strategic cam-

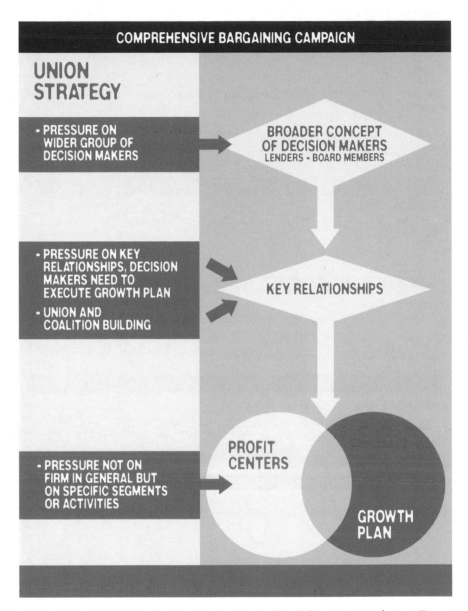

Fig. 5 Comprehensive campaign. Developed by Tom Juravich with design assistance from Art Torres.

paign itself and serve as part of the campaign planning process. Figure 6 is a calendar that uses these core concepts to plan out a campaign over a number of months. The idea here is that actions in each of the four core areas should escalate each month as the campaign builds. Note that an

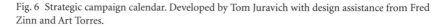

STRATEGIC CAMPAIGN CALENDAR

MONTH:

PROFIT CENTER

GROWTH PLAN

DECISION MAKERS

KEY RELATIONSHIPS

WORKERS / UNION

Fig. 6 Strategic campaign calendar. Developed by Tom Juravich with design assistance from Fred Zinn and Art Torres.

additional category referring to workers/union has been included in the campaign calendar. Although workers should be involved in every aspect of the campaign, it is also important to specify worker/union issues in each monthly cycle.

As globalization continues, unions will need to broaden their use of strategic research and strategic campaigns if they hope to remain a viable institution for workers in their struggle for justice and dignity. While unions in the United States and around the world have demonstrated the power of these campaigns, they are still infrequently used, with labor too often remaining mired in earlier methods for organizing and bargaining that stand little chance of success.

To succeed, the labor movement worldwide will need to ramp up its capacity for strategic research and comprehensive strategic campaigns. Strategic research and campaigns should not just be the purview of a small cadre of researchers and campaigners; rather, efforts should be made to train and mentor a whole new generation of researchers and campaigners at all levels of the labor movement around the globe.

To do this we need more research, analysis, and teaching materials about both strategic research and comprehensive campaigns. We need to greatly expand the literature with more in-depth and critical analysis of both successful and unsuccessful campaigns that goes beyond the basic materials on the Internet and uncritical reports by campaign participants. Equally important is the expansion of teaching materials that not only guide basic strategic research but demonstrate how this research sets the foundation for comprehensive campaigns. Both university-based programs and NGOs have an important role to play in providing objective analysis and in spearheading the broad dissemination of materials across industries, employers, and countries.

For strategic research and comprehensive campaigns to begin to reach their potential they must become more than just defensive actions when unions have their backs to the wall against major employers. Instead, they need to become integral to organizing and bargaining campaigns at all levels of the labor movement, with employers both large and small. Rather than being seen as special tools used only occasionally, strategic research and comprehensive campaigns need to become part of day-to-day practice if labor is to have any hope of winning against global firms.

2. "DUE DILIGENCE" AT APM-MAERSK

From Malaysian Industrial Dispute to Danish Cross-Border Campaign

PETER WAD

Denmark could be described as a society of small business and big unions because of its industrial structure, dominated by small and medium-sized firms, and industrial relations characterized by a very high level of union density, nationwide and craft-based unions, a hybrid of comprehensive centralized and decentralized collective bargaining, and neocorporate-based trade union influence. However, Denmark has homegrown transnational companies, the largest of which is A.P.Moller-Maersk Group (henceforth APM-Maersk) with a labor force of more than seventy thousand employees working in more than 125 countries (Maersk 2005). APM-Maersk is among the largest Nordic corporations and one of the two hundred largest companies in the world (Maersk 2005). Its subsidiary, Maersk Line, formerly known as Maersk Sealand, is a global market leader in container services. Moreover, APM-Maersk operates a very successful retail business in Denmark as the joint venture Danish Supermarket Group and owns approximately 20 percent of the largest bank in Denmark, Danske Bank.

APM-Maersk has enormous economic and even some political power in Denmark (Benson, Lambek, and Ørskov 2004). The dominant owner, Maersk McKinney Moller, took over as CEO and chairman of APM-Maersk from his

This chapter is partly based on research carried out with financial support from the Danish Council for Development Research and the Danish Social Science Research Council. It draws on experiences of, interviews with, and/or feedback from trade unionists and labor activists from Malaysia and Denmark, especially Francis Xavier, K. Veeriah, Sallma Mustafa, Tian Chua, Anna Diemer, Christian Juhl, Flemming Carlsen, and Ib Maltesen. I thank all of them—including two anonymous reviewers and the editor of this book—very much for sharing their time and views with me. The responsibility for mistakes and misinterpretations rests with the author alone.

father in 1965, retired as CEO in 1993, and stepped down as chairman in 2003. He has a close relationship with Danish royalty and leading politicians. His motto, which he learned from his father, Arnold Peter Moller, the founder of APM-Maersk, was "due diligence," understood as preventive and timely cost reduction, not corporate social responsibility.

In 1998 Maersk Medical, a manufacturing subsidiary of APM-Maersk, acquired the Malaysian-based company Euromedical Industries Sdn. Bhd. (henceforth Euromedical), which is located in an industrial area in the northwestern part of Peninsular Malaysia. Through this purchase, the Danish giant became involved in a long-standing industrial conflict in which the Malaysian workers and their union, the National Union of Employees in Companies Manufacturing Rubber Products (NUECMRP), had been fighting for the right to organize and bargain collectively since 1975.

This chapter aims to investigate how and why the APM-Maersk Corporation avoided granting union recognition during its five years of management and what made the organizing campaign successful after APM-Maersk divested Maersk Medical, including Euromedical, to a Nordic venture company, Nordic Capital. The Euromedical case is interesting because the Malaysian unionists expected that APM-Maersk, based in a country with a strong trade union movement, would rectify the breach of international labor rights at the factory, yet that did not occur. Nor was it the specific national Danish trade union representing workers at Maersk Medical that took the lead in the international solidarity campaign for the Euromedical workers. Instead, an informal group of labor activists initiated a cross-border campaign within the framework of a Danish nongovernmental organization (NGO), in which Danish unions played a dominant role.

Malaysia, with a union density rate of only about 10 percent, is known for its pro-foreign-direct-investment policy, extremely detailed and restrictive industrial relations legislation, and its failure to ratify the International Labor Organization (ILO) covenant on the right to form free and independent trade unions (Todd, Lansbury, and Davis 2004; Kuruvilla and Erickson 2002; ILOLEX 2006). Yet why did the Malaysian judiciary system finally sustain the union case and force the company to the bargaining table?

The basic assumption of this chapter is that the traditional industrial relations perspective, with its national-oriented focus, is ineffective for understanding the dynamics of union cross-border campaigns in the current environment. With globalization, transnational corporations have gained increased leverage in the north and the south. Trade unions have to operate across borders at multiple levels and with new partners, such as NGOs and national and international union federations, to counter the power and strategic initiatives of transnational corporations (Harrod and O'Brien 2002). There were two working hypotheses. The first was that transnational corporations with their cross-border production chains exploit the weakest links in national industrial relations terms (e.g., Malaysia), while the trade unions rely on the strongest links (e.g., Denmark). The second hypothesis was that cross-border campaigns targeting transnational corporations depend on the strength and perseverance of the active organizations together with the directly involved members and the combined leverage they are able to generate across borders. The first hypothesis was not corroborated by the case considered, but the second withstood the test.

The empirical evidence underpinning the analysis is generated from several sources: reports from the NUECMRP, field visits to the industrial area of Euromedical, meetings and interviews with trade unionists, press reports, and company sources. The author has not visited the company nor met the management. He has kept in touch with union leaders and staff involved in the campaign and has researched the trade union movement in Malaysia on and off since 1984 and as recently as September 2005. Because of space requirements and the international perspective applied, the chapter omits an analysis of the internal politics of the NUECMRP and the Malaysian Trades Union Congress (MTUC), although these union politics influenced union practices during the industrial dispute. Suffice it to say, first, that NUECMRP was in arrears with dues to MTUC and hence could not count on the support of the peak labor center, and second, that the leadership of the NUECMRP was contested and shifted between two conflicting groups, while the Danish union activists collaborated primarily with the industrial relations officer of the union administration.

The chapter tells the story of the industrial dispute embedded in the corporate and Malaysian context. It details the emergence of a local group of a Danish NGO that got involved in the Euromedical industrial dispute, the industrial actions at Euromedical by the end of 2001, and the international campaign initiated by the Danish NGO, including its use of the Danish National Contact Point of the Organization for Economic Co-operation and Development (OECD), and lessons learned by the Danish campaigners. The chapter ends with an explanation of the labor-management struggle and the outcome of the Euromedical campaign.

The Industrial Dispute in Its Corporate and Malaysian Context

Euromedical was incorporated in 1973 as a private limited joint venture between Euromedical Industries Ltd. in the United Kingdom and two Malaysian partners, Plantation Agencies Sdn. Bhd. and the Kedah State Development Corporation (PKNK), owned by the state government of Kedah, located in the northwest of Peninsular Malaysia (NUECMRP 2001). Production of medical equipment began the following year. In 1976 the German corporation Hoechst acquired Euromedical Industries Ltd., and in 1978 Hoechst also acquired the Plantation Agencies' shares. In 1985 Hoechst sold a controlling share to American Hospital

Supply. Finally, Maersk Medical acquired 75 percent of the equity in 1998, leaving PKNK with 25 percent of the share capital (Yap 2002; NUECMRP 2003).

Maersk Medical grew out of a small entrepreneurial Danish company, Pharma-Plast, incorporated as a limited company in 1964 with the mission to manufacture low-cost, single-use medical items (Unomedical 2005). The APM-Maersk Group acquired the company in 1968. Maersk Medical was incorporated in 1996, underscoring the linkage to APM-Maersk and consolidating all Pharma-Plast companies into one concern, which aimed to be a global brand supplying medical equipment (Ellemose 2004, 307). This consolidation enabled Maersk Medical to expand its Danish facilities and to continue its internationalization. Maersk Medical became the world's largest manufacturer of Foley catheters when it acquired the share majority of Euromedical Industries Sdn. Bhd. in 1998. A major restructuring and focusing of the APM-Maersk business group, aimed at divesting its manufacturing companies, began in 2002. In April 2002, APM-Maersk announced that Maersk Medical was up for sale, and in December 2002 it concluded a transaction with Nordic Capital, a private equity company headquartered in Sweden. In accordance with the new ownership, Maersk Medical changed its name to Unomedical in 2003. Unomedical had four thousand employees worldwide, with a turnover of 1.8 billion DKr ($329 million in 2004) of which 98 percent was earned outside Denmark in 2004 (Unomedical 2005, 5).

Euromedical has always had a predominantly female workforce. It started out with about 100 employees, growing to reach 1,050 employees in 2001, of which 800 (76 percent) were women (NUECMRP 2001).

Shortly after production started in the middle of the 1970s, the long struggle for union organization and collective bargaining began when the first national industrial union claimed recognition as the representative for Euromedical workers. According to the Malaysian Industrial Relations Act of 1967, a trade union can claim recognition by an employer if the union is a legally registered union, is competent to register the employees concerned, is the appropriate union, and is sufficiently representative of the employees by way of having at least 51 percent of the employees as members (Ayadurai 1992, 74–75). The fight over union jurisdiction with the company and the Ministry of Labor (today the Ministry of Human Resources) continued from 1975 to 1988, involving several industrial unions and even an attempt by Euromedical employees to form a new industrial union when the Department of Trade Unions (DTU) disqualified the alternatives. Finally, the NUECMRP applied to the DTU to amend its constitution to include medical products in the union's domain of jurisdiction, and the DTU surprisingly approved this amendment in January 1988. The workers of Euromedical subsequently withdrew their application for the registration of the new union. What is surprising is that just prior to the decision of the authorities, the union reported attempts to form an in-house union (otherwise known as a company union) at Euromedical. In-house unionism was the type of trade unionism preferred by the Malaysian government, although the concept of in-house unionism did not exist in the Trade Union Act and regulations before 1989 (Wad 1997, 2004). Hence, in the Euromedical case the DTU followed the regulations and not the policy of the government.

While the NUECMRP was recognized as the competent union by the Ministry of Labor, the struggle with U.S.-controlled Euromedical for management recognition and collective bargaining within the industrial relations system of the Malaysian state continued until 1994, with a detour into the civil court system. During this period, the NUECMRP made several claims for union recognition because the management refused to accept the prounion stance of the workforce and complained to the ministry about incorrect membership forms, falsification of signatures, and misleading information by the union. The response of the NUECMRP was that the procedure for union approval had been followed and the company was wrong in all respects.

A third claim for union recognition was served in June 1989, followed by the union's fourth recognition claim in 1990. Due to a pending civil court case filed by the NUECMRP after the rejection of its third claim of union recognition, in 1993 the DTU carried out a membership check at the request of the Department of Industrial Relations. Nearly 60 percent of the employees voted for the NUECMRP. Again the company rejected the union's claim for recognition, but this time the ministry confirmed that the union had the right to be recognized. The company appealed to the minister of human resources, but the minister confirmed the decision of the DTU and directed the company to recognize the union and start collective bargaining. This happened in February 1994, nearly twenty years after the employees of Euromedical joined a union in order to organize and engage the company in collective bargaining and reach a collective agreement (NUECMRP 2001).

From 1994 until 2004 the struggle was transferred to the civilian court system, with the company now complaining to the High Court about the administrative procedure. After a four-year process, the High Court declared in March of 1998 that the minister's directive to the company to recognize the union and start collective bargaining was null and void. The union, which had become a party to the High Court case in 1994 on the initiative of the attorney general, reacted by taking the case to the Court of Appeal. More than five years after the appeal, the court handed down its decision in November 2003, quashing the decision of the High Court (Francis Xavier, e-mail to author, 2003). However, the Nordic Capital/Unomedical-controlled management continued to pursue the strategy of legal action begun by the former U.S. and Danish owners, and appealed to the highest court of Malaysia, the Federal Court (formerly Supreme Court). The Federal Court considered the appeal of the union within a year and on August 2, 2004, upheld the decision of the Court of Appeal, which approved the order of the minister of human resources directing the company to recognize the NUECMRP and take up collective negotiations with the union (Francis Xavier, e-mail to author, 2004).

Having lost the case in the civil court system, the management of Euromedical abstained from engaging in collective bargaining with the union. In response to a complaint by the NUECMRP, the Department of Industrial Relations called the union and the management of Euromedical to a meeting in March 2005 in which the department directed the company to start negotiations within a month. Dragging its feet, the management finally commenced negotiations in April 2005, a few days after the deadline provided by the department.

The Euromedical case stands out for the following reasons. First, the industrial conflict took place at a predominantly female workplace, contradicting the old notion of Asian female workers as docile employees who formed a structurally weak workforce underpinning the rapid labor-intensive industrialization of East Asia (Deyo 1989). Second, it was carried out by workplace union activists who, with the support of the national industrial union and a global cross-border solidarity campaign organized by a Danish labor NGO, won a three-decade fight for freedom of association and collective bargaining against the employer. Third, the company has been controlled by European, U.S., and Nordic parent companies for the past three decades, yet each of the foreign managers, despite differences in the industrial relations background and training they brought with them from their home countries, converged on the same goal: avoiding trade union recognition with all legal means at their disposal in Malaysia. And fourth, it demonstrated the powerful commitment of local trade unionists to the struggle for their own labor rights, as expressed by a leading female union activist at Euromedical: "We just wanted our rights to be respected" (Sallma Mustafa, interview by author, 2002).

The Danish Malaysia Group

When Maersk Medical acquired control of Euromedical in 1998, connecting companies and workplaces in Denmark and Malaysia, the corporation also created a basis for international cooperation between Malaysian and Danish unions and NGOs. In 1999, a Danish study circle on globalization was formed to discuss globalization from a local (Danish) angle. Its members were drawn from the International Forum of the Labor Movement (AIF), the Female Workers' Union of Denmark (KAD), and shop stewards from Maersk Medical's factories in Haarlev and Osted (AIF 2003, 6). The AIF was established in 1989 as a member organization dominated by the Danish Confederation of Trade Unions (National Organization, or LO) and most of its affiliate national unions and other national trade unions, as well as the Danish Social

Democratic Party and fifteen hundred individual members (AIF 2006). AIF operated with relatively autonomous local branches.

The group organized four informational meetings. These highlighted that the proportion of Maersk Medical goods being produced in Denmark had steadily declined from 100 percent in 1985 to 50 percent in 2000 and was forecast to be 35 percent in 2005, and that the company confirmed it was complying with rules, legislation, and collective agreements in offshore locations. The meetings also determined that Maersk Medical was part of a labor struggle for organizing at Euromedical. After these meetings the group decided to continue the work with a focus on Malaysia and the industrial struggle for union recognition and collective bargaining.

The group was known to the public as the Malaysia Group and was based at the local branch of the AIF in Roskilde, because the two Maersk Medical factories were covered under the jurisdiction of AIF Roskilde. In March 2001 the Malaysia Group secured financial means from a fund, various trade unions, and the AIF for a study tour to Malaysia to visit Euromedical and the NUECMRP.[1] The group informed Ole Weiling, the CEO of Maersk Medical, about the employees' fight for union organizing and collective bargaining at the Malaysian subsidiary of Maersk Medical. The CEO did not know about the case and argued that the companies in the local industrial area had a community of interest and that the Danish company would itself be castigated as a scab if it deviated from the norm (AIF 2003, 7).

Although the KAD representatives supported the idea that the Malaysia Group should operate within the framework of the Danish labor NGO (AIF), the KAD invited two labor representatives from Malaysia to its congress in 2001 in order to expose the Malaysia case to a Danish public. When Sallma Mustafa, a production worker and union activist, and K. Veeriah, the industrial relations officer of the NUECMRP, visited Denmark, the AIF organized a meeting between the CEO of Maersk Medical and the Malaysian representatives. The CEO stated that the issue of industrial relations was within the orbit of the local management of the subsidiary and not headquarters but that he would discuss the matter with the local manager, which he did not do.

The Danish group visited Euromedical and participated in an off-factory general meeting with five hundred out of eight hundred employees. The next day the group met with the managing director, Rolf Bladt, and the meeting turned into negotiations on a new process of union recognition, in which the employees would be offered a choice between the NUECMRP and an in-house union. However, Rolf Bladt changed his mind and denied that any agreement

---

[1] Flemming Carlsen, member of the AIF Roskilde and a union teacher in international labor issues, knew Malaysian trade unionists of NUECMRP and other unions from several trips to Malaysia with Danish shop stewards from the General Workers Union of Denmark (SID).

had been reached. He was soon taken off the case, and his contract with Euromedical was terminated before its expiration. This event convinced the Danish Malaysia group that the industrial relations issue would not be decided by the local management but by the headquarters of Maersk Medical.

Industrial Actions at Euromedical

At the end of 2001, things had worsened dramatically in Malaysia. After the visit of the Danish group of trade unionists, the core group of Malaysian unionists met in August 2001 with Peter Ring, the new Danish managing director of Euromedical, and discussed, among other things, the year-end bonus issue. The meeting appeared to go well and the director agreed to meet with them again in October, but the group learned that the company's human resources department had formed its own hand-picked committee of workers, and management refused to meet the union activists. As reported in a union flyer from that time: "Our reps tell us that there was no confidence amongst the workers, generally, in the committee formed by the company. Discontentment began to build from September 2001. When it was clearly known that bonus for 2001 was not going to be paid by the company, this dissatisfaction manifested itself in the lay down of tools on 27.12.2001 and 31.12.2001" (NUECMRP 2002, 3).

The annual bonus was the norm at Euromedical and in the local industrial area and Malaysia in general. It was part of the household budget expectations of Malaysian families, and its unilateral cancellation created anger and triggered a wildcat strike among the workers of Euromedical, starting with the morning shift December 27. The union recounts what happened:

> About 350 workers reporting to work did not commence work but demonstrated *peacefully* demanding for the minimum of one (1) [month's] bonus. Some workers, returning home after working the previous night shift (i.e. 11:00 p.m. 12.26.2001 to 7:00 a.m. 12.27.2001) also stayed-on.
>
> The Human Resource Manager (Zulkefli Pa'wan), the Plant Manager (Kenny Ho) and the Managing Director (Peter Ring) were amongst the managerial representatives who met the workers. Later they also met representatives of the workers including those from our core group. Thereafter, there was intervention by officers of the Ministry of Human Resources and also one officer from the special Branch of the local police. However, the [worker's] demands were not met and the stand-off continued until about 3:00 p.m. (NUECMRP 2002, 1)

The management of Euromedical suspended all participating workers for two weeks and announced a plant shutdown (lockout) from 3:00 p.m. until

December 30, which was the Sunday day off. When another shift of workers reported for work at 7:00 a.m. on Monday, December 31, the industrial action was repeated. Management suspended the workers again. The following shift, arriving at 3:00 p.m., renewed the action until 5:00 p.m., when they started work. This group was given a written final warning for undertaking an illegal strike and the breaking of company disciplinary rules. The management ordered all workers to report for work before 12:00 a.m. on January 2, 2002, and when this happened most employees were given a final warning letter and asked to begin work. Fifteen workers were kept on suspension, including the core group of union activists and other workers who had exposed themselves during the illegal strike by way of speaking out or being in the front line of the action. Four of the fifteen suspended workers were finally dismissed, including Sallma Mustafa (K. Veeriah, interview by author, 2002; NUECMRP 2002).

Francis Xavier, labor activist and former executive secretary of the NUECMRP, described the changing climate at Maersk Medical by pointing out that while in the two decades from 1978 to 1998 only two union leaders had been kicked out by the company, the company dismissed four union leaders between 1998 and 2002 (Francis Xavier, interview by author, 2005). The dismissed Euromedical union activists were concerned whether the pressure of the Danish labor movement was strong enough to make Maersk Medical back down (Ex-Euromedical employees, interview by author, 2002).

The International Solidarity Campaign in Denmark

The events around New Year 2002 triggered a larger campaign in Denmark in support of the dismissed workers and their fight for organizing and collective bargaining rights (AIF 2003, 8–11). The Malaysia Group held a fund-raiser in the winter and spring of 2002, which raised around 35,000 Danish kroner (about $6,600 in 2002). The AIF Roskilde lodged a complaint against Maersk Medical for breach of the OECD Guidelines for Multinational Companies at the OECD National Contact Point in Denmark in February 2002; this complaint, signed by the AIF Roskilde chairperson, was the first ever received by the National Contact Point. The Malaysia Group started an information campaign under the logo of the "Mouse and the Elephant," handing out information at street stalls along with Go-cards (free passes) to cafés, while the AIF published a booklet about the Euromedical case (AIF 2003). A demonstration was held at the APM-Maersk annual shareholder meeting after the association's "Critical Shareholders" had been mobilized to deliver the message to the other shareholders.

As part of the information campaign in 2002–3, a member of parliament from the Social Democratic Party directed questions about the Euromedical case to the minister of foreign affairs and the minister of employment. The minister of foreign affairs agreed that Danish and other transnational corporations should comply with the guidelines of the OECD but governments should not enforce the rules because they were voluntary norms, not legal regulations. The minister also declined to condemn Maersk Medical for breaching the OECD guidelines in Malaysia because the case was pending at the Court of Appeal. When the AIF group noticed that the acquisition of Euromedical by Nordic Capital had been approved in early 2003, they wrote to Nordic Capital informing the new management about the union recognition case and its solution and proposed a meeting. Nordic Capital responded immediately that as long as the case was being processed by the National Contact point, the firm would not discuss the matter. In February 2004, the AIF group organized an e-mail action in which an estimated four to five hundred e-mails about the Euromedical case were sent to Nordic Capital and two journalists (Anna Diemer, e-mail to author, 2005).

Two AIF groups, AIF Roskilde and AIF Silkeborg, joined hands and produced a film about two interconnected cases in which they had been involved: Euromedical and the case of the Malaysian Labor Resource Center (LRC) and its leader, Tian Chua, who was imprisoned in Malaysia under the Internal Security Act (ISA) from 2001 until 2003. AIF Silkeborg had supported the LRC since 1997 and campaigned to get Tian Chua released from prison. The film cost 300,000 DKr ($48,000) and was financially supported by a range of Danish labor organizations, with the Competence Center of the Trade Union Movement paying half the expenses (Anna Diemer, interview by author, 2005).[2]

The AIF support groups also linked up with Malaysian unionists and activists. They invited Sallma Mustafa and Francis Xavier to Denmark to attend the alternative ASEM4People Meeting in Copenhagen in September 2002. Mustafa and the general secretary of the NUECMRP, Zamri bin Abdullah Rahman, visited Denmark in the autumn of 2003, and Nordic Capital declined to meet them. Sallma Mustafa and Tian Chua received the Rose Award from AIF in 2003 and the Malaysian Suaram Human Rights Award in 2004. The AIF Silkeborg collected $3,000 to support Mustafa and her three other colleagues in their legal case against Euromedical for unjustified dismissal. Two dismissal cases had been settled out of court with the intervention of NUECMRP but at a level unacceptable to the two remaining dismissed workers.

Finally, the LRC affiliated Mustafa as a voluntary activist promoting the right of trade unionism and the right to organize and bargain collectively in the industrial area where Euromedical (now Unomedical) is located. Although unemployed and blacklisted, she uses her energy pursuing the cause of

---

[2] In order to make the film accessible to an international audience English translations have been added. All inquiries regarding the film should be sent to Anna Diemer's home mail (anna@diemer.dk).

labor and setting an inspiring example. From her viewpoint the case is clear: "Look at Euromedical—it can be done even if it takes thirty years" (Tian Chua, interview by author, 2005).

The OECD National Contact Point in Denmark

The OECD National Contact Point, which is a tripartite body monitoring the OECD Guidelines for Multinational Enterprises, administratively linked to the Danish Ministry of Employment, agreed to handle the complaint in April 2002—the same month that Maersk Medical came up for public sale. At a meeting in January 2003 organized by the National Contact Point and its associated NGO forum, it was disclosed that nothing had happened because of a missing case number in the Malaysian legal case regarding Euromedical. In the end AIF Roskilde took action and resolved the matter in February 2003 (Flemming Carlsen, interview by author, 2006).

The complaint to the National Contact Point was finally concluded in the spring of 2005 after the Federal Court of Malaysia decided in favor of the NUECMRP. Nordic Capital informed the National Contact Point that it would comply with the order of the minister of human resources in Malaysia and initiate collective bargaining with the NUECMRP. The National Contact Point took note of the company's intention. It has no mechanism for monitoring the behavior of Unomedical's Malaysian subsidiary, but the parties of the National Contact Point can reopen the case on their own initiative if they deem it appropriate (Kontaktpunkt 2005; Ib Maltesen, interview by author, 2006). Considering that according to the LO representative, in practice "postponing labor rights is equal to denying labor rights," the Nordic companies' conduct is a breach of the core ILO convention of the right to organize and to bargain collectively (Ib Maltesen, interview by author, 2006).

Lessons Learned by Danish Campaigners

This cross-border campaign, while it involved Danish unions on the one hand and the legalistic Malaysian industrial relations and judiciary route on the other, cannot be considered a traditional global union campaign driven and run by national and international trade unions (see Tom Juravich's distinction between traditional and comprehensive strategic campaigns, chapter 1). Instead it was a broader, stakeholder-oriented campaign, which may be termed a rudimentary comprehensive strategic campaign, in which the leading role was played by what we call a labor NGO, an organization where labor activists undertook the activities of the campaign although the organization was heavily dominated by national labor unions and labor federations, along with political and community allies sympathetic to labor. This peculiarity is explained by one of the key campaigners in Denmark and chairperson of the AIF Roskilde branch, Anna Diemer:

KAD and their local union officers and shopstewards were part of the project from the very beginning, but it was very early pointed out clearly and in a proper way that it was an AIF project. It was our project. But they supported the project morally and it happened that we got a few pennies in between or help to organize a meeting in one of their rooms and whatever could be on. They backed up the project very much. And this [outcome] has some advantages and some disadvantages.... Let's say that it had been run as a KAD project or another trade union project, then the trade union has to make up its mind to what degree it wants to quarrel with its employer, its counterpart. And it is a counterpart with which it has a reasonable relationship in this country [Denmark]. How much do you want to put at risk to support some women in Malaysia? I have never asked them this question, but you have to reflect on this issue. One of the lessons experienced here is that it is benefiting the trade union and the case letting a NGO, a labor grassroots organization, running the project. Because we can put some other questions, and he [the employer] can be so furious he wants toward us, because we are not counterpart in a collective negotiation. We play another role, and we can intervene and make noise. (Anna Diemer and Christian Juhl, interview by author 2005)

Yet the disadvantage of an NGO's substituting for direct union involvement, even one as dominated by the trade unions as AIF, is that the NGO may be in a weaker position than the union. Christian Juhl, chairperson of AIF Silkeborg, describes the risk involved:

I think that there is no doubt about that if the shop stewards and the trade union have the courage, then they have more leverage. They have to tell [the employer], what the hell do you do? It's us you are working with, and we have a trade union and they must have such an organization, too. It is them who can say, so far and no longer.... However, we shall not underestimate that in such a case like this one [Maersk Medical] and probably in all cases with transnational corporations the fear of retrenchment will be huge because they offshore so much. (Anna Diemer and Christian Juhl, interview by author, 2005)

The Danish campaigners agree that if the Danish unions had participated more strongly and visibly in the campaign, the Danish side might have been able to contribute significantly to the outcome. Still, they do consider the international campaign to have been a success in Denmark as well as in Malaysia because they gained insight and they generated this insight themselves. The story is a very useful remedy against the attitude that "nothing happens"; the AIF film conveys the message that although there are victims, there are also heroes, and that it makes a difference to act locally and internationally. The involvement of both stakeholder groups—unions and NGOs—at all levels of the campaign is also in keeping with the comprehensive cross-border campaign model as outlined by Tom Juravich in chapter 1, which relies on workers and their allies in other unions and in NGOs to leverage employers by interfering with key relationships between the company decision makers, profit centers, and growth strategies, which to some degree were essential elements of the Euromedical case.

Explaining the Euromedical Case

Within Denmark, Maersk Medical complied with the Danish industrial relations model, including the acceptance of unionization and collective bargaining at its Danish subsidiaries. APM-Maersk has a blurred track record of industrial relations abroad, indicated not only by the Euromedical case but also by its disputes with American dockers, truckers, and the Teamsters union and its most recent debacle where it seized control of Khor az-Zubayr industrial harbor in Iraq, alienating both Iraqi authorities and local trade unions until it was kicked out in 2005 (Lambek 2002; Ørskov and Lambek 2003; Kaarsholm, Aagaard, and Al-Habahbeh 2005). Hence, the corporation may care about its social reputation in its home country but not abroad, and particularly not in developing countries. When Maersk Medical was taken to task in the AIF group's complaint to the OECD National Contact Point, the company announced it was up for sale. Its timing may have been coincidental; the APM-Maersk strategy for divesting its manufacturing activities and focusing its activities on shipping and oil and gas (the growth centers of APM-Maersk) was already set. Maersk Medical was considered a "loss center," marginal to the core activities of the business group. Management was unhappy about its earnings, which included an outright deficit in 2001 (Ellemose 2004, 307, 316–17). However, the direct impact of a high-profile union-busting case on the share price and its indirect impact on the corporate reputation of APM-Maersk might have created a kind of urgency or tension, activating the principle of due diligence, implying "sell now." Thus, although the Danish Malaysia Group was not consciously following a comprehensive campaign strategy, its appeal to the OECD National Contact Point was in effect interfering with the key relationship between a decision maker (APM-Maersk) and the company's overall growth strategy, which included a substrategy of divestment of business activities considered relatively unprofitable by the APM-Maersk headquarters but doing so with "due diligence," which meant obtaining the best price for these assets.

The withdrawal of Danish trade unions from direct industrial actions in support of the Euromedical workers in Malaysia, while they still supported the Danish labor NGO and its international campaign, may be conditioned by the Danish industrial relations model. Danish unions cannot take legitimate action against an employer who is complying with Danish collective agreements. Moreover the KAD, in organizing semiskilled female workers, faced a very strong business group employing workers in sectors unionized by male-dominated unions within the manufacturing sector. Together these unions were bound by an industry-wide collective agreement, in which KAD did not play the dominant role. Finally, and contrary to the tactics of the AIF, the union tactic toward APM-Maersk would be to keep the issue and bargaining outside public exposure and negotiate the case along internal lines in order to avoid the anger of APM-Maersk and secure consent for an agreement (Former KAD staffer, interview by author, 2006). The same framing by industrial relations rules and regulations also applied to the position of the LO in the OECD National Contact Point. Cases against Danish transnational corporations that comply with local laws and regulations, as Maersk Medical/Euromedical did during 1998–2002 because of the pending civil court case, are considered lost cases that do not improve the standing of the institution in the eyes of the unions, even though the exercise may be part of a learning process (Ib Maltesen, interview by author 2006).

APM-Maersk controls a very successful retail discount chain in Denmark, which has provided it with considerable profit and liquidity, enabling it to invest and acquire assets within its core business. Recently, the retail chain has been elevated to a core activity of the corporation. Targeting this cash cow (profit center) of APM-Maersk could have increased the pressure on Maersk Medical through the headquarters of APM-Maersk and affected the global corporate brand that the founding fathers of the business group continue to hold in high regard. However, a consumer campaign was never used or considered by the campaigners, although such campaigns of political consumerism have been effective in several other cases such as the Union of Needletrades, Industrial and Textile Employees UNITE's targeting of Gucci and others in the Brylane campaign (Clean Clothes Campaign 2002). As explained in chapter 1, using alliances between workers and consumer groups to interfere with relationships between key decision makers (APM-Maersk) and profit centers (discount retail chain) can be one of the most effective tools in a comprehensive campaign strategy and might have enabled the workers at Euromedical to attain victory much more quickly.

The industrial dispute could be internationalized by way of mobilizing the global union federations (GUFs) of APM-Maersk. The General Workers Union of Denmark (SID) did in fact involve the International Transport Federation (ITF) in their fight for improving working conditions of APM-Maersk employees in 2003, and ITF aired the idea of engaging APM-Maersk in negotiations and the signing of an international framework agreement (IFA) (Ørskov and Lambek 2003; for IFAs, see Tørres and Gunnes 2003). However, APM-Maersk has not entered any IFA with ITF, nor did the corporation commit itself to a code of corporate social responsibility while it controlled Euromedical (today it has taken on a code of corporate citizenship). Christian Juhl reasoned that GUFs are not strong enough to ensure transnational corporations' commitment to the IFA; the national unions in the home country of the transnational corporation's headquarters need to be the driving force. Hence, in global container shipping, where APM-Maersk is now the market leader, Denmark would be the proper place for the amalgamated United Federation of Danish Workers (3F) of KAD and SID to persuade APM-Maersk to enter an IFA with the ITF regarding transport activities. Given APM-Maersk's expansion in the retail sector, it is worth noting that IFAs on core labor rights and other issues have also been agreed upon in the food industry. The first of these was the agreement of the International Union of Food, Agricultural, Hotel, Restaurant, Catering, Tobacco and Allied Workers' Associations (IUFs) with the French global food processing firm, Danone, followed by the agreement between IUF and a regional coalition of Latin American trade unions with the U.S. company, Chiquita (see Frundt chapter 5; Riisgaard 2005).

The legalistic and proceduralistic Malaysian industrial relations framework, embedded in the overall judiciary system of the country, played a crucial role in prolonging the dispute and the final outcome at Euromedical. Hence, what mattered most was the Malaysian, not the Danish, institutions, power structure, and political-economic system. The slow working of the Malaysian system postponed and hence denied the achievement of labor rights at Euromedical for three decades, but the claims of Euromedical workers and the Malaysian union were kept on track by committed local unionists and activists. The conflict between capital and labor interests at the micro level spilled over into the local and federal level of political and judiciary power and turned into a conflict between a Malaysian minister's authority and the noncompliance of a foreign-controlled company. Moreover, the foreign company was located in an industry that was marginal compared with the strategic and foreign-owned electronics sector of Malaysia, where Malaysia's government has undertaken a policy that is extremely friendly to foreign direct investment (FDI), including measures against the formation of an electronics industrial union.

In the Euromedical case the Danish labor unions and Malaysian unions were connected by a labor NGO, which relied on the support and collaboration of the trade unions concerned. The Malaysian union and Euromedical workers fought for their labor rights in a very legally oriented industrial relations system that integrated industrial and civil law within a highly politicized judiciary system. Surprisingly, the industrial relations and civilian judiciary systems supported the union's case in the end, but only after thirty years of union activity. Hence, the industrial dispute was primarily fought and won by Malaysian organizations and institutions in what is considered a weak industrial relations system from a union perspective.

Instead of direct connection at the company industrial relations level, the Danish labor unions and labor federations took a rather passive role in the campaign as a coalition partner in a labor-dominated NGO in which local committees of trade union activists were drivers of international solidarity work like the Euromedical campaign. The relevant Danish trade unions were constrained by the comprehensive collective bargaining system covering workplaces in Denmark. Yet regardless of how the connection was made, the outcome was still the same: a labor dispute with a transnational firm required a global campaign involving a coalition of actors from labor, NGOs, and governmental organizations putting escalating pressure on multiple fronts and interfering with key relationships in the company. Facing the combined pressure of a rudimentary comprehensive strategic campaign with the transnational corporation's own strategy for disinvestment of non-core business activities, the largest Danish corporation retreated with due diligence from the Malaysian industrial dispute—a dispute that had become globalized thanks to the perseverance of trade unionists in weakly unionized Malaysia and their connections with trade unionists in strongly unionized Denmark during a critical juncture of the decade-long industrial dispute. Finally, the exit of APM-Maersk and the entrance of Nordic Capital as the owner of Euromedical transferred Euromedical from a loss center to a profit and growth center of a private equity company, whereby the industrial conflict that had been internationalized through a comprehensive campaign could put the medium-term profitability of its acquisition strategy at risk. When the legal case turned against the employer in Malaysia, the company gave in reluctantly and commenced collective bargaining.

After the successful outcome of the Euromedical campaign, the Danish trade unions closed the AIF down in April 2006. This decision was a response to increasing financial constraints due to the Danish government's reduction of grants for development education in Denmark and to declining union membership in the LO-affiliated trade unions (Rasmussen 2006). The LO wanted to make international solidarity work an integrated part of its international activities and incorporate core components of the AIF in the LO structure. Few union activists aired criticism of this decision in public, but one of them was Christian Juhl, who feared that the local solidarity work of the past twelve to fourteen years would crumble away.

In fact, the Danish trade unions did not directly take responsibility or make use of their clout to put pressure on Maersk Medical and AMP-Maersk in the Euromedical case. Although the unions now aim to enter the center stage of global labor campaigning, they may not be able to inspire the motivation, energy, and perseverance of labor NGOs like the AIF, and the dilemma of such campaigns, articulated by the chairperson of the AIF Roskilde branch, Anna Diemer, persists: "How much do you want to put at risk to support some women in Malaysia?" Or stated more generally, how do national trade unions mobilize support at all levels in the home country of transnational corporations when these corporation deny basic labor rights of employees in foreign subsidiaries while recognizing such rights for their home-country employees? The IFA mechanism of the global union federations is a relatively new device that enables international union organizations and transnational corporations to establish global codes of corporate conduct. But, as described in chapter 9, IFAs are largely ineffective if they are not actively supported by comprehensive campaigns driven by the level of commitment and cross-border networks of union activists demonstrated in the Euromedical case.

3. INDIAN LABOR LEGISLATION AND CROSS-BORDER SOLIDARITY IN HISTORICAL CONTEXT

ASHWINI SUKTHANKAR AND KEVIN KOLBEN

It has been suggested that "the history of labour legislation in India[1] is naturally interwoven with the history of British colonialism" (Mathew 2003). If that is true of the history of laws regulating workers in India, it is equally true of the history of laws and policies that not only regulate how Indian workers are able to engage with the world and how the world's workers are able to engage with India but also shape their willingness to do so. This chapter analyzes the historical and legal context and potential of cross-border organizing and international solidarity in India, with an eye to demonstrating that successful collaborations with India must be cognizant of this background. Our ultimate goal is to suggest what kinds of campaigns have succeeded and why. We propose to show by way of two case studies that narrowly tailored cooperation between allies in the Global North and Indian partners can be successful when there is direct engagement and when competing and complementary interests are carefully defined and negotiated.

We begin by analyzing colonial attempts to regulate the welfare and duties of Indian workers, in the context of often conflicting interests, including workers and employers in Britain, employers in India, and indigenous and white workers encountered by Indians who migrated in search of employment. We believe that this is a useful process for two reasons. First, a precise examination of the racism, exclusions, and differential treatment practiced in that period

---

[1] We use "India" here, even though the historical portion of this chapter is concerned with a larger geographic entity coterminous with British India and thus including today's Pakistan and Bangladesh. For reasons of space, we cannot address in any depth the contemporary legislation and policies of other countries in the region.

encourages a more nuanced understanding of particular areas where the Indian labor movement today may express real cynicism about international solidarity, whether expressed through trade-labor linkages or by pressuring brands through a discourse on corporate social responsibility. Second, the legal system that governs these same issues today is very much an inherited framework. The occasional, rarely implemented, amendments that are made to these laws are for the most part much less relevant than the preceding two centuries of remarkably unaltered policy and practice. It is therefore important to understand the historical context within which contemporary legislation was created.

In the second part of this chapter, we use two brief case studies to illustrate recent instances of cross-border collaboration linked specifically to one brand: Hindustan Lever Limited (HLL), a subsidiary of Unilever. We focus on HLL because it is one of the few Indian employers that have been subject to cross-border campaigns developed with real input from Indian workers and unions, rather than through the imposition of discourses and strategies from unions in the Global North. We believe that case studies such as those in this chapter, as well as the historical analysis preceding them, should assist all of us in developing a set of conclusions regarding best practices for labor movements in India and their potential allies as they engage with each other, in older as well as emerging industries.

Indian Workers and State Regulation: A Brief History of Laws, Policies, and Practice

We begin our analysis in the mid-nineteenth century. Until 1858, the East India Company exercised primary control over the subcontinent. We address this historical period for two reasons. First, looking at the position of workers within what can be considered the world's first transnational firm illustrates instances of worker resistance that are instructive for contemporary industry- and company-specific campaigns. Second, it is interesting to note that even then, labor struggles had to have a cross-border consciousness, given that many decisions that directly affected workers' lives were made by actors in imperial Britain.

Legislation, to the extent that there was any, was one example. The British colonial regime was the pioneer of at least two of the policies that have been the central focus of many cross-border campaigns. First, it introduced the idea that labor policy should be determined "locally" while much else, from productivity standards to quality standards, could be uniform across operations. The central focus of imperial legislation, at this point, was primarily on promoting security of investment through rule making about contracts and property rights. There was, as M.R. Anderson describes it, "a stubborn refusal of the legal establishment to recognize worker welfare as an object of state concern" (1993, 91). These legislative priorities were justified on the basis of the questionable argument that while labor relations were already integrated within traditional systems of caste, religion, etc. that ought not to be disrupted, there were no preexisting norms or practices surrounding contract and property rights (as imperial Britain chose to understand them).

An example of imperial Britain's exploitation of the local/universal division was its development of the reprehensible idea of "statute labor." Here colonial authorities could order their subjects to perform public works, ranging from military transport to the construction of roads, entirely without compensation, on the basis of the principle that indigenous rulers also demanded uncompensated work in the name of the public good. Colonial powers, while extracting benefit from the system, still organized it through traditional intermediaries. Thus, legislation such as the Madras Compulsory Labour Act of 1858 states that "any person bound by ... [local] custom to contribute labour" would be fined for refusal, and anyone refusing to work on the order of the village head in an emergency would be fined or imprisoned (Anderson 1993, 98–99). This is particularly noteworthy since the British Empire had, in 1833, abolished slavery in all colonies except those in the possession of the East India Company.

Second, and closely related, is the practice of subcontracting, which has emerged as a major global labor-rights issue. Imperial Britain co-opted the indigenous *sardari* labor system, in which numerous subcontractors recruited, managed, and paid the workers. But in applying it to mines and plantations, imperial Britain utilized it to an extent and at a scale previously unknown. From the earliest years of imperial Britain's version of this practice, workers voiced opposition to rule by an absent and therefore unaccountable employer. They called for more direct engagement with the imperial employer, and though direct protests were relatively unsuccessful, the strategy is noteworthy. Workers argued that if the imperial regime's mission was, at least in part, to "civilize" and protect the exploited, then it should critique exploitative labor practices rather than benefit from them.

The transfer of authority from the East India Company to the British Crown in 1858 did not interrupt or redirect a regulatory approach that focused on the protection of contract and property rights yet avoided the regulation of the employment relationship. For example, the first piece of legislation enacted after the transition was the Workmen's Breach of Contract Act of 1859, which imposed criminal penalties for breach of an employment contract. This preceded by over fifty years the passage of protective legislation that addressed employment security or wage fixation (ILO 1996).

The state's lack of interest in worker welfare was not confined to its colonies. In Britain, criminal penalties for contract breach were still in force through the Master and Servant Act. That law would be repealed in 1875, while India had to wait another fifty years for repeal of the Breach of Contract Act. This comparison between workers in imperial Britain and workers in British India is crucial because it demonstrates how the interests of workers in Britain and workers in British India sometimes coincided and sometimes diverged when confronted with British labor policies. It would be a mistake to assume that the interests of British workers and the British state were always the same, just as it would be to assume that the interests of British and Indian workers were the same.

Late colonialism finally brought a number of pieces of ostensibly protective legislation for workers in India. However, upon closer inspection these were complicated by somewhat less benign motivations. First, as employers' complaints of labor shortages grew, there was grudging recognition of the need for regulations that would ensure a steady, stable supply of workers, both within India and in other colonies. Second, the rise of industrialization in India, especially the textile industry, prompted British industrialists such as cotton-weaving interests in Lancashire and the workers in those industries to complain that Indian industry, with its reliance on long hours of toil by women and children, had an unfair advantage. In response, Britain set up a Factory Commission, whose report resulted in the Factories Act of 1881, which limited the hours of work for women and children in large operations using mechanical power. Explicitly excluded from the reach of the law were sites producing raw materials to be used in British industries—plantations and mines—where the British had an incentive to keep costs low.

An examination of the regulation of Indian workers abroad also sheds light on the contradiction between seemingly protective legislation and its more complicated motivations. Indentured Indian laborers had been traveling to former slave-holding colonies such as British Guiana, Jamaica, and Trinidad ever since the abolition of slavery (Mohapatra 2006). For several decades these workers were regulated only through the so-called coolie ordinances passed in the receiving colonies in the 1840s, which imposed criminal penalties of imprisonment and fines for breach of contract by the worker, although not by the employer. The employers complained that the absence of similar legislation in India allowed workers to break their contracts and attempt to renegotiate them with impunity before departure for the colonies. The legislation drafted in India in the 1860s to supplement the colonial ordinances addressed criminal penalties in India for breach *before* departure for the plantations and also began imposing tentative, though minor, obligations on employers and recruiters in terms of conditions of employment.

It should also be noted, however, that while there were significant protectionist and proemployer motivations behind the early labor legislation, greater regulation of the workplace was desperately sought by workers. For example, over five thousand organized workers from the Bombay mills presented a petition to the Factories Commission in 1889 demanding that the law be amended to provide for even greater protections such as shorter hours, holidays, meal breaks, and injury compensation, and that it apply to all workers, not just women and children (Anderson 1993, 115).

Similarly, in the 1880s, Indian workers in the West Indies began asserting demands, not for an end to the exploitative indenture system but for greater regulation of it. Specifically, they asked the colonial government to legally provide for the retention and settlement of workers rather than their repatriation, allowing them to live and work in their host country indefinitely.

The reaction from the colonial authorities to the demands for retention reinforced these conflicting interests in ways that exemplified British policies of "divide and conquer," exploiting the economic fears of local workers to create distinct categories that were easier to control. In 1880, British Guiana barred Indian workers from engaging in any other form of labor except on sugar plantations; in Australia in 1884, the state of Queensland blocked the participation of Indians in any form of skilled labor; in the 1890s, Natal Province in South Africa created a formal, unequal status for Indian workers who had stayed after the end of their contract of indenture, with measures that included the imposition of a special tax (Mohapatra 2006). Through these policies, the colonial legal regime managed conflict between workers and their interests while limiting the possibility of the emergence of solidarity. The colonial regime also took deliberate measures to thwart solidarity, as we see in the creation of laws and policies that were not racial on their face but placed restrictions on international unions, sympathy strikes, secondary boycotts, and other measures by which workers in different legal jurisdictions could support one another. There is a tension between these policies and the central role of imperial Britain, as well as British India, in founding the International Labor Organization (ILO) in 1919, given that the ILO was intended to promote the international harmonization of labor law as well as dialogue between worker groups.

Imperial Britain's reluctance to change its divisive and opportunistic labor policies in India played a part in fundamentally compromising both of these goals. With respect to the first of these, membership in the ILO brought pressure to bear on imperial Britain to reform the colonial regime's labor regulations and to bring them into conformity with ILO conventions. Yet much of the pressure related to the vital issues of work hours and the labor of women and children—already a point of conflict at the level of the Factories Acts, as we have described—was deflected by imperial Britain's insistence on limiting language in the text of the conventions.

Looking at conventions passed during 1919, the ILO's first year, illustrates this. Convention 1, Hours of Work (Industry), extended the protection of a sixty-hour workweek to certain specified Indian industries but stated that "[i]n other respects the provisions of this Convention shall not apply to India" (article 10). The now-defunct Night Work (Women) Convention (convention 4) provided for suspension of the provisions restricting women's late-night work for British India, as required. The Minimum Age (Industry) Convention (convention 5) and Night Work of Young Persons (Industry) Convention (convention 6) offered substantially truncated protections for Indian children, covering a smaller set of industries deemed to be particularly hazardous and only younger children (ILOLEX 2006).

These special exceptions within conventions that were intended to be universal should serve to remind potential allies of the Indian labor movement that there is historical cause for doubting the sincerity with which the West develops and deploys international norms. The failure to take this history into account contributed to the lack of cooperation around such issues as the inclusion of the workers' rights clause in the World Trade Organization (WTO) and other initiatives that called for compliance with universal standards, such as antisweatshop campaigns. For example, as one Indian opponent of the workers' rights clause described it, the lack of transparent debate over what constituted core or minimum labor standards that would have to be complied with, and western activists' "assumption of universality" with respect to those standards, resulted in a widespread perception that the West was simply continuing to propagate systems that were secretly skewed in its own favor. As a result, "[a]s long as symmetry of obligations does not exist in the proposed social clause, the moral argument will remain one-sided and opposition to it undiminished" (Chaulia 2002).

With respect to the second issue—increased dialogue between worker groups through the ILO—differential treatment by imperial Britain played in a role in stunting the development of any solidarity between British unions and Indian workers. Forging solidarity proved difficult in part because the perceived economic interests of many British workers were closely allied to the protectionist interests of British industry and the trade agenda of the imperial British state. The differential treatment of agriculture on the one hand and textiles and steel on the other is one example. The colonial regime continued to avoid protections for Indian workers in agriculture while responding to demands for further reductions in unfair competition from "sweated labor" in textile and steel from a British union movement with increasing political and membership strength. British unions demanded that the excise duty on Indian cotton textile manufacturers not be lifted and urged that if it were, it would have to be replaced by "countervailing labour legislation" (Gupta 2002, 42).[2] The British unions were largely silent about poverty-level wages and harsh conditions on Indian cotton plantations, however, since as noted before there was a significant

---

[2]   A countervailing duty is a duty placed on an import that has received an illegal subsidy from the exporting country.

interest in keeping prices low for the raw materials required for the Lancashire weaving mills. In any case, the excise duties on Indian textile exports remained, and little happened in the sphere of labor legislation, since trade barriers were already doing the relevant work of protecting British economic interests.

Trade barriers and labor legislation were mobilized in basically interchangeable ways by imperial Britain during this period; the Indian labor movement has thus had many years to question the operation of overt and covert linkage— particularly in textile production, as noted above. The relative lack of support in India for the antisweatshop campaigns of the 1990s, with their focus on garments and textiles, was one example of resistance to an analysis focusing on export production and trade relationships to advance labor rights. The veiled or overt references to the "unfair competitive advantage" of countries with low labor standards in the sector were also not helpful, and proposals from the Global North for collaboration in this sector were generally met with demands that northern groups also take a position on restricted access to northern markets for Indian goods through the operation of tariffs and quotas. However, NGOs and unions were by and large reluctant to do so and were also reluctant to give up on the sweeping rhetoric of the anti-antisweatshop campaigns in favor of more narrow, negotiated bases for a shared platform that would have acknowledged the shared interest in supporting organizing and unions in India.[3]

The passage of the Indian Trade Unions Act (1926), which is still on the books today, marked a turning point in Indian and British trade union cooperation. In 1921, The British Trades Union Congress (TUC) proposed that Indian labor regulation be amended to grant Indian unions immunity from prosecution for certain industrial actions, legislation similar to what already existed in Britain (Gupta 2002, 48). This was, in part, in response to an appeal from the Madras Textile Labor Union, whose leaders were facing prosecution for interference with employment contracts between the owner of Binny & Co. and his employees (Misra 2002, 43). The British India office opposed such legislative protections for trade union activity on the grounds that picketing ought to remain illegal because in India it was indistinguishable from a boycott for political (usually nationalist) motives (Gupta 2002, 48). Ultimately, with support from the British unions and in the face of strong resistance from employers of Indian workers, the Trade Unions Act was passed in 1926. That year marked another important labor law reform, the repeal of the Workmen's Breach of Contract Act, finally bringing an end to the criminal penalties for breach of employment contract that the TUC and the Indians had lobbied against for years.

---

[3] Conclusions based on conversations with Indian labor-rights activists and trade unionists Gayatri Singh and Apoorva Kaiwar, Girni Kamgar Sangharsh Samiti; Mohan Mani and Gautam Mody, New Trade Union Initiative; J. John, Centre for Education and Communication (2002–3).

But the relationship between British and Indian unions was also subject to disagreement and tension, particularly surrounding issues of national self-determination. At the same time as the passage of the Trade Unions Act, the All-India Trade Union Congress (AITUC) approached the TUC for organizers from four British industries to come and work in India for one year each, to train local organizers and share industry-specific expertise. The TUC rejected the proposal, however, on the grounds that it would be "too expensive" (Gupta 2002, 109). But there were at least two other reasons for the TUC's hesitation to lend tangible support to an organization, such as the AITUC, that explicitly called for Indian self-determination. Some of this hesitation from British unionists came from self-proclaimed imperialists, while others opposed "home rule" for India on the grounds that it would not be in the interest of the Indian working class, which would be as powerless as ever when the upper-middle-class nationalists took over from the British.

Some also argue that solidarity between British unions and Indian workers during this period was reliable only when it came to core workplace issues, such as those that led to the passage of the Trade Unions Act. These included criminal and civil penalties for trade union activity and the use of violence in strike breaking. However, dialogue and cooperation were much less robust when it came to negotiating the broader processes of industrialization in India, for these issues potentially placed British jobs in jeopardy through the threat of increased competition with Indian workers.

This is not to say that all solidarity relationships require broad, unconditional acceptance of an ally's full agenda. However, it is necessary to emphasize an issue that has been clear to the Indian labor movement for a long time: the distinction between narrowly defined solidarity that comes at minimal cost to the supporting union and a more profound solidarity that requires compromise and sacrifice of real interests. The distinction is all too rarely made explicit, and Indian unions have argued, with some justification, that the former type of solidarity (useful in its own right) frequently masquerades as the latter, as in the case of the garment industry campaigns.

In the late 1920s, two major debates took place that had serious bearing on the ability of workers to engage in cross-border activities. The first ultimately led to the restriction of sympathy and general strikes. In 1928, several industries in India, including the railways, ironworks, and textiles, experienced a series of crippling strikes that resulted in the loss of millions of work hours. The Royal Commission on Labour, a group of five Indians and six Britons brought together in part to analyze the phenomenon and propose reforms at the level of law and policy, was in general very sympathetic to Indian labor, arguing, among other things, that the Trade Unions Act should be amended to require employers to bargain with registered unions. However, on two issues central to the legislative framework for cross-border solidarity there was much greater ambivalence. When addressing the rash of strikes, the commission speculated that at least some had been organized by nationalist leaders, were prompted by the spread of Communism, or had been instigated by those seeking to influence the commodities or share markets. The commission applied the distinction that the British Trade Disputes Act of 1927 had just drawn between "acceptable" actions, designed to advance workers' own economic interests, and "unacceptable" actions, taken for the interests of other workers or other movements through general strikes and sympathy strikes, which were outlawed. Compared with the rate at which labor-related norms generally flowed from Britain to its colonies, this one traveled with great speed. The Trade Disputes Act of 1929, like the British law, banned general strikes and sympathy strikes in India. The commission—and, in turn, the legislation that was its outcome—thus took a position against one of the most crucial strategies of cross-border worker support, since industrial action to bolster workers' struggles in a different legal jurisdiction, even if those workers had the same employer, was now barred (Royal Labour Commission 1929, chap. 18).

The other contentious issue addressed by the commission was the question of whether working conditions in India ought to be prescribed by statutory means, as advocated by proworker commissioners, or through voluntary action. The commissioners who proposed more extensive regulation were running counter to a long history of minimal protective labor legislation for British India. The Trade Disputes Act of 1929, which regulated labor relations and dispute settlement, was one of the areas of compromise in that debate. In order to reduce the number of strikes taking place in India, the act required that all industrial disputes be settled through conciliation and private arbitration, minimizing the role of the judiciary. The basic framework of this act survives into the present as the Industrial Disputes Act of 1947.

This issue is relevant to contemporary questions of cross-border organizing that rely on appeals to corporate social responsibility (CSR), such as codes of conduct. It would be difficult to grasp the specific contours of Indian unions' general distrust of private or voluntary mechanisms, which have played a significant role in cross-border organizing strategies in recent years (given the lack of accommodation for international solidarity action in most domestic labor law regimes), without understanding this background. It is important to keep in mind the particular resonance that calls for CSR have in the Indian context, where protective labor legislation was the result of hard-fought battles against both Indian employers and colonial interests.

The culminating event of the late 1920s with respect to cross-border solidarity was the beginning of the Meerut Conspiracy Trials. Three British unionists who were working in the Indian union movement and twenty-four Indian unionists were tried on charges of attempting to "deprive the King Emperor of his sovereignty of British India" under section 121A of the Indian Penal Code

(IPC) by, in part, being linked to the Communist International and organizing trade union activity (Noorani 2005). While the Trade Unions Act of 1926 had afforded unions and union leaders some protection from section 120 of the IPC, which addresses criminal conspiracy, it did not provide immunity from laws of sedition as the British Trade Unions Act of 1906 did. In fact, the court explicitly cited the "internationalism" of the efforts as evidence of sedition. The Meerut case is generally read as holding that Indian unions are creatures of the state and that by accepting cross-border support they assert a challenge to state sovereignty. The principle survives in contemporary rules restricting Indian trade unions from accepting funds from foreign donors.

The TUC was at that time unable to reach agreement within itself about how to support the unions crippled by the Meerut Conspiracy Trials and was not able to develop a uniform position on supporting or opposing the three-year boycott of British textiles by Indian unions and nationalists that eventually ended in 1931, and that had proved ruinous to British manufacturers and workers since India was a primary market. But in the process, the TUC began to arrive at a principled set of resolutions about solidarity with Indian workers. In 1932, British steelworker and textile union leaders began to reorganize the industry, rather than join with employers in continued lobbying against the Indian competition. With respect to steel, for example, there was recognition that even if the import of Indian pig iron resulted in loss of employment in Scottish ironworks, it increased employment with steel-plate manufacturers (Gupta 2002, 229).

The regulation of Indians working abroad during the period after the First World War also shows how colonial law intervened to inhibit cross-border solidarity in ways that have certainly left their mark. The story of Indian Tamil workers who were imported to Ceylon, now Sri Lanka, from the 1860s onward to work on the tea plantations is a case in point. Imperial Britain, though ruling both Ceylon and India as Crown colonies, justified different regulations for tea plantation workers in the two regions. As articulated by Victor Sassoon of the Royal Commission on Labour, it was justifiable to set minimum wage levels in Ceylon so that the government of India could be satisfied about the well-being of Indian migrant workers abroad, but no such guarantees were required for the migrant workers who were recruited for the Assam tea estates in the Northeast, since "this province and the areas from which the Assam tea industry draws its labour force are both under the Central Government of India" (Sassoon 1929). As noted above, uniform legal protections had been a key demand of Indian workers, who pointed to the availability of certain protections for workers traveling abroad.

Reliance on sometimes arbitrary political borders to contain, discipline, and segregate workers was central to the colonial strategy, as was the use of restrictions on citizenship and franchise. Thus, for example, during the mid-1930s, as the price of tea was falling and radical union activists from India were making inroads into the plantations, defying the trespass laws intended to keep them out, the colonial office announced at the behest of the planters that Indian Tamils had status in Ceylon only so long as they were employed. If they were not, then they would have to return to India. Postindependence Sri Lanka has continued to try to control the so-called estate Tamils this way—revoking citizenship, negotiating the repatriation of more than two hundred thousand to India, and so on. The unintended consequence has been to reinforce the ties between Tamils in Sri Lanka and Tamils in India, and this connection has been the core of the campaign for justice for workers on tea plantations around the world, as we describe at length below.

Another important factor in shaping cross-border organizing strategies is the politics of migration. In South Africa and other regions of the empire with white settlers, the end of indenture in 1920 was intended, in part, to freeze the rising Indian population, which was by and large refusing repatriation at the end of the indenture period. This created a new source of anxiety about competition from postindenture Indian workers. Not only did white unions not challenge the "color bar" that ensured them a monopoly on skilled jobs, but they did not support nonwhite workers in their acts of labor militancy, uneasy perhaps about the relationship to racial militancy (Mantzaris 1995). British unions were reluctant to intervene in the racial politics of South African labor. Thus, at the first Commonwealth Labour Conference in 1924, the South African Labour Party sent a white-only union, and the TUC failed to object.

The exclusion and discrimination experienced by indentured and post-indenture workers helped to create a unified category of racially oppressed Indian workers across a wide geographic area, offering Indian unions a motivation for cross-border mobilization and solidarity. At the 1924 conference, for example, the AITUC raised the issue of Indian labor in the colonies and was alone in attacking the South African union that was present for being unrepresentative of the Indian workforce. The AITUC proposed a joint conference with the South African Labor Party to discuss the status of Indian workers in South Africa, but the offer was rejected.[4]

Over these last pages, we have tried to highlight particular elements of the colonial effort to regulate Indian labor and laborers in ways that often served to privilege the economic interests of the British state, its employers, and/or its workers. These regulations also, sometimes incidentally, discouraged solidarity between Indian workers and their foreign counterparts. In this discussion our goal was not to provide a checklist of steps and missteps for potential allies of Indian labor seeking to forge successful cross-border union campaigns. Rather,

---

[4]   Some of the connections between unions in India and Indian workers' unions in South Africa have been explored through histories of M. K. Gandhi, who attempted to develop and promote an understanding of the similar conditions faced by low-wage Indian laborers across the colonies under colonial rule and rule making.

our aim was to examine through a narrative history the numerous ways in which the period of colonial rule, and its legacy of legislation, policy, and experience, has helped shape Indian labor movements and their attitude toward solidarity. In order to illustrate the contemporary relevance of the insights gleaned from this history, we have developed two case studies describing recent cross-border collaborations, based primarily on reports produced by Indian and international NGOs and supplemented by our own knowledge of and involvement in these campaigns. Both involve one particular Indian company with transnational links, Hindustan Lever Ltd.

Challenging "Backdoor Labor Reforms" at Hindustan Lever

A 51 percent-owned Indian subsidiary of the Anglo-Dutch Unilever, HLL is India's largest manufacturer of fast-moving consumer goods (FMCGs), such as shampoo, detergent, toothpaste, shaving cream, and soap. After a merger with Brooke Bond Lipton in 1996, HLL also became the largest producer of tea in India and the largest company in the Indian private sector as measured by market capitalization (Banaji 1996, 191). Of the two case histories that follow, the first analyzes the long-standing dispute between HLL and its employee unions at manufacturing facilities for FMCGs, particularly with respect to employment practices and trade union rights. The cross-border support in that instance involved interventions by the international affairs arm of the Dutch union federation, Federatie Nederlandse Vakbeweging (FNV), as part of its broader efforts to bring targeted pressure to bear on Dutch transnational firms. In our second case study, we discuss the role of Indian activists in a collaborative effort targeting Unilever in its capacity as the world's largest tea company. In this example, Indian and international unions, as well as NGOs, came together to confront the impact of the radical fall in tea prices on the world commodities market and to analyze the responsibility of brands to address the devastation of tea plantation workers.

Our case studies suggest that contemporary campaigns are rarely concerned with questions of legal compliance. As was true in the colonial period, the looming issues are of employers exploiting the *gaps* in legislation. Years of policy and practice may sometimes dovetail with and at other times conflict with the law, but it is the practice on which we will focus; in that respect, much of the practice of contemporary employers will be resonant with the historical narrative.

The practices of HLL that became the target of international campaigns took place in this context, a multiplicity of gaps within a legislative framework that has, in any case, failed to keep pace with changing economic realities. Thus, the unions focused less on HLL's defiance of labor law than on the company's attempts to achieve what Rob Jenkins (2000) has called "'back door' labour reform." He notes, with respect to HLL, three particular strategies: the use of voluntary retirement schemes (VRS), the substitution of regular workers with contract workers, and the shifting of production from strongly unionized facilities to others that do not fall under the coverage of the Industrial Disputes Act (IDA) in a move that was claimed to be part of a larger "corporate restructuring" process (193). We would add another strategy to this set—that of not bargaining with or even acknowledging the industry-wide All-India Council of Unilever Unions but dealing only at the level of individual plants, if at all.[5] We will address each of these in order.

Under the VRS process employees continue to receive the bulk of their salary if they agree to retire early. Initially developed by the government in the 1980s to increase productivity in public-sector undertakings where technology was reducing the need for labor, the VRS process is increasingly being used by private enterprises following the institution in 1991 of the "new economic policies" in the context of restrictions in the IDA on layoffs and retrenchment. Access to voluntary retirement is not a matter of right for employees but is offered selectively by the employer to categories of workers, who technically have the right of refusal. However, in the face of verbal threats to close facilities and/or shift workers to other facilities, the degree of volition has often been in question, and HLL, like a number of other companies, has thus been able to use VRS to whittle down its unions.

HLL has also replaced large numbers of regular workers with contract workers, either on fixed daily wages or on project-based contracts with a lump sum payable at the end of the project. Furthermore, since establishments and contractors employing fewer than twenty contract workers escape legislative scrutiny,[6] HLL, like many other employers, has engaged with multiple subcontractors, each employing no more than eighteen or nineteen workers. This strategy, strongly reminiscent of the colonial use of multiple labor recruiters and managers, has also reduced union strength in key facilities in cities such as Bombay and Calcutta.

The shifting of production to rural areas, taking advantage of tax breaks and government subsidies while escaping unions, has been somewhat easier to challenge, with some industrial courts and high courts willing to assert that even if moving production is a standard "managerial function," notice to workers is still required under the IDA (Hindustan Lever Employees Union

---

[5] The Trade Unions Act does not require an employer to bargain with a recognized union.

[6] The Contract Labour (Regulation and Abolition) Act of 1970 places restrictions on the contracting out of labor, forces employers to register their workers, and requires them to provide access to government inspectors. However, as noted, the act applies only to employers with twenty workers or more.

2005). In general, however, there has been little questioning. While some have criticized the company's unions, including Bombay's Hindustan Lever Employees Union (HLEU),[7] for some amount of apathy and paralysis with respect to organizing relocated facilities and subcontracted workers (Sherlock 2001, 161), it is important to recognize the long history of policies that have permitted and framed the practice of subcontracting. From the perspective of workers there is not much of a distinction between subcontracted labor and subcontracted production. The strategy chosen by the unions—of opposition and protest and of insistence on a direct relationship rather than accepting indirect management—must be read in the context of a long history of indirect labor management in India and of the experienced futility of dealing with ever-shifting intermediaries. Successful support efforts have understood the salience of this trade union priority and have identified the core problem: that HLL refuses to negotiate its labor issues on a national level and will bargain only at the level of individual units. This is so, even though Unilever encourages national bargaining in most of the countries where it operates (ExpressTextile 2004).

Indeed, one of the peculiarities of transnational firms dealing with India is the extent to which colonial Britain's practice of considering labor policy intensely local and governed by local rules continues to govern labor relations. While, as FNV chairman Lodewijk de Waal noted, there is nothing noteworthy today about the fact that " [a]t McDonalds, the recipe for ketchup is laid down by headquarters, but the personnel policy is a local matter" (*FNV Company Monitor* 2003, 5), the distinction is exaggerated in India, where the accretion of centuries of practice in this regard has meant that companies routinely expect minimal opposition. At the same time, certain disciplinary/labor control policies are also proliferating as part of global policymaking, as FNV notes of Unilever, among other Dutch companies: "In recent years, the companies have divested themselves of a large number of units and then proceeded to recontract them. The same applies to the workers: greater use is made of temporary personnel, who have far fewer rights and lower wages than the permanent staff" (10).

As Bennet D'Costa of the HLEU noted, the result is that labor conditions are worse than they were in earlier years of the company's functioning. "If a worker has a problem on the shop floor and it can't be solved, then he takes it to the factory manager, who now has only as much power as the worker used to have. He merely carries out instructions and no longer takes decisions. For

---

[7]   India's trade union movement is made up primarily of five major trade union centers that are affiliated, or closely associated, with political parties. There are also smaller independent unions, such as HLEU in Bombay, which are not affiliated with political parties. The recently-formed New Trade Union Initiative (NTUI) has begun to serve as a coalition of many of these independent trade unions.

that, you have to go to the international management.... In the days when we took our problems to the factory manager, it wasn't as an individual.... But a local union nowadays has only as much power as the individual worker used to in the old days" (*FNV Company Monitor* 2003, 19). The HLEU concluded, then, that global organizing was the only way to counter the globalization of control, with the intermediate goal of organizing bargaining at the national level in India.

This was not the first time that HLEU had articulated the need for a single unified body that could bargain for workers across all the Indian units. Comparing the situation of workers within HLL to those at an Indian firm, the HLEU's Ramanathan noted in 1987,

> Look at TOMCO (The Tata Oil Mills Company) which is HLL's nearest competitor in the consumer goods market. Our turnover is three times that of TOMCO, employee strength almost double, profits ten times higher and per-employee profitability nearly five times that of TOMCO. And yet our salaries are lower than those of our counterparts there. This is because TOMCO employees have a single unified federation as a combined union to fight for its rights. (Rajabali 1987).

In any case, FNV's solidarity efforts did not impose an international agenda on HLEU but sought to internationalize long-standing local and national campaigns. Pushing for national-level bargaining became the core of FNV's support for workers at HLL, picking up on workers' own demands that dealings happen through the All India Council of Unilever Unions. Earlier cross-border support, including that initiated by the global union federation (GUF), the International Union of Food, Agricultural, Hotel, Restaurant, Catering, Tobacco and Allied Workers' Associations (IUF), had focused on support for individual unions through lockouts and strikes and had achieved much, though little at the big-picture level where Indian workers were concerned.[8] FNV saw that it had leverage, however, through the discovery of pervasive child labor in cottonseed production in agricultural facilities partly owned by HLL in the state of Andhra Pradesh. The Dutch federation met repeatedly with Unilever to discuss the issue, along with Dutch NGOs such as the India Committee of the Netherlands. FNV used the child labor issue to press Unilever on issues that it saw as more fundamental, such as the need for national-level bargaining as a systemic solution for child labor and other concerns.

---

[8]   Interestingly, IUF had mobilized a significant campaign against Unilever in the late 1980s when the company was closing plants and moving production out of Europe. The IUF had attempted to force the company to negotiate with international, not just national, unions. However, Unilever argued that it had no legal obligation to recognize the GUF and refused to do so (Lamb and Percy 1987).

The insistence of HLL on a strategy of dividing and segregating workers is strongly reminiscent of colonial practices that mobilized unrelated or arbitrary categories, such as race, to prevent workers from coming together. The Indian firm TOMCO's willingness to engage in national-level bargaining was hardly an instance of nationalist resistance to colonial practice. However, HLL's purchase of TOMCO in 1993, leading to further deterioration of labor standards in the sector, is certainly an example of the ways in which colonial experiments in labor management expanded in India and around the world, overwhelming and co-opting alternatives.

Recent debates in India about the ability of CSR initiatives to effect change for Indian workers seem to echo colonial-era conversations comparing the benefit of voluntary initiatives by employers with regulation by the state. The skepticism of many Indians is further nuanced by the memory of protectionist motives in colonial-era cross-border appeals citing the interests of Indian workers, as well as more contemporary and universal fears that CSR, as a discourse, is all too often offered as an alternative to unionization. As Bennet D'Costa has suggested, in contrast to worker organizing, "culturally ... and ideologically biased" elements of CSR merely "burnish a company's reputation in the eyes of insufficiently informed Western consumers" (Bais 2005, 14). However, in this instance the FNV approach mobilized incidents of child labor, a hot-button issue for western consumers, to address the agenda of Indian unions, rather than simply acceding to the interests of unions in the West that had frequently used stories of third-world child labor to advance narrow protectionist interests.

Despite FNV's support, HLEU was not successful. While HLL pulled out of the cottonseed venture in Andhra Pradesh, there was little progress on the issues of trade union rights, outsourcing, and subcontracting. According to the mainstream press, the outcome of the conversations between FNV and HLL was, ultimately, that the latter "agreed to disagree" with the suggestion that union and labor issues should be negotiated on a national level and asserted that it would merely "follow the legal norm with respect to outsourcing and subcontracting" (ExpressTextile 2004).

However, in other ways, the campaign had marked outcomes. For the Indian unions at HLL facilities, as well as for FNV, it produced a different perspective on international collaboration. HLEU was one of the very few unions to break with the rest of the Indian labor movement and tentatively support the idea of a social clause in the WTO, in part because of the degree of trust that had developed and the emerging sense that first-world unions could actually exert themselves for the genuine interests of third-world workers. HLEU, in turn, has developed into one of the key players in the World Wide Network of Unilever Unions, participating in the shaping of multilateral strategies rather than simple two-way relationships.

Crisis in the Tea Industry

Our second case study takes place in the context of commodity price manipulation by brands in the tea industry. Initially, vertical integration in tea production made such manipulation possible: Thomas Lipton, who pioneered the marketing of tea to the middle classes, bought estates in Ceylon in 1890 and engaged in the preparation, shipping, and packaging of the tea himself. Unilever bought Lipton in 1930 and in the process refined and expanded the model considerably. The total control of production and distribution was temporarily disrupted in Sri Lanka when the plantations were nationalized in 1975. Under pressure from international financial institutions, however, the plantations were privatized in 1992, and Unilever Ceylon led the way in promoting many of the subsequent erosions in worker welfare documented by local activists: the privatization of social security for plantation workers, resulting in reduced or eliminated benefits, "premature retirement" (similar to VRS in India, described above), and casualization through subcontracting (Centre for Education and Communication 2005a, 47).

There were numerous similarities between the structure of the tea industry in Sri Lanka and that in South India, including the central role of the domestic Unilever subsidies in their respective contexts, as explained in detail below. Furthermore, the fact that Unilever's various tea brands were cooperating at the international level to depress commodity prices (while keeping retail prices high) made the company a natural target for campaigns in tea-producing countries where, as a labor-support NGO in India phrased it, "there is disintegration and disengagement at the plantation level and consolidation at the brand level" (Centre for Education and Communication 2005b).

In considering the conditions for tea plantation workers in India, it is worth exploring the specifics of a background that includes the usual tale of outdated and poorly enforced legislation. The Plantation Labour Act of 1951 provides for very minor fines for the violation of its provisions on health and safety, social welfare, facilities, etc., and contains no provision for limitations on child labor, except to note that children must have a certificate of fitness in order to work. But law, as is often the case in India, plays only a small part in the story. Child labor on tea plantations is certainly a part of the legacy of colonial patterns of recruitment; in Assam, in the northeast, which produces more than half of the tea grown in India today, workers are the descendants of indentured migrants from central India, who were brought to the region in the late nineteenth century with their families and housed on the estates. Then, as now, the entire family is involved in the work. There are high levels of unionization in the tea plantations of the Northeast, but given the restrictions on workers' mobility and contact with each other and the feudal relationships that prevail, workers have seen few benefits of union membership.

In the plantations of South India, the workers are Tamils whose families also moved there when the plantations were British-owned, as is the case with the Sri Lankan plantations. Unions were much stronger in the south of India than elsewhere in the country, and higher prevailing wages there had been at the heart of the Northeast workers' campaign for wage increases. Until 2003, workers in the South received the equivalent of $1.80 per day, compared with U$1.00 in the Northeast; however, plantation owners in the Nilgiri Hills in the South, citing adverse market conditions, were able to negotiate wages down by an average of 10 percent, as well as higher leaf-plucking quotas (Devraj 2003). South Indian unions were thus faced with the prospect of leading a race to the bottom, and they began the process of identifying targets against whom to launch a counterattack. HLL had long been a key player, even at the level of plantations, continuing to either own or control several in the South. It had been centrally involved in the process of wage erosion, having served notice to workers at one of its estates that wages would be reduced still further, to the equivalent of $1.30 and that there would be penalties for failing to meet quotas (Devraj 2003).

Unilever tried to use some of the colonial strategies of divide and conquer through its subsidiaries in the tea-producing former colonies. In 1998, workers in Sri Lanka mobilized against the changes brought by privatization, with a massive strike that led to a collective agreement that workers would be guaranteed three hundred days of work per year and that their wages would be increased after two years (Centre for Education and Communication 2005a, 48). Subsequently, Unilever Ceylon tried to avoid its obligations under this agreement. In 2001, citing the India-Sri Lanka Free Trade Agreement (1999) that reduced tariffs on tea, it tried to pit Indian workers against workers in Sri Lanka, with its subsidiaries in each country blaming cheap imports from the other for a drop in prices that would not only render wage increases impossible but require actual reductions. Unilever Ceylon further threatened to end all tea production in Sri Lanka, citing union disruption, and asserted that it would simply bring in Indian tea to sell in Sri Lanka. Unions mobilized in both countries to counter the strategy, sharing information about the practices of the respective Unilever subsidiaries. They noted that not only was Sri Lanka a negligible market for Unilever Ceylon, which exported almost all the tea it packaged, but also that the company had lobbied strongly for the trade agreement, seeking India as a new market. Unilever Ceylon, with the connivance of HLL, was hoping to expand the potential of its export labels essentially by buying the bulk of its tea from India and then re-exporting it as a blend with a little Sri Lankan tea, as the CEO acknowledged in 2003, noting that the plan had been blocked by the Sri Lankan government under pressure from plantation unions (Malik 2003, 4).

South Indian and Sri Lankan unions cooperated to call the bluff of Unilever Ceylon. In this instance, the collaboration between the unions was an easy one, given strong connections dating back many years. These connections are primarily ethnic. Tamil plantation workers in Ceylon were organized in 1939 by Indian unionists as the Ceylon Indian Congress (later, the Ceylon Workers' Congress). The ties were only strengthened by the periodic postindependence limitations on the citizenship and franchise of "estate Tamils" in Sri Lanka, and their interests were consolidated until, as current Sri Lankan prime minister Mahinda Rajapaksa noted, "There are few countries in the world where an ethnic group, a trade union, a political party and a specific industry are so closely inter-twined, as in the case of tea plantation labour in Sri Lanka" (Rajapaksa 2004). These unions became the nucleus of an international campaign that later coalesced around demands that included an end to such "unethical and unhealthy competitiveness" (Centre for Education and Communication 2006, 37).

The strong ties between South Indian tea plantation unions and the Ceylon Workers' Congress in Sri Lanka might have had no broader relevance had it not been for the need for extensive mobilization to counter the problems faced by tea plantation workers around the world. In the early period of the tea crisis, codes of conduct had been tried and had failed. The IUF, for example, had prepared a draft code in 1995, focusing not only on core labor rights, but also on living wages, housing, water, hours of work, and health and safety (IUF 1995). However, the industry came back with its own initiative in 1997, and the "Ethical Tea Partnership" (of which Unilever was a founding member), while superficial in both content and process, successfully blocked IUF's code from being adopted widely.

Ultimately, in part through the World Social Forum process, a number of NGOs with close ties to the labor movement began bringing together unions throughout the tea-producing world; at the core of the effort were those who organized ethnic Tamil workers in Malaysia's Cameron Highlands, East Africa, Sri Lanka, and South India. In Delhi, one NGO organized international meetings on December 15, 2005, designated International Tea Day. The international NGO Action Aid devoted a report to the tea crisis, pointing out the role played by the brands by noting that buyer cooperation on the auction floor had kept prices artificially low, even though retail prices were rising. The research focused entirely on a South Indian estate owned by HLL and zeroed in on the particular responsibility of this one brand, noting, for example, that it controlled 39 percent of the packaged tea market in India and bought 10 percent of all the tea produced in the country (Action Aid 2005, 8). Mindful of prevailing suspicions of voluntary and private mechanisms such as boycotts or preferential purchases that relied entirely on consumer sentiment, the report instead called for the U.K. government to take action against its own companies, by seeking legislation in the United Kingdom that would impose a legal duty of care toward plantation workers on companies such as Unilever (3). The report called for further legislative action on the part of the Indian government as well, through a stronger competition law that would make it more difficult for companies to manipulate prices, and it even advocated for trade and labor linkages, but through a nonpunitive clause that would ensure protection for the agricultural sector (9). With all of these elements that were attentive to the particularity of Indian history, the most important factor, it must be acknowledged, was beyond the control of international allies: India, after all, is a *market* for tea, not just a producer, and so the dynamic was very different from that in the campaigns that had focused on labor rights in purely export-oriented industries.

The next step, then, incorporated many of the lessons of CSR initiatives that had initially served only to alienate the Indian labor movement but placed in the foreground the experiences of local workers and activists. Armed with an analysis of supply chains and consumer awareness provided by international allies accustomed to campaigns around imports into their countries, Indian partners recognized the need to expand local strategies beyond trade union mobilization alone. A multistakeholder initiative seemed critical; it would have to address the interests of small-scale tea growers—equally victimized by the brands—and would have to commit itself to educating some portion of the Indian population that consumes 80 percent of the tea grown in the country. The project, Just Tea, is jointly managed by an Indian labor-support NGO and European groups with expertise in fair trade and economic development, thus taking on the full economic context for the deteriorating conditions for workers on tea plantations in India (Just Tea 2005).

India's rapid economic growth and integration into the world economy means that solidarity with Indian unions will become increasingly important. We suggest that effective cross-border campaigns with Indian workers and their organizations require a richer version of solidarity than is normally found—one that is attuned to the historical background against which Indian labor operates. While certainly not completely determinative, the colonial encounter and the strategies that colonial Britain wielded in its laws and policies to maintain control over the labor of its subjects provide an important frame through which Indian labor views western efforts at solidarity. This history has helped nurture a skepticism that informs Indian unions' approaches to everything ranging from relationships with western unions to policy debates over trade and labor linkage. In addition, an understanding of the fraught histories of migration within and from South Asia, shaped as well as inhibited by colonial law, will help develop a solidarity between the Global North and Global South that takes advantage of existing patterns of collaboration, and not just competition, between workers across the Global South. In concrete terms, this would mean, for example, harnessing the potential of existing relationships between workers in India and workers of Indian descent elsewhere.

Therefore, a deep solidarity requires an explicit acknowledgment of the protectionism and racism that have sometimes informed previous attempts at cooperation, as well as an understanding that some issues, such as child labor, while deeply important to western unionists and consumers, are often viewed with some measure of pragmatism by Indian counterparts. It requires that groups and unions from the Global North initiate direct contact and conversation with local activists and workers and an ongoing self-reflexive process to ensure that Northern allies not treat Southern partners simply as instruments to achieve purely self-interested ends.

4. STRUGGLE, PERSEVERANCE, AND ORGANIZATION IN SRI LANKA'S EXPORT PROCESSING ZONES

SAMANTHI GUNAWARDANA

> Unions are necessary. I like unions. But I have to think about my job.
> When you join a union, you get dismissed.
>
> North Sails factory female worker, interview by author, 2003

The aim of this chapter is to examine the forms of organizing that have been possible in Sri Lankan export processing zones (EPZs),[1] where young women drawn from the rural poor make up approximately 85 percent of all workers (BOI 2003b). This analysis is framed by a close reading of the local context of struggle pertaining to social relations in which workers, labor movements, and labor-management practices are constructed and embedded (Polanyi 1957, 43–55; Munck 2004, 258), with a view to understanding the importance of, and possibilities for, global trade union campaigns.

EPZs are crucial areas of study, as they are deeply entrenched in transnational commodity chains through direct investment, business alliances, or subcontracting relations (Gereffi 1994; Gordon 2000, 66). These zones are state-demarcated production spaces where imported materials undergo some degree of processing before being re-exported. They are designed to attract foreign investment and operate under preferential investment policies, financial inducements, and other special legal and political policies (ILO 2004).

The author thanks the following people for their assistance: Dr. Darryn Snell, Monash University, and Dr. Kate Bronfenbrenner, Cornell University, for their comments on earlier drafts of this chapter; two anonymous reviewers for their comments; Anton Marcus and Padmini Weerasoorriya for their assistance in conducting and participating in this research; the workers of the Katunayake zone who participated in this research; and all the other interviewees.

[1]   The term "EPZ" has been used interchangeably with "free trade zone," "free economic zone," "free ports special economic zone," "single industry zone," "single commodity zone," and "free trade geographical border." Single enterprises can also be granted EPZ status.

The number of these zones has grown exponentially over the past forty years with the growth of export-oriented industrialization among developing countries. In 2004, the International Labor Organization (ILO) documented that there were 5,174 EPZs worldwide, employing 41,934,133 people, mostly in Asia (ILO 2004).

While EPZ workers on the whole are geographically, structurally, and culturally diverse, an important commonality across all zones is that gendered assumptions about women's purportedly submissive nature and seeming physiological predisposition for work requiring rapid hand-eye dexterity have long made them the employees of choice for zone enterprises (Elson and Pearson 1981; Heyzer 1986; Ong 1987; Ghosh 2001; Elias 2004; Hewamanne 2003). Forty percent to 90 percent of zone workers are poor or lower-middle-class women, who are disproportionately represented in semiskilled and unskilled positions (ILO 2004).

Although EPZ work has enabled the inclusion of women into formal work, workers commonly face "low wages, poor working conditions and underdeveloped labor-relations systems" (ILO 1998), where freedom of association, collective bargaining, and the right to organize have been constrained largely through the nonenforcement of labor laws (Gordon 2000). In addition, EPZ women are subject to social stigma and violence in many communities (Garwood 2002; Fine and Howard 1995; Safa 1981).

For global organizing, the challenge lies in finding and articulating a common context for struggle while accommodating local group-based needs and desires (Jonasdottir 1988). This is particularly important when discussing women workers in EPZs, whose shared experiences are "useful only if they are generated through local, contextual analysis" in order to avoid a "false sense of the commonality of oppressions, interests and the struggles between and among women globally" (Mohanty 2004, 36). This approach enables us to identify material and historic bases shared among EPZ workers while recognizing women's subjective experience of multiple identities and accompanying contradictory consciousness, which ultimately influences the issues women organize and protest around and how and when they do (Mohanty 2004; Chhachhi and Pittin 1996).

This chapter is organized as follows. I first outline the context for struggle and worker characteristics in Sri Lanka. I then examine the challenge for organizing Sri Lankan EPZs and summarize some of the key challenges in global organizing. In the third section, I examine a successful global campaign at Jaqalanka Pty. Ltd., an apparel manufacturer in the Katunayake EPZ (KEPZ). This involved a partnership between the democratic Free Trade Zone Workers Union (FTZWU) and a grassroots women's collective, the Women's Centre. This global campaign centered on the struggle for freedom of association and the right to organize. In the following section, I examine the two groups in turn and discuss their organizing strategies and tactics. Finally, I draw upon the previous discussion to present lessons learned and offer some conclusions.

This chapter is based on ethnographic research since 2001. Ethnographic research methods allow close discernment of human values, beliefs, and practices, and can have an important place in strategic global research, particularly in outlining possibilities for grassroots action and global linkages. The main portion of research was carried out during twelve months of participant observation in 2003. I lived in a worker boarding house for twelve months and worked as an unskilled worker in an apparel garment factory in the KEPZ for eleven months. Here, the factory is referred to as "Factory X." I also engaged in research with several nongovernmental organizations (NGOs) and trade unions working with women workers in the zone. Subsequent interviews were conducted with the Women's Centre and FTZWU in 2006. I have omitted the names of individual workers, factory managers, and senior government officials for reasons of confidentiality.

The Creation of a Gendered Working Class

In 1978, the United National Party (UNP) in Sri Lanka established the first EPZ at Katunayake, twenty kilometers north of Colombo, as part of a wider program of economic liberalization. This represented a vast policy realignment of the postindependence era, toward export-oriented industrialization underpinned by neoliberal economic policy. By 2003, there were nine EPZs and two industrial parks in Sri Lanka employing approximately 139,000 workers (BOI 2003b). Much of the investment into the zones originates from Japan, the United States, the United Kingdom, Australia, India, and Germany, while the main export markets are the United States, Europe, and Southeast Asia. Apparel sector manufacturing dominates exports, with enterprises producing goods for a range of products for transnational firms such as Victoria's Secret, the Gap, Tommy Hilfiger, Liz Claiborne, and Nike.

Eighty-five percent of workers are poor women, the majority of whom are unmarried and ethnically Sinhalese and identify themselves as Buddhist. Most are between nineteen and twenty-six years old, with a relatively high level of educational attainment. EPZ firms rely on cultural assumptions about the disposition of these young rural women, who are typecast as *ahinsaka* (innocent), disciplined, and filial. In addition, they are expected to display *laja-baya* (shame-fear),[2] which is perceived as preventing women from being vociferous.

---

[2]   In the socialialization of young men and women in Sri Lanka "shame (*laja*) and fear (*baya*)" is internalized and acts as a self-disciplining moral mechanism (Obeyesekere 1984).

Such gendered ideas have informed the recruitment strategies of firms undertaking export-oriented manufacturing elsewhere, in both the formal and informal sectors (Standing 1999; Arrigo 1980; Salaff 1981; R. Gallin 1990; Elias 2005; Pearson 1995; Fussell 2000; Nash and Fernández-Kelly 1983; Rowbotham and Mitter 1994). The pervasive belief that women are on the whole more docile and nimble-fingered than men persists (Elson and Pearson 1981), although preferences as to marital status, race, and age have varied across contexts (see for example, Lee 1998; Elias 2005). As Joan Ackers argues, gender is utilized as a resource for global capital whereby women are integrated into transnational production and existing local gender relations are viewed as a resource for both local and global capital (2004).

In Sri Lanka, women workers typically remain in the EPZ for a period of five years before returning to their village or moving on to other forms of employment such as domestic service. They reside in crude row houses built by residents in the areas surrounding the EPZs. Anywhere between two and twenty women share small cramped spaces, in which they sleep, eat, cook, and store their possessions. Amenities such as security, waste disposal, sanitation, and medical centers are poor, and violence such as rape and sexual harassment has also been reported (KEPZ police, interview by author, 2003; Hemalie Fernando, interviews by author, 2003, 2005).

Given the nature of transnational sourcing strategies and global competition within commodity chains, EPZ firms compete over cost efficiencies, quality, and lead time. In Factory X, for example, a forty-five-day lead time was promoted regardless of order size.[3] Workers labored between sixty-nine and seventy-seven hours a week. In addition, competition over quality resulted in strict surveillance of adherence to quality standards, with penalties for lapses, including wage deductions and warning letters.

Work intensification is experienced in multiple ways. Workers might be assigned two machines consecutively in one assembly line but be held to the same production targets as those operating only one machine; production targets can be increased; and workers may have to work longer and more varied hours, including nights. The constant scolding and verbal pressure is one of the most stressful aspects of their work. Workers often voluntarily skip meal and break times and refrain from using the bathroom to meet targets and fix quality problems, leading to numerous health problems and exhaustion. Indeed, worker burnout is an endemic problem (Samarasinghe and Ismail 2000).

Despite the stress and degradation of the factory system, women reported feeling pride in their work and empowered through earning an independent income. In 2003, sewing machine operators from a number of different

---

[3] Apparel orders can range anywhere from five thousand to sixty thousand garments or more.

factories in the Katunayake EPZ reported earning an average monthly wage between a minimum of 5,500 rupees ($58) and 6,500 rupees ($68, with incentives and bonuses)[4]. Workers receive wages that are usually higher than those outside the zone (see also Ratnayake 1984). For example, in the case of wages for garment workers (the apparel industry dominates EPZ production in Sri Lanka) outside the zone, the centralized wages board set the minimum wage for a grade A garment worker at 3,025–3,165 rupees in 2003 (Ministry of Employment and Labor 2003, 78). Although EPZ wages were higher, the rising cost of living was unsustainable for EPZ workers, particularly if they were supporting their families in the village. As a consequence, workers relied heavily on overtime income and bonuses.

Outside the workplace, EPZs workers have become marked as a distinct group for their lifestyle, which includes the consumption of clothes and jewelry, along with a shift toward "unrespectable" sexual behavior that has purportedly resulted in unwanted pregnancies and unsanitary abortions (Hewamanne 2003). The EPZ has been referred to disparagingly as *Stripura* (City of Women) and *Vesa Kalapaya* (Zone of Prostitutes). However, workers have maintained a positive, albeit stigmatized, collective cultural identity as industrial workers, which has enabled the creation of a "critical space" in which women subvert middle-class cultural hegemonies (Hewamanne 2003).

This subversion of the *ahinsaka* village girl ideal is also enacted in the workplace. The regularity of labor protest in the EPZs has been persistent, albeit uneven. During the period 1994–2003, there were a recorded 155 work stoppages (at least one per month) in the Katunayake EPZ (BOI 2003a)[5], and there has been a history of spontaneous strikes in the zone and informal habits of resistance (Rosa 1994) at the workplace level over issues such as the denial of annual bonuses, nonpayment of wages, management harassment, and the arbitrary dismissal of coworkers (Industrial Relations Department 2003a, 2003b).

Struggle: The Challenges of Organizing Workers

While Sri Lankan labor law guarantees freedom of association, the right to organize, and the right to collectively bargain, by 2003 only 4 percent of EPZ factories had recognized trade unions with varying degrees of functionality, and a collective agreement has yet to be reached. The challenges facing trade unions are outlined below.

---

[4]   Workers in the private sector received a thousand-rupee increase in 2005, which, according to trade union officials, has since been implemented in a number of EPZ factories.

[5]   This register, accessed in the BOI industrial relations offices, was incomplete and listed disputes only from 1994 onward.

First, the government has constrained trade union activity through the invocation of special laws. The Public Security Ordinance has been used to ban trade union activities. Although established as an act to counter terrorism, it can be invoked to ban demonstrations, pickets, strikes, and certain categories of meetings, and it has been utilized to prevent picketing at the Fine Lanka factory in the KEPZ.

Second, the government has enabled a system of industrial relations containment through the setting up of the Board of Investments (BOI), as well as banning May Day parades in Colombo. The BOI is a sophisticated central authority, which reports directly to the president, through which all investors negotiate without ever needing to contact any other authority in Sri Lanka. It is responsible for administering national labor law, as well as establishing and monitoring guidelines for investors, on such issues as labor rights and the operation of enterprise-level workers' councils (BOI 2006).

The ultimate authority over entry rests with the BOI. Stringent security at the zone keeps "outsiders" out. The perimeter of the KEPZ, for example, is ringed by barbed-wire fencing, and in certain locations armed security personnel stand guard; everyone entering the zone must have both a factory identity card and a BOI-authorized pass. In the past, the identity cards of workers engaged in trade union activities have been confiscated, and workers have been refused reissuing of cards (Gunatilaka 1999).

Each zone has an industrial relations department, whose role it is to "foster harmonious working relationships" (BOI senior industrial relations official, interview by author, 2003). This has been in the form of diversion away from traditional arbitration mechanisms (Rosa 1994, 84). In the 155 stoppages at the KEPZ over the period from 1994 to 2003, the BOIs were the first point of call when a dispute arose. Direct mediation between managers and workers has been encouraged so that disputes can be settled internally and swiftly without "politicization" (KEPZ senior industrial relations official, interview by author, 2003).

In addition, enterprise-level alternatives to trade unions have been created. The formation of in-house workers' councils was initiated after the 1994 presidential election, following mass labor agitation for trade union rights. This has reportedly resulted in a decline in stoppages because of direct and timely dialogue between workers and managers (BOI senior industrial relations official, interview by author, 2003).

However, workers' council representatives have limited influence. Senior positions on councils are often held by senior staff members while workers hold committee positions. Meetings are generally called when management requires them, and concerns about food, uniforms, and other issues pertaining to worker welfare are raised, along with questions—depending on the factory—about holidays or overtime hours; collective bargaining over wages and conditions, however, does not occur. Success is predicated upon individual worker representatives and their confidence in negotiating with managers. Members may have little prior experience or training in negotiating directly with managers, although workers commonly select other workers who "can speak well, are not scared and know what they are talking about" (Factory X sewing machine operator, interview by author, 2003).

Beyond state action, the organization of production itself prevents political action. For example, competition between groups of workers is enhanced through the incentive system, which rewards line performance. Within the line, the dependency of the assembly-line system breeds argument and tension, particularly when workers are absent.

Although never explicitly stating that union membership is prohibited, management engages in direct and indirect ways of minimizing union involvement. These include instigating emotional bonds between workers and supervisors, providing anonymous complaints boxes, and having counselors who listen to worker problems. These techniques not only appear to be giving a voice to workers but also have the effect of providing convenient surveillance methods. Other indirect strategies include selective recruitment socialization and the provision of services such as libraries, beauty competitions, parties, and annual factory-funded trips. Direct strategies include asking workers to sign contracts stating that they will not engage in, or encourage others to engage in, disruptive behavior; harassment and intimidation of union members; and their outright dismissal (Field notes, 2001, 2003; Prices Candles KEPZ female factory worker, interview by author, 2003).

Another set of challenges in organizing involves the relationship between workers and trade unions. When faced with a large body of workers in one location, living and working in close proximity to one another, trade unionists believed that collectivism would be a natural outcome (Anton Marcus, FTZWU, interview by author, 2003). Indeed, workers were highly conscious of their exploitation, self-evaluation of their labor was high, and they displayed a common identity as EPZ workers, which propelled enterprise-level protest and collectivism (Knoke 1990). However, all the activists interviewed for this research reported being frustrated by their inability to garner support for a consistent, continual labor movement.

While the masculinist orientation of political trade unionism in Sri Lanka traditionally hindered women from participation and leadership positions (Caspersz 1998; Rosa 1994), EPZ workers did not join trade unions in great numbers or take an active part in them because of cultural and time restrictions and the rationalization that they would be there for only a short period of time (Rosa 1994). Fear of job loss (as the opening quote indicates) and factory closure were also important considerations, as many had observed union members being dismissed and factories being closed after organizing attempts.

This structural vulnerability was combined with a sense of cynicism about trade union (and NGO) political interests. This did not however, mean that women workers were ideologically opposed to trade unions, nor did it preclude them from taking part in the activities of labor-based organizations on a selective basis.

Fundamentally, however, it was only when they could not resolve their grievances at the factory level that workers sought to join trade unions or take part in organization. Workers felt that they could access internal avenues to express their concerns without being penalized. It was only when these internal avenues of resistance (which might include work stoppage) and negotiation failed, or if the job was already lost, that workers approached trade unions. Thus, for EPZ women workers, trade union membership and action were viewed instrumentally as tactics of last resort.

This discussion of challenges to local-level organizing must be placed in the context of global union solidarity and campaigns. Challenges include divergence in labor laws, systems of industrial relations, and trade union structures, which are compounded by concern over timely communication and coordination (Garwood 2005, 23). In addition, the precarious nature of employment and the lack of employment security, as well as local laws pertaining to solidarity actions such as sympathy striking, can make cross-border campaigns precarious. Finally, global organizing requires sustained global solidarity, which can be difficult to foster owing to competition and diverging local interests. As Shae Garwood (2005, 23) explains, "[T]he challenge faced by activists, regardless of their own location in the global economy, is to create cross-border relationships and networks which avoid pitting poor women against each other as regional opponents in the global labor market, and which honor the depth of complexity of individual difference."

In summary, the challenges for organizing are manifold in EPZs, where local-level constraints combine with the challenge of coordinating and campaigning globally. While the discussion to this point has focused on the challenges posed for trade unions and activists, the following section examines a case of successful trade union organizing.

Freedom of Association and Organizing at Jaqalanka Apparels Pvt Ltd.

Jaqalanka Ltd. operates three factories in Sri Lanka, two of which are situated in the Katunayaka Free Trade Zone (KFTZ), while another is located in rural Balangoda. The KFTZ factory was first established in 1978, making it one of the oldest in the zone. It is a British-owned company, which has several Sri Lankan expatriates on its board and Sri Lankan managers on site. At the time of the dispute, there were four hundred workers. Until this particular dispute, the BOI work stoppages register does not record any disputes between 1994 and 2003.

At the time, the factory was producing jackets for RedKap, which is owned by VF Workwear, a large transnational that distributes safety equipment and clothing in the United States. The parent company, VF Corporation, also owns several brands such as Lee, Wrangler, Rustler, Riders, Britannia, Chic, and Gitano, which account for 25 percent of the U.S. jeans market. Jaqalanka also produced Columbia Sportswear, underwear for the New Time label, and underwear samples for Nike.

The Dispute

As part of its remuneration system the factory had paid all workers an annual Aluth Avurudda (New Year, in April) bonus since its establishment. New Year has a special significance in Sri Lanka, and this bonus is common among factories in the EPZs. The EPZ factories shut down for a period of five to ten days as workers returned to their villages. Many workers relied on this bonus not only to supplement the income for day-to-day living expenses but also to purchase New Year gifts for their families.

In March 2003, the factory announced that the company was operating at a loss and would not be able to pay this bonus. Workers were surprised and angered by this announcement, as there had been no change in production. Indeed, in the following October Daniel Ortiz, the joint managing director, stated that "during the time in question, we did not have any major financial losses" (Juriansz 2003). The issue was raised internally with the workers' council, but discussions failed. The reason for this decision therefore was never made clear. Instead, the point of conflict would later become the role of the local branch union of the FTZWU.

By April the company still maintained that it would not "pay even a single cent as a bonus for this year" (Anton Marcus, FTZWU, interview by author, 2003). As a result, the production sections stopped work after lunch and went on a half-day strike (FTZWU branch union secretary, interview by author, 2003).

The BOI was informed, and senior officials from the BOI engaged in a discussion with the workers' council. The BOI attempted to mediate between workers and managers, with management informing the BOI (but not the workers) that the company was running at a 300 million-rupee loss in profits.[6] The managing director was out of the country, and the BOI attempted to convince workers to wait until he returned. Workers refused and stopped work

---

[6] This was never confirmed by management.

for the rest of the day (KEPZ senior industrial relations official, interview by author, 2003).

Trade Union Formation

Several of the women workers had been taking part in the activities of the Women's Centre (FTZWU branch union secretary, interview by author, 2003). At this point, a number of workers approached the FTZWU at the Katunayake Centre and decided to form a branch union of the FTZWU at Jaqalanka. Two hundred twenty members, a little over half of the total workforce, joined the trade union and elected officers, consisting of both men and women.

Workers returned to work the next day but were refused entry into the factory (Anton Marcus, FTZWU, interview by author, 2003). The workers wrote a letter advising that they had become members of the trade union; they requested to be taken back, stating that they wished to settle the dispute. At the same time, the union requested intervention from the commissioner of labor and industrial relations, and the district commissioner, Negombo, who was responsible for EPZ labor disputes.

Later that week when workers reported for work, management asked them to sign a letter of condition asking for management's forgiveness and admitting that they had engaged in an illegal strike. Workers refused to sign this letter but signed an amended letter stating that they regretted any inconvenience caused by their action. Management agreed to take the workers back effective April 8, 2003 (TIE-Asia 2003), at which point workers requested that managers deal with the branch union. The factory went on the New Year holiday on April 11 with a bonus that equaled one-quarter of the usual annual bonus.

Work resumed on April 21. Management refused to engage with the union, attend meetings with the assistant commissioner of labor, or give leave for workers to attend the meeting (Anton Marcus, FTZWU, interview by author, 2003). Union members were verbally harassed and intimidated. The union then requested a referendum to be arranged under the provision of section 56 of the 1999 Industrial Disputes Amendment Act for recognition of the union in the factory.

The Global Campaign

Both the BOI chairman and Labor Department officials visited the factory and allegedly insisted members speak with management directly. The assistant commissioner of labor, for example, allegedly had a discussion with selected workers from each section and told them not to work with outsiders and to try to settle these matters directly with the management. A subsequent letter from the BOI chairman stated that he had "advised the newly elected members of the executive committee not to resort to any unilateral action, but to seek solutions to problems through dialogue and consultation with managers" (Connor and Dent 2006, 22).

A date for a referendum on the union was set with the labor commissioner, after which workers reported that a steady campaign was waged by managers to dissuade union membership. The union officers and their respective work sections were verbally abused and harassed to sign letters of resignation (TIE-Asia 2003). The loyalty that workers felt for their organization and individual personnel was manipulated. For example, workers reported that the packing and ironing section manager told the workers that if they were going to vote for the union, he was going to resign, and if they loved him they shouldn't vote for the union. The union was categorized as a group of outsiders who were instilling dissent against the factory that "look[ed] after you for 25 years as your parents" (TIE-Asia 2003). Workers reported that fear of factory closure was repeatedly provoked and they were "requested" to disassociate themselves from the trade union.

When Nike sent a regular auditor to the factory, rumors circulated that because of the union, the factory had lost some orders from Nike and therefore might have to close. However, both the FTZWU and an Oxfam Australia report praised Nike and Columbia auditors for playing a positive and cooperative role with the union and workers (Connor and Dent 2006).

At this time, the FTZWU, supported by Transnational Information Exchange Asia (TIE-Asia), requested and received support from the Clean Clothes Campaign, the Maquila Solidarity Network, No Sweat, the International Textile Garments and Leatherworker Federation (ITGLWF), and other international solidarity alliances (Connor and Dent 2006, 22). They also received solidarity support from the Sri Lankan office of the American Council for International Solidarity (ACILS). Support included publicizing the campaign among their constituents, advocacy support in the case of the ITGLWF, and research and mediation from ACILS. Clean Clothes incorporated the struggle into its global campaign, publicizing it through online appeals and directing attention to Jaqalanka within its network. In addition, the Committee for Asian Women (CAW) set up a regional workshop on organizing strategies for activists and women workers in Sri Lanka. At this workshop, women workers from Jaqalanka shared their experiences and a petition was prepared and endorsed by all the representatives of South Asian trade unions and women's labor groups who were present.

The trade union still faced difficulty in accessing and talking to workers at Jaqalanka to encourage them to take part in the referendum. To overcome this, the Women's Centre, along with trade union members, visited the boarding houses of Jaqalanka workers and distributed a letter outlining the situation to date.

Despite this, Jaqalanka workers still faced a struggle. On the day of the referendum, June 9, 2003, a number of international observers from U.S. and European labor groups were present. A report by the observers from the Fair Labor Association (FLA) concluded that "the election was marred by the clumsiest of employer intimidation. The government of Sri Lanka did nothing about it" (Connor and Dent 2006, 23). Only 17 workers, out of a total of 402, voted.

Management publicly rejected the workers' harassment claims described above, saying that they had always looked after their workers through the creation of a safe work environment that respected worker rights, the provision of training, and the arrangement of annual trips (Juriansz 2003; Kasturisinghe 2003).

Intensification of the Campaign

The Clean Clothes Campaign, global trade unions, and other international organizations managed a sustained letter-writing campaign in both Europe and the United States, targeting both Jaqalanka and its international brand-name clients, such as Nike and Vanity Fair. These two brands advocated a balanced settlement between the parties. With the help of ACILS, the FTWU lodged a petition to the EU and the U.S. government, asking for the granting of trade preferences under the Generalized System of Preferences (which was being negotiated at the time), a plan to remedy violations of core labor standards, with specific reference to the Jaqalanka case and trade union rights (Anton Marcus, FTZWU, interview by author, 2003). The issue was thus bought to the attention of the investing countries from which factories like Jaqalanka received their orders. The possibility of interruption and cessation of orders, as well as the negative reputation that was developing among investor countries, was publicized in the popular press (Samath 2003; Juriansz 2003). The international publicity intensified when the ITGLWF, at the World Trade Organization (WTO) ministerial meeting in Cancun, Mexico, accused the company of abusing workers' rights, undermining development, and putting in jeopardy the future of the country's textile clothing industry. This forced the management to make a number of public statements confirming that "damaging emails from locals and foreigners" had been received (De Mel, finance director, cited in Juriansz 2003) and that the "Fair Labor Organisation [sic] needs to be educated on the matter; it is comparing us to the Dominican Republic" (De Mel, finance director, cited in Juriansz 2003).

At the local level, on the factory floor, workers spoke out to auditors. For example, on September 18, 2003, auditors from the brand label Columbia visited the Jaqalanka factory and interviewed workers. Many workers spoke about the continual intimidation by management and other issues such as being forced to work after they had punched out for the day and being forced to work overtime. The day after workers met with the Columbia auditors, more threats were made inside and outside the factory, threatening violence, including threats to murder an officer (Connor and Dent, 2006, 23; TIE-Asia 2003; Anton Marcus, FTZWU, interview by author, 2003).

The Women's Centre provided a safe and open space for workers to meet and discuss the campaign. Previous training and ongoing work with the center and the FTZWU enabled them to sustain their struggle.

Resolution

Both the FTWU and Nike lodged a request with the FLA, and subsequently FLA engaged with all key stakeholders to pursue "an amicable non-confrontational resolution." They engaged a local NGO, the Center for Policy Alternatives (CPA), to convene a roundtable discussion. In mid-October, a discussion was held between FTZWU representatives, factory management, Nike, Columbia Sportswear, the ILO, ACILS, the CPA, and FLA (Connor and Dent 2006; FLA 2004). The factory branch was recognized as "representing the concerns of its members at Jaqalanka" (FLA 2004). The union then called off the global campaign.

Workers and management were further supported with training in freedom of association and workers' rights. This was supported by the FLA and implemented by the local CPA. Currently, the union functions and is working with management, which now allows union meetings in the factory (Conner and Dent 2006, 24), and union dues are being deducted by the factory. Discussions have been instituted toward forming a collective agreement, the first such agreement for the Sri Lankan EPZs since their inception in 1978 (Anton Marcus, FTZWU, interview by author, 2006).

This case has led to a number of other positive outcomes for labor in the EPZs. The BOI released a new set of labor guidelines incorporating freedom of association and collective bargaining rights in 2004 (BOI 2004), and the Labor Department tries to settle disputes and recognize unions without recourse to referendums (Connor and Dent 2006, 24). The FTZWU was also able to form a functioning trade union at Sinotex garments in the KEPZ.

Perseverance: Understanding Forms of Organizing Found in Sri Lankan EPZs

The previous section presents a case study of a successful organizing attempt. To explain why the campaign was successful, I now examine how local trade unions and other groups have engaged in sustained organizing efforts to reach out and inform workers of their rights while supporting workers who wanted to form unions. I also highlight the role of cross-border solidarity and action.

Women Organizing Women: The Importance of Women's Labor Groups

Women's organizations were among the first in Sri Lanka to work directly with EPZ workers. They have persistently worked with one another and other regional and international women's groups to articulate a common interest among Asian women workers, through a shared understanding of and confrontation of gender inequality as a basis for political action in the workplace. In doing so, they have focused on issues that have been overlooked by traditional Sri Lankan unions. While these groups have not attempted to engage directly in bargaining with employers, they are significant because they provide space for workers, information, referral networks, education, and training and hence possibilities for the action-oriented empowerment of women workers (CAW 1998).

Early groups that attempted to assist women were the Women's Liberation movement of Sri Lanka (*Pacific and Asian Women's Network Newsletter* 1993); the Katunayake Women's Group; local religious centers, such as Catholic churches and Buddhist temples, who assisted women in integrating into their new neighborhoods, created educational opportunities, and offered support in times of crisis such as unwanted pregnancy; and a legal advice center that provided intervention, information, seminars, and discussions. These groups also formed local alliances in the 1980s around issues such as sexual harassment and violence (Rosa 1994; Jayakody and Goonatilake 1988).

From these early ad hoc beginnings, organized groups began to emerge. These include the Women's Centre, the *Da Bindu* (Drops of Sweat) Collective, and *Kalape Api* (We in the Zone). All three of these groups are led either solely or jointly by women, some of whom have been workers themselves. These centers are located within the residential areas of workers, making them easily accessible, and are open during workers' days off.

Most are funded externally by international NGOs in the Global North and supported by regional groups such as CAW, Asia Monitor Resource Center (AMRC), and Asian Labor Exchange (ALE), which have served as coordinating-type umbrella bodies. These groups enable linkages between disparate women's labor organizations in the region and facilitate information sharing, capacity building of local activists, and the development of alternative methods of organizing.

The most proactive of the groups in Sri Lanka's EPZs is the Women's Centre, which originated from a strike at the Polytex garments factory in 1982 on an industrial estate next to the KEPZ. This strike was led by young women workers who instigated a community-based campaign, supported by local activists and other organizations, and faced off a coalition of police, state agents, management, and hired thugs (Jayakody and Goonatilake 1988). At this time a partnership was formed with the Industrial Transport and General Workers Union (ITGWU). The center was born from the workers' need to create a space to meet and plan their actions. From the mid-1980s, it has been led by Padmini Weerasooriya, who was an EPZ worker in the early 1980s; she was later joined by Sriya Ahangamage, a worker who gained leadership skills through her association with the Women's Centre (Padmini Weerasooriya, interview by author, 2003).

Currently, the center provides legal and medical assistance, library facilities, training, seminars, discussions, and education, as well as a much-needed space for women workers. Its aims and objectives are based on a discursive reorientation of women's work as a valuable service to the national economy. They do this by ensuring that all of the materials they put out in the public sphere, both in the language used and in the way women are described, promotes the value of women's work. A key aim is to counter derogatory societal attitudes toward women through organization and collectivism. In addition to Katunayake, there are centers at the Biyagama and Koggala EPZ, and the center is currently in the process of reaching out to workers in all the other EPZs and industrial parks (Padmini Weerasooriya, interview by author, 2006).

The Women's Centre engages in solidarity action with regional women's groups and trade unions and facilitates exchanges with other local women's labor groups, such as those working with migrant domestic workers and plantation workers, regardless of ethnic, religious, or caste differences. For example, in 2003, a number of Women's Centre workers journeyed to eastern Sri Lanka, where EPZ workers shared experiences with Tamil women workers from this area.[7] The center also takes part in male-dominated May Day rallies and International Women's Day rallies with other women's organizations (Biyanwila 2006).

What differentiates this center from other NGOs mentioned above is that it seeks to actively involve its members in union activities; the center identifies and trains potential trade union leaders. According to Padmini Weerasooriya, the Women's Centre seeks to "develop leadership opportunities among women, and provide opportunities for them to become leaders and branch presidents of the plant-level trade unions" (interview by author, 2003). This occurs through a gradual process of participation, confidence building, and raising awareness.

[7]   Sri Lanka has been in a state of civil war since 1983. There was a ceasefire in 2003. The north and east are predominately ethnic Tamil and Muslim areas. Many of the young EPZ women had boyfriends or brothers in the Sri Lankan army who were fighting for the state against Tamil rebels.

Because many women are neophyte workers, creative expression through writing and performance has been instrumental to the success of these groups. These practices seek to reorient workers as active agents. Worker poems and other creative works such as short stories are published in independent worker-centered newspapers, giving voice to constituents who, especially in the early days of zone operation, had none. They have also served to hold companies publicly accountable (Samanmalie, Da Bindu coordinator, interview by author, 2003). Issues of sexual harassment; the lack of labor rights, including freedom of association; and problems of substandard housing, sexual and reproductive health, and violence that workers face day to day—topics never broached by traditional unions—are addressed in these papers.

Another form of creative expression that has been used by women's groups is the traditional *vedi natya* (street drama), which enables workers to express their grievances in an accessible and nonconfrontational, albeit powerful and expressive way. For example, the street drama called *Avashyathavaya* (Our Needs), written and performed by the Women's Centre's *Kantha Shakthi* (Women's Strength) group of workers, tells of the workers' problems and the hypocrisy of management. The drama group was established in 1989 in the KEPZ and in the Koggala EPZ in 1998. This play was performed at the CAW-organized Asian Women Workers' Festival held in Bangkok in 2002. Taking part in such experiences enables workers not only to gain confidence, self-awareness, and knowledge but also to engage in cross-cultural exchange with other workers. The festival featured women's labor groups from Korea, the Philippines, Japan, Nepal, Hong Kong, Indonesia, and Thailand, who shared their situations through different performances such as song, dance, music, and drama (CAW 2003, 15) and expressed solidarity toward one another. Such events enable workers to share everyday experiences, highlighting and strengthening the need for international solidarity. It is noteworthy that these international events are targeted at and inclusive of the grassroots level, not only the peak leadership.

Another area where women's groups have worked together across borders is in conducting strategic localized research that has in turn contributed to global campaigns. Organizations such as Da Bindu and the Women's Centre have been instrumental in documenting the conditions of not only EPZ workers but also other peripheral workers such as home-based workers in transnational commodity chains. For example, in 1999 the U.K.-based Women Working Worldwide (WWW), Da Bindu, and the Women's Centre began to look at transnational codes of conduct in an effort to explore possibilities for rights enforcement and to inform workers about these codes. One localized outcome of the research project was workshops organized by the FTZWU for identified women worker leaders. They were attended by 426 workers, of whom 90 percent were women, more than half were from FTZs, and more than 80 percent were garment workers (WWW 2002). Positive outcomes from these training sessions included requests by workers for more of such programs. They wanted to learn more about the labels/brand names that they were sewing and about a company code of conduct that had been previously unknown to them. However, even with such initiatives, time restrictions and fear of job loss played a major role, as it was difficult to get workers to attend consecutive sessions (WWW 2002).

A global outcome was that this research and other country-based research formed the basis for a global initiative established by Women Working Worldwide, called the Ethical Trading Initiative (ETI). The ETI is a U.K.-based alliance of trade unions, NGOs, and firms that seek to enforce transnational codes of conduct.

The Women's Centre is also involved in global alliances such as the global Clean Clothes Campaign solidarity network, which also encompasses consumer-based activism. Locally it is part of the Oxfam initiative Apparel Industrial Labor Rights Movement (ALARM), which is made up of trade unions and NGOs.

The Trade Union Movement

The first union to substantially concentrate on organizing EPZ workers as a distinct group was the ITGWU. It began to organize workers outside the EPZs in nearby industrial areas, while simultaneously campaigning for organizing rights in the EPZs. The union offered informal worker education and training programs for EPZ workers in conjunction with the Women's Centre. Because of the repressive political context in which the ITGWU and the Women's Centre were organizing, workers' rights were also expressed as human rights (see Biyanwila 2006 for extended analysis). The partnership with the Women's Centre enabled the union to highlight women's rights issues such as sexual harassment and living conditions in boarding houses through the 1990s, bringing them into the domain of trade union concern (Anton Marcus, FTZWU, interview by author, 2003).

The ITGWU utilized existing mechanisms such as workers' councils while campaigning for trade union rights (Anton Marcus, FTZWU, interview by author, 2001). On June 30, 1996, the Joint Association of Workers and Workers' Councils of the Export Processing Zones was launched as a politically independent organization that would work with unions, labor, and NGOs. The association functioned as a trade union, organizing a strike in Hong Kong Knitters Ltd., for example. In 1999 the joint council decided to take advantage of the 1999 amendment to the Industrial Disputes Act strengthening the recognition of unions. The politically independent FTZWU of Sri Lanka was formed, drawing a membership base from all three EPZs (Dent 2000, 3). In 2003 the ITGWU merged with the FTZWU.

In 2003 the FTZWU had six thousand members (Anton Marcus, FTZWU, interview by author, 2003), 90 percent of whom were women. At present, women make up more than 85 percent of the fourteen thousand members (Anton Marcus, FTZWU, interview by author, 2006). There are joint male and female presidents and male and female secretaries, three of whom were employed in factories. Anton Marcus, the joint secretary for the FTZWU, explains that for the union "the main object is to help the women workers in the EPZ to take up their issues with the employers and to create a good relationship between the employers and the workers as well as educate the workers about their rights and the social issues" (Anton Marcus, interview by author, 2003). The union also organizes women in factories producing for export outside the zones.

The union targets three strategic levels: the factory, the local/national, and the international. At the factory level the union, along with the Women's Centre, concentrates on identifying potential leaders and lobbying and agitating for the implementation of existing labor law and enforcement of ILO conventions 87 and 89. The union also attempts to utilize workers' councils, because although these are not legal bodies, the union believes the councils can be representative of workers. The union seeks to educate and provide awareness of labor law to workers who are members of the workers' councils outside the factory (Anton Marcus, FTZWU, interview by author, 2003).

At the national level, the FTZWU engages in advocacy for labor law reform. With the linkage with the Women's Centre remaining at the center, the union also engages in building solidarity links with other workers, such as workers in the plantation sector, and in people's movements. In addition, the FTZWU has attempted to influence trade negotiations with the EU regarding access to apparel markets and concessions for Sri Lankan producers.

It is also part of a wider group of transnational trade union alliances and networks of NGOs. These networks include other local, regional, and international women's groups; trade union bodies; and human rights activists, such as the Southern Initiative on Globalization and Trade Union Rights (SIGTUR). These groups were vital to the success of the Jaqalanka case.

A key partner has been TIE-Asia, which encourages and supports the development of trade unions and democratic worker organizations, with particular emphasis on women-centered, export-oriented industries of South and Southeast Asia (TIE-Asia 2005). Other partners have been global groups that employ consumer-based pressure campaigns such as No Sweat and Clean Clothes Campaign, the latter in particular providing much-needed support during a number of campaigns.

In terms of strategic research, the FTZWU has maintained a database with information about garment factories operating in the EPZs. This database is supported by the American Solidarity Center and includes information based on research as well as the testimony of workers.

Lessons Learned from the Sri Lankan Experience

The successful partnership between the Women's Centre and FTZWU and their strategic mobilization of international networks in the Jaqalanka case offer insight into the possibilities for cross-border organizing. It is clear that timely support offered by trade unions and consumers in the Global North has been important. This included support for corporate research and capacity building even before the case came to the forefront, as well as mobilizing international networks in solidarity. Anton Marcus reports that success was possible "not because of labor department intervention, but because of the pressure from buyers, and the global unions and the consumer campaigns" (Anton Marcus, FTZWU, interview by author, 2006). This was also the case in the union's subsequent (successful) campaigns at Polytex garments in Koggala EPZ and Sinotex in the KEPZ.

One concern with the top-down strategy of engaging the Global North is that although international pressure campaigns can generate quick results, they do not resolve the issue of maintaining worker organization at the local level. Empowerment of workers in workplaces and worker communities is vital (AMRC 2006) particularly where organizing is constrained. This strategy has been embraced by the Women's Centre in empowering women workers through an understanding of gender inequalities in wider society as well as in the workplace. Specifically in the Jaqalanka case, the Women's Centre provided localized support in reaching workers and sustaining the campaign. Subsequent training programs stressed the importance of remaining organized and enhanced the leadership capabilities of workers.

Furthermore, as I noted at the beginning of the chapter, it is essential to consider local needs while articulating global interests, particularly in global spaces such as EPZs. In Sri Lanka, for example, trade unions were viewed as a strategy of last resort because of the material conditions under which workers labored; the threat of job loss in particular was a major limitation. Global trade unions attempting to organize such workers must take these factors into consideration.

One way of being active globally and responsive locally is through the development of direct worker-to-worker networks in addition to those involving only trade union officials and leaders. Here workers themselves can gain an understanding of their shared experiences, differences, and global connection. In South Asia, for example, women workers face similar cultural assumptions about femininity but differing laws and workplace conditions. The Women's Centre and other such groups in the region have been able to successfully form worker-to-worker networks on a small scale, despite language difficulties.

The local-global nexus is also important in considering the position of local firms such as Jaqalanka. For example, the pressure that was applied through trade talks was successful because of the inherent structural inequality of trade in the global apparel sector. Local firms such as Jaqalanka find themselves in a precarious position with regard to global capital. Sri Lanka was at the time facing the imminent phaseout of the Multi-Fibre Agreement (MFA), which had shaped the character of export markets for two decades, and garment manufacturers were worried about competition from China and India; Sri Lanka's labor cost was higher and productivity lower relative to these countries. Consequently, national trade talks were being held to maintain favorable access to markets in the European Union. The trade-labor standards link therefore was important to the Jaqalanka campaign because of the threat that withdrawal of tariff concessions would impair market access.

This link has not been missed by local producers. Three years after the Jaqalanka case, the Sri Lankan apparel industry formally adopted this stance by marketing itself with the slogan "Garments without Guilt" (Joint Apparel Association 2006). Apparel manufacturers linked higher labor standards to better quality and "guilt-free" products, which seemingly detached Sri Lankan products from the labor price war (Weeraratne 2005). However, violations of labor law and standards persist (Lanka Business Online 2006).

These cases also highlight the potential for partnership between trade unions and other labor organizations. Women workers remain underrepresented in Sri Lankan union leadership, and the partnership between the Women's Centre and the FTZWU enabled the development of women leaders in workers' councils and in trade union activities and campaigns. In addition, the center's innovative and creative methods were able to reach and access women when the trade union could not. Notably, workers were actively encouraged to think of themselves as active political agents. In a wider global context, trade unions and NGOs need to consider areas of commonality and contradiction in such partnerships and the possibility for further action. I mention "contradiction" because NGOs and trade unions have customarily viewed each other with suspicion and questions of legitimacy (Compa 2006).

We do need to question how we can move from case studies such as this to sustained global unions. Here we can look at the example of transnational regional women's labor networks that have been important for cross-border solidarity in two ways. First, transnational networks have facilitated solidarity action between labor groups in different South and Southeast Asian countries. Second, regional organizations such as CAW, TIE-Asia, and WWW are uniquely placed to bring together workers, facilitate exchange, provide information, provide resources, and, most important, engage in capacity building at the grass roots. These networks engage activists, trade unionists, and workers. AMRC, for example, began in 2003 to build a regional network through which labor organizations in different Asian countries can "pursue concrete solidarity actions to improve working conditions in Asian Transnationals" (AMRC 2006).

Finally, a persistent theme in this chapter has been the relationship between the local and the global. Authors like Steve McKay (2005) point out that while global organizing is important to meet the pressures of global capital, it is at the local level that labor control is constituted and reconstituted. He argues that in the case of the Philippine EPZ organizing, "*strategic* trans-national solidarity that puts local unionization and organization-building first" was a key to success (60). Thus we can conclude that in order to work successfully within and overcome these repressive environments that are found at the nexus of globalized production systems, global action is a necessity. Yet global action alone is insufficient in sustaining trade union rights and the betterment of workers' lives. Organizations such as the FTZWU and Women's Centre demonstrate how being responsive to, and working in and with, the wider communities in which workers' lives are situated is important to understanding and articulating local and global interests, as well as formulating multidirectional campaigns. The success at Jaqalanka should be viewed as a decisive moment in the struggle for labor rights in Sri Lanka's EPZs and an important illustration of the need for locally responsive global solidarity action.

5. ORGANIZING IN THE BANANA SECTOR

HENRY FRUNDT

Bananas do not rank highly among labor's strategic organizing targets in the global economy. Nevertheless, in developing nations, banana workers have achieved notable organizing success, gaining a unionization rate of 30 percent or more between 1960 and 1985. This rate declined in the 1990s as banana organizing faced major obstacles. However, in the new millennium local unions are struggling to overcome these barriers with U.S., European, and Canadian support. Their battle offers instructive lessons for cross-border efforts in other sectors. Key aspects of this effort include differential strategies for organizing transnational banana firms, such as Chiquita, Dole, and Del Monte; collaborative efforts with small-farmer associations and nongovernmental organizations (NGOs) to confront changing trade regimes, especially those in Europe; and collaborative action with small farmers and northern supporters to promote a retail marketing strategy that clarifies the benefits of various product certification schemes, supermarket approaches, and alignment with the Fair Trade movement.

The identification of these strategies and the descriptions of union organizing activity and global campaigns are based on a grounded theory approach that included fieldwork observations, secondary data analysis, and interviews with banana workers and company officials. This study began with the author's four-month stint in Central America in 1995, followed by subsequent biennial visits of several months over a ten-year period. In summarizing the results, this chapter will first briefly review historical efforts at banana organizing. The second section will examine different corporate strategies. All three transnational firms have banana unions, but they increasingly are also handling nonunion bananas, especially from Ecuador and most recently from Brazil, where unions are very limited. The third section will briefly lay out the stakes involved in rapidly changing banana trade patterns—from a quota-guaranteed system to a tariff-only system. Finally, with bananas going on the open market, unions and small-farmer allies are stepping up their direct appeals to consumers to support worker rights and livelihoods. Transnational firms and supermarkets have countered with a variety of schemes to certify the "quality" of their bananas as demonstrated by their brand's sustainable environmental and social practices. The last section will briefly outline the union consequence of the supermarket/transnational certification battle via auditing programs like the Rainforest Alliance, SA8000, EurepGAP, and Fair Trade. The Regional Coordination of Latin American Banana Workers' Unions (COLSIBA) and TransFair USA, the distributor of Fair Trade Labeled bananas in the United States, have agreed to promote union-approved fruit. However, Dole, which handles some Fair Trade bananas, is being targeted for its antiunion practices.

A History of Banana Organizing

The evolution of banana unions in Latin America and the Caribbean is an inspiring story that has been ably told by many skilled narrators (e.g., Dosal 1993; Euraque 1996; Grossman 1998; Jenkins 2000; Kepner 1936; Langley and Schoonover 1995; Striffler and Moberg 2003). Several key events in that history are particularly relevant to this chapter. Early in the twentieth century, as United Fruit absorbed more and more banana companies, it showed little sympathy for workers. A major confrontation came in 1928 when Colombian army officials acting under United Fruit's influence murdered four hundred striking employees. But in 1933, the local Costa Rican Communist Party led Atlantic-zone banana workers in a massive strike that resulted in the Confederation of Costa Rican Workers. Similar movements developed strong banana unions throughout Central America and Colombia. Political conditions also aided the workers as market conditions·improved.

During the middle decades of the twentieth century, transnational banana firms began to tolerate unions. Besides facing vociferous workers, they had to contend with skeptical government officials, stricter shipping schedules, and consolidated sales outlets. To avoid bottlenecks, they reluctantly negotiated contracts and increased wages and benefits. There were notable exceptions, such as Guatemala, where United Fruit rebuffed militant worker demands in the late 1940s and in 1954 aided the CIA's overthrow of a democratic government, forcing its workers to take refuge within a U.S.-backed labor confederation (Frundt and Chinchilla 1987). Yet when U.S. antitrust laws forced United Fruit/Chiquita to sell Guatemalan properties, the workers kept their Union of Banana Workers of Izabal (SITRABI), currently the nation's oldest existing union, for dealing with Del Monte. Although it never became politically militant, SITRABI gained solid contracts with Del Monte that provided housing, sports facilities, schools, transport, health services, and a livable wage (Frundt 1995). In Honduras in 1954, fifty thousand workers from United, Standard Fruit, and related companies inaugurated a sixty-nine-day "Great Banana Strike" that shut down half the country and precipitated the formation of the Federation of National Workers of Honduras (Argueta 1992). Recalling Guatemala, U.S. officials advised United Fruit to negotiate with the Union of Workers of the Tela Railroad Company (SITRATERCO), which stimulated the growth of other unions and passage of a national labor code. By the 1970s, banana workers in Colombia and Panama had also gained sufficient protective legislation to fit a Fordist model of labor relations that brought improved pay with managerial controls (Harari 2005). Honduras and Costa Rica had also made advances, inspiring numerous company stratagems to undermine union strength, ranging from in-house associations to protective arrangements with local "independent" producers. Most of these efforts failed.

However, in the early 1980s, when banana companies launched expansion plans to meet anticipated markets, they decided to confront militant unions head on. The transnational firms chose the largest exporter, Costa Rica, where they created "solidarista associations" as a sophisticated legal alternative to unions (Flores 1993). Costa Rican workers boldly resisted with several lengthy banana strikes, but the companies fired labor activists en masse and vilified unions and contracts in the media. Finally, struggling union leaders in Costa Rica and Honduras established COLSIBA as a regional response, which also included affiliates from Colombia, Panama, and Guatemala (G. Bermúdez, interview by author, 1999).

Organizing since 1998: Transnational Firms in Crisis

Since COLSIBA's origin in 1992, its unions have gained beneficial agreements in most Latin producing countries. SITRABI and the independent Union of Workers of Guatemala (UNSITRAGUA) won contracts in Guatemala, as did the National Union of Agribusiness Workers (SINTRAINAGRO) in Colombia. Two Costa Rican unions negotiated with Chiquita in the Sixaola region, and another organized near Nicaragua. Among COLSIBA's thirty thousand members, its five thousand women earned special protections as Frank (2005) engagingly elaborates. Two other aspects of COLSIBA's coordinated efforts are notable: its strategy to achieve global framework agreements on labor rights and its NGO collaboration. COLSIBA's efforts with Del Monte in Costa Rica and Guatemala and its major accord with Chiquita illustrate both strategies.

Following steps described by Tom Juravich in chapter 1, they also demonstrate how unions take advantage of "points of leverage" for building a comprehensive campaign.

In 1997 Costa Rican unions working with NGOs mounted an international publicity campaign to highlight insidious solidarista practices in Costa Rica. As a result, a COLSIBA affiliate union gained an accord with Del Monte/BANDECO. The agreement endorsed "respect for free unionization"; it allowed organizers access to each plantation and "the right of the worker to his/her free election of choice."[1] In October 1998, however, Hurricane Mitch dealt a shattering blow to Guatemala, Honduras, and Nicaragua. Extensive flooding in banana-producing areas cost an estimated nine thousand lives and more than $9 billion in damages (Thompson and Fathi 2005). Export production in nonunionized Ecuador rose to meet world demand. Then in late 1999, world demand peaked (Perillo 2000). The subsequent banana glut inspired the companies to demand major labor concessions.

Unions in each country felt the brunt, if in somewhat different ways. In Honduras, Chiquita insisted that SITRATERCO, the union that had inaugurated the country's national labor movement, modify its contracts and accept layoffs. In Nicaragua, banana unions from the Sandinista years struggled as Dole, the only transnational investor, left the country. Panamanian workers barely survived their lengthy strike in 1999. In Colombia, where an internal war was taking its toll, feisty banana unions faced demands for higher productivity as transnational firms curtailed purchases.

In Guatemala in 1999, hired goons vehemently attacked the stalwart union that represented Del Monte workers (SITRABI). The company had just subleased three major plantations and terminated more than nine hundred workers. As SITRABI planned a legal work stoppage in response, it suddenly faced a squad of two hundred armed thugs encouraged by Del Monte's independent producers. Company henchmen dragged SITRABI leaders from their beds in the middle of the night and threatened them with death if they did not renounce the union, call off actions, and accept layoffs and lower salaries. However, the union quickly notified the U.S./Labor Education in the Americas Project (US/LEAP), the European Banana Action Network (EUROBAN), and other organizations, which mounted an intense international campaign and induced Del Monte to sign an agreement with SITRABI and the International Union of Food, Agricultural, Hotel, Restaurant, Catering, Tobacco and Allied Workers' Association (IUF). Although the workers had to accept a 70 percent

---

[1]   A campaign by the World Development Movement, Banana Link, and the SITRAP union persuaded Del Monte-CR to sign a framework agreement in December 1997. SITRAP held the "majority in 1/3 of the elected permanent committees of Del Monte's 24 plantations, and ... rose to over 20 percent of Del Monte's total workforce of 4300"(Banana Link / War on Want 2003).

cut in health benefits, a 30 percent wage reduction, and some losses in education and housing, it was a major victory for SITRABI, which gained a master contract for more than six hundred workers and an unprecedented trial for the attackers (*US/LEAP* 2000).

Despite this accomplishment, transnational firms cited Hurricane Mitch as justification for replanting the Caribbean coast with African palm, which absorbed only a tenth as many workers (Perillo and Trejos 2000, 4). Chiquita also set up nonunion banana operations on Guatemala's Pacific coast, where work conditions reflected those in Ecuador.[2] Joint national-international union efforts could not alter the market glut caused by Ecuadorian producers, whose government permitted employers to quash organizing and violently evict unionized strikers (Human Rights Watch 2002).

COLSIBA mobilized to protect jobs. It leveraged Chiquita's profit center rooted in its "quality" image, its growth strategy built on responsiveness, and its key relationships and decision makers who were seeking to move the company in a fresh direction (Taylor and Scharlin 2004).[3] A coordinated campaign across Europe, Latin America, and the United States contacted supermarkets to urge Chiquita to honor its policy on corporate social responsibility, worker rights, and the environment. Locally, Chiquita labor leaders requested meetings with plantation managers. Finally, in June 2001, with its stock hanging in the balance, Chiquita signed a historic framework agreement with COLSIBA unions and the IUF, the first of its kind in the agricultural sector. A similar agreement was signed at the local level in Central America. EUROBAN and US/LEAP helped facilitate the accord. Chiquita promised to follow International Labor Organization (ILO) conventions in all countries *and* to ensure that its independent producers did so as well. It reaffirmed its commitment to address worker health and environmental concerns and agreed to engage with the unions when it had to relocate operations. Finally, all signatories assented to a biannual monitoring process (www.chiquita.com 2006). The accord represented a major achievement in the fight for banana worker rights. While

[2]   Chiquita gradually phased out its Atlantic operations. One contractor abruptly closed his Alabama/Arizona plantations, precipitating an eighteen-month worker occupation supported by UNSITRAGUA. After further pressure from US/LEAP and others, Chiquita finally hired 110 of the workers on its own lands. Lacking an overall strategy, however, UNSITRAGUA subsequently lost five of its nine Chiquita unions.

[3]   Following protests from Foro Emaús, the union-NGO coalition in Costa Rica, and pressure from the 1992 Earth Summit, Chiquita gradually committed itself to produce environmentally and socially responsible bananas in a new marketing strategy via the Rainforest Alliance. After unions and NGO supporters in the European Banana Action Network (EUROBAN) organized the first international banana conference in Brussels in May 1998 to scrutinize corporate performance, Chiquita quickly agreed to direct discussions. In consultation with COLSIBA, US/LEAP exerted additional leverage on key relationships and company decision makers via communications and publicity.

Chiquita had admittedly sought to undermine unions throughout its history, the company now aspired to a leadership position in worker relations. Some local union leaders remained skeptical—with its stock prices at an all-time low, Chiquita was promoting corporate responsibility and labor relations as its hope for salvation. They predicted trouble once salvation arrived.

Results of the framework agreement have been mixed. Union officials acknowledge that Chiquita has honored its commitments to an extent and in many ways is much better than its competitors. Since 2001 the company has allowed greater access to union organizers and has set up local commissions to resolve labor disputes. According to COLSIBA's vice coordinator, Gilberth Bermúdez, after Chiquita sold its operations in Colombia in 2004, "the agreement enabled the transfer of unions so that the new owners respect free unionization. In Ecuador, it facilitated discussions between Chiquita's contractor Reybanpac and the National Federation of Small Farmers and Indigenous Community Organizations of Ecuador (FENACLE). In Costa Rica, Chiquita became less antiunion than it had been in 1996–97. In Guatemala, however, the company transferred production to the south coast, an area that is very antiunion" (interview by author, 2004). In 2007, COLSIBA accused Chiquita of violent breaches overall.

Unions faced a challenge, however, as they sought to convert their members' historically bitter mind-set toward Chiquita into a more rational and pragmatic effort to engage local management and transform specific antiworker and antienvironmental practices. At the same time, where it has not closed *fincas* (plantations), Chiquita continued to demand major work changes. In Honduras and Guatemala it imposed *caja integral*, a new method for paying workers based on the amount of exported product rather than on the amount of picked fruit. In Honduras and Sixaola, Costa Rica, it removed cable motors that transported the fruit to packing sheds, forcing workers to hand-carry the huge stems. During 2005, strikes occurred at a number of Chiquita plantations. Following Hurricane Gamma in November 2005, Chiquita terminated its new Surco *finca* in Honduras and laid off a thousand workers elsewhere without consultation. Following scathing union publicity in Honduras and IUF intervention, it subsequently contracted with Surco as an independent producer and rehired the workers, but union rights there remained weak (*US/LEAP* 2006).

Del Monte and Dole have shown even less willingness to consider a global rights accord. Del Monte boasts of improved union dealings in Guatemala. According to local head Marco Garcia, since 2002 Del Monte has "stressed our labor-management relations ... [and] signed collective agreements in record time" (interview by author, 2005). But Del Monte subverted its 1997 agreement in Costa Rica and freely sources nonunion bananas from various countries.

Dole, which has been the least communicative with the unions, claims to support a rigid verification process for worker freedom of association but has been virtually silent about worker violations in Ecuador, where it obtains a third of its Latin bananas and where banana workers usually receive 30 percent of the wages earned by unionized workers, with no benefits (Perillo and Trejos 2000; see also the following discussion). Such a "comparative advantage" entices companies to enhance their Ecuadorian banana procurement, but it devastates worker standards in Central America, Colombia, and other traditional banana-producing areas.

To stem the expansion among nonunion banana firms in 2001, labor attempted to organize the 225,000 Ecuadorian banana workers. In February 2002, 1,400 workers represented by FENACLE inaugurated a job action at seven plantations producing for Noboa (Bonita), the largest independent. When FENACLE gained union recognition, Noboa accelerated its firings. When the union called a broad strike, the company hired thugs to terrorize the workers, sending nine to the hospital with gun wounds. FENACLE called for an international campaign, coordinated by US/LEAP and EUROBAN, to persuade Alvaro Noboa, then a candidate in the Ecuadorian presidential election, to negotiate a contract (*US/LEAP* 2002, 3). The campaign was only minimally successful. Subsequently, FENACLE and the IUF inaugurated a new organizing project that targeted Reybanpac, a Chiquita supplier.

Unions praise Chiquita for being the only transnational that has signed a global framework agreement, thereby exposing itself to criticism for an inevitably imperfect record of fulfillment. Nevertheless, many of Chiquita's actions and those of other companies show a pattern of persisting subversion of labor rights. According to German Zepeda, COLSIBA's coordinator, "between 1993 and 2004, 10,000 unionized workers were laid off in the region as a result of closures, large-scale dismissals and disease problems.... . Trade union attempts to organize workers have provoked a shift of production" that continues (2005).

Zepeda and other labor leaders complain that Chiquita and other transnational firms are engaging in specific strategies to escalate the global race to the bottom in their industries. These include the following:

1. Shifting their growing operations to national producers both to avoid dealing with union issues and to lower pay scales, since national producers often pay workers less than minimum wage.

2. Increasing the use of labor contractors to skirt wage and benefits obligations.

3. Imposing piecework formulas that force additional work for lower salaries.

4. Eliminating traditional benefits such as housing and schools.

5. Giving lip service to inequities and health problems faced by women workers.

6. Sporadically enforcing environmental regulations (see Frundt 2004b for elaboration).

At the same time COLSIBA has called upon transnational and national firms to reverse this race to the bottom in wages, benefits, and working standards. It is also expanding contacts with international NGOs to encourage greater understanding and support for the problems workers face when attempting to exercise their rights to organize in an openly competitive trade environment (Eade 2004).

The Common Effort to Defeat a (High) Tariff-Only System

A second area of dynamic organizing is the collaborative actions COLSIBA has taken toward trade policy. Historically, the banana sector enjoyed certain protections that benefited unions and small holders. As these protections began to erode dramatically in the early 1990s, COLSIBA joined with European activists and small farmers to prevent race-to-the-bottom competition. In 2005 the alliance struggled to prevent a tariff-only system in Europe that would eliminate supports to national markets.

Background

During much of the twentieth century, as U.S. transnational firms expanded their Latin plantations to ship bananas around the globe, European governments created alternate marketing opportunities for small holders in their own colonies. Seeking political stability, Britain, France, Spain, and Portugal each offered inducements to banana cultivators in island territories, and the yellow fruit frequently became a major source of income and employment. In 1975, via the Lomé Convention, nine European nations assured forty-five countries from Asia, the Caribbean, and the Pacific (ACP region) that they would maintain their banana industries, a commitment they periodically renewed until the end of the century. The nine nations also assigned licenses to transnational shippers from Latin America that guaranteed higher-priced banana sales in European venues.

In 1993 the countries of the European Union (EU) combined their individual national import regimes into a single system. The EU had been purchasing 40 percent of the world's bananas via two separate arrangements: the United Kingdom, France, and Spain paid higher prices to producers in current and former ACP colonies, while others, such as Germany, purchased bananas on the open market. Under its unified market in 1993, EU Regulation 404 allowed some of both arrangements under a complicated mix of licenses and quotas (Sutton 1997, 14f).

Agricultural ministers from the United Kingdom, France, and Spain persuasively argued that, as the Lomé Convention specified, colonies and ACP countries should not be adversely affected by any new banana import regime. Retaining their quotas would help preserve the small-holder way of life without wreaking ecological havoc on the land. It also would retard drug production and immigration. The European public supported protecting the imports from former colonies. In the end, the 1993 EU trade regime represented a compromise that retained some protections and phased out others, with severe effects on certain farmers and workers. Nevertheless, the United States was conspicuously unhappy with *any* protective quotas, a point it pursued in the newly established World Trade Organization (WTO) that it dominated (Grossman 1998; Myers 2004; Perillo and Trejos 2000; Raynolds 2003; Sutton 1997). United States transnational firms, especially Chiquita, claimed that the EU's 1993 import system had brought a dramatic 65 percent drop in its prior share of the European market. Leading the other transnational firms, it invoked section 301 of the U.S. Trade Act of 1974, which required an official trade-impact study (Frundt 2005). Chiquita's intervention appeared to pit Latin union interests against peasant banana producers.

The Battle in the WTO

Caribbean representatives vehemently disputed Chiquita's action. They claimed the company had dramatically increased production in the early 1990s, hoping to also earn a higher base for its EU market license allocation. It also had experienced lost profits and market share *before* the new system had been implemented. Finally, in disregarding their vulnerable economies, Chiquita "ignored the fact that ACP bananas were a great deal less profitable to import ... cost twice as much at point of origin, cost more to ship" (Myers 2004, 78, 128).

Nevertheless, Chiquita pressured the U.S. government to file suit under WTO regulations, successfully arguing that penalties should be imposed on Europe to assure equity. The Europeans repeatedly appealed to have the decision revoked, arguing that the United States was acting as spokesperson for the U.S.-based transnational banana companies. The United States warned that under the guise of aiding former colonies and small producers, the EU was actually protecting its own banana-trading companies and middlemen. However, unions and small holders advocated a third perspective: the thirty-five thousand workers represented by COLSIBA handled 40 percent of Latin bananas (outside Ecuador). If Chiquita folded, they would lose at least two-thirds of their members and weaken their negotiating power elsewhere. Through the umbrella EUROBAN network, COLSIBA and small Caribbean producers each opposed the WTO for undercutting European efforts to support fairer trade, both with former colonies and with Latin America. Finally, in April 2000, the WTO's Dispute Settlement Body reduced the U.S. claim by nearly two-thirds to $191.4 million but said the aggrieved could levy these penalties on imports from the European Union (WTO 1999).

A series of agreements temporarily resolved the burgeoning trade conflicts. First, European and ACP nations signed a successor accord to the Lomé Convention at Cotonou, Fiji, that made a somewhat weaker commitment to ensure "the continued viability" of national banana export industries in former colonies. Second, new faces in Washington negotiated an agreement with the EU that accepted the 1994–96 reference period proposed by Chiquita for determining customary markets. Although import guarantees for specific Latin countries would end immediately, the overall quota for Latin American producers would hold until 2006, granting unionized producers in Central America temporary relief. Then the quota would sunset and a tariff-only system would begin. For their part, ACP countries kept their protections until 2008 (Joint United States-European Union Release 2001; Josling and Taylor 2003).

The Subsequent Common Struggle

Despite a limited respite, banana workers and small farmers painfully witnessed "open trade" erode past protections. In 2000, for example, more than 100 million pounds of nonunion Latin bananas entered Europe on forged licenses, further depressing prices. Unions also had to contend with the growing power of supermarkets that formed major alliances to contract directly with nonunion producers and engaged in discount battles that undersold unionized and small-holder bananas. Windward producers saw their shipments to the United Kingdom decline from 238,000 tons in 1993 to 99,000 tons in 2002, and the number of farmers dropped from 27,000 to 7,000 (Myers 2004). The Windward Islands Farmers Association (WINFA) made common cause with Latin banana unions to stave off the complete elimination of EU banana import quotas. In 2005, unionists and island producers convened with EUROBAN in a second major banana conference to confront the banana race to the bottom. They predicted that Europe's change to a tariff-only system in 2006 would have a severe impact on unionized bananas and large segments of small-holder production. It would motivate transnational firms and others to increase exports from Brazil and West Africa. COLSIBA, WINFA, and EUROBAN called for "a continuation of the current system ... until a system that enables sustainable production can be introduced" (Parker 2005; EUROBAN et al. 2005).

COLSIBA coordinator German Zepeda said, "The resulting increase would dramatically affect Costa Rica and Honduras. Ecuador would ship more fruit to the US, causing a build-up of fruit in the other Latin countries as happened in the 1990s. . . . I see a huge impact on workers in the ACP countries. Even the Canary Islands producers have joined us with their concerns, shifting 360 degrees" (2005). COLSIBA affiliates and support groups had already begun to lobby government officials throughout Latin America and the Caribbean, in opposition to the high tariff-only plan. Banana workers such as Jiménez Guerra, Auria Vargas Castañeda, and Florintino Chavez, from Sixaola, Costa Rica, articulated their worries about banana sales. "The loss of our quotas [guaranteed sales to Europe] will reduce wages, with big ramifications for the economy here," complained Chavez. "They are saying we can handle a tax of 75 euros a box, but if it is higher, it will hurt us considerably. As a union, we are organizing to prevent this" (interview by author, 2004). Likewise, WINFA also mobilized a demonstration of two thousand farmers, trade unions, and support groups in St. Lucia and subsequent rallies in Dominica and St. Vincent (WINFA 2005a and 2005b). Caribbean Community (CARICOM) officials invited the organizers in to discuss their views, as both COLSIBA and WINFA worked to minimize divisions between CARICOM and Latin banana producers.

In 2006, the EU imposed the high tariff system of 176 euros per ton. Marcelino García, president of the Nicaraguan Union of Banana Plantation Workers (TRABANIC), has urged Nicaragua and Honduras to join Ecuador, Colombia, Panama, and the United States as they seek WTO arbitration of the high EU tariff. He viewed it as discriminatory against Latin American countries (Fresh Plaza 2007). As individual nations considered appeals, the unions and small holders also devoted attention to new policies that would recycle tariff funds to aid vulnerable economies such as those in the Caribbean. Whatever its final outcome, the trade battle offered an opportunity for both unions and small holders to join forces in a fresh collaboration that also set the stage for an integrated approach to brand certification.

Building Consumer Relations via Certification and Fair Trade

A third approach banana unions have taken to oppose the neoliberal onslaught has been their own "free market" appeal to the purchasing public. This parallels the corporate effort to hire third-party monitors who certify that their banana production meets certain environmental and social standards. As certification programs proliferated over the past decade, unions questioned the validity of these occasional "snapshot" audits. Just as important, they charged that companies and retailers were exploiting the monitoring process to polish their public image while simultaneously undercutting collective bargaining to gain competitive advantage. In the new millennium, however, unions have adopted a more nuanced stance, with certain certification programs such as Fair Trade.

The Union Critique

Beginning in 1993, labor began to question the way Chiquita was promulgating its endorsements by the Rainforest Alliance's Sustainable Agriculture Program for meeting environmental, and especially social, conditions. While the alliance program acknowledged the right of association, it did not properly recognize the freedom to bargain collectively. Even more suspect was how Dole and Del Monte applied the ISO 14001 environmental management system, which gave companies considerable latitude to create their own benchmarks and virtually bypass social impacts.[4] Because of such criticisms, newer certification plans sought greater social legitimacy, such as the United Kingdom's Ethical Trade Initiative and Social Accountability International (SAI)'s SA8000 standards that referenced core ILO labor conventions.[5]

Workers have welcomed initiatives that address social standards since they help brake a banana market's race to the bottom. Nevertheless, while acknowledging cosmetic improvements, labor openly challenges business claims about better social conditions. This is especially true concerning company disregard of labor's freedom of association to form unions and negotiate contracts, despite code references to ILO conventions 87 and 98.

Unions present six arguments that detail their questions about certification: (1) corporations adopt codes primarily as a marketing tool; (2) codes can be used to substitute for local laws; (3) codes are fundamentally designed to protect the corporate image; (4) outside monitoring of codes risks interfering in bona fide union activities; (5) most workers have little knowledge about codes, rendering them ineffective; and finally, (6) the "single snapshot" approach taken by code certifiers has not offered an adequate picture of company behavior, and lip service to freedom of association has not made it happen (Frundt 2004a; Longley 2005).

Some companies have responded by calling for dialogue. In the banana sector, from 2001 to 2006, union-company exchanges grew increasingly sophisticated, as corporate representatives appeared to reasonably negotiate with unions on the one hand but to brutally threaten employees and close large operations on the other. Where unions existed, some plantation officials agreed to improvements. But "in plantations where there was no trade union at the time of certification, certification has not led to freedom of association" (Chambron 2005, 105).

---

[4]   ISO 14001 arose in 1996 as an application of the international standards management approach codified under ISO 9000. It encouraged safer corporate environmental practices but contained no environmental benchmarks (Krut and Gleckman 1998). On Chiquita, see Taylor and Scharlin 2002.

[5]   Giant supermarkets have also developed codes such as EurepGAP, but they do not cover labor rights. In a 2005 campaign, Banana Link convinced Tesco to source union bananas.

Suspicious about codes, certain agricultural unions have preferred to promote union-produced products, as the UFW has done with lettuce, grapes, and strawberries in the United States. However, both the strategy and the logistics of developing a union-label campaign are fraught with difficulties (Frank 1998). In addition, all banana companies, including Chiquita, strongly resist a union label (it could necessitate that *all* bananas of a certain brand be unionized). Equally problematic is the supermarkets' effort to bypass their traditional dependence on transnational firms and forge their own direct arrangements with banana producers, such as the Nuboa (Bonita brand) from Ecuador and "Lola" from Guatemala's southern coast that are virtually nonunion.

Unionized Fair Trade?

For bananas, however, a different type of code has emerged that offers fresh possibilities: Fair Trade. The idea of Fair Trade labeling originated with small farmers in Mexico who thought consumers would be willing to pay a bit more for their coffee if they could be assured that those producing it would earn a sustainable livelihood. In the late 1980s, the Max Havelaar Foundation in the Netherlands helped Mexican farmers in Oaxaca establish a program that applied a "Fair Trade" label to coffee in order to assure a fair price to growers and pickers. Thus, the Fair Trade movement's primary objective was to improve living standards for small agricultural producers by making certain that their market price covered costs and livelihood. Purchasers also pay a small additional premium to the local community.

In 1997 participants founded Fair Labeling Organizations International (FLO) to standardize Fair Trade audits. In comparison with other certification approaches, FLO's cost accounting measures have gained high ratings for ensuring farmers a livable wage. In addition, FLO has developed well-articulated rules for preserving biodiversity, preventing soil depletion, and handling waste. As the only certification program to directly address commodity price declines, FLO has enabled at least 2,500 small producers in the Windward Islands to survive (Chambron 2005, 106). The U.N. Food and Agricultural Organization (FAO) has shown that, besides FLO's higher price premium, its benefits include better organization, bargaining position, creditworthiness, capacity building, guaranteed markets, access to international markets, and learning-by-doing export programs (FAO, cited by Chambron 2005, 102). Despite FLO's superior approach, some market coordination difficulties remain—supply has sometimes been higher than demand, so the premium has not always directly improved income (Bastian 2006).[6]

---

[6]   Moberg (2005) also documents participation and earnings problems for Caribbean farmers.

In the new millennium, FLO created standards for plantation workers that paralleled its requirements for small farmers. FLO claimed to perform a rigorous audit of freedom of association. Workers who petitioned would be guaranteed the right to collectively bargain. FLO also insisted that the social premium be distributed democratically. Besides being assured a livable wage, workers would receive the social premium via their union. These mechanisms potentially offered strong encouragement for forming unions within the intent of ILO conventions 87 and 98.

However, just as they had questioned other certification programs, labor leaders also expressed reservations about Fair Trade. First, the various Fair Trade organizations hold divergent positions on trade policy and social conditions. Notable advocates of alternative small-farmer production such as the Latin American Campesino Movement (CLAC) are reluctant to endorse transnational companies that have a history of environmental and labor abuse (in this, they do not differ from many union leaders). European FLO organizations remain divided about how to assess union claims concerning violations of freedom of association, especially in regard to cooperative banana producers that hire outside workers. Second, and more daunting, FLO *has* certified some plantations and cooperatives where questionable labor practices persist, including some that hire low-wage workers and lack unions. Virtually all FLO-approved shipments from Ecuador are nonunion, and union leaders such as Guillermo Touma from Ecuador insist that "Comercio Justo no es justo"— "Fair Trade is not fair" (2005). By not giving sufficient attention to labor rights while encouraging consumer purchases of Fair Trade produce from Ecuador, FLO may be actually undercutting union-produced bananas.[7]

FLO members are correct that establishing detailed international standards for working conditions is a major challenge. Wages vary substantially by region, and legislating common procedures for monitoring pay and safety conditions remains problematic. Nevertheless, since cultural differences affect how basic standards are best applied within globally competitive economic conditions, local organizations such as farmers' associations and independent unions are in the most advantageous position to assess what is appropriate for their own situation.

Finally, unions point out that just before FLO and other certifiers conduct their biannual visits, rules are observed and treatment improves, but

---

[7] Fair Trade bananas constitute important market segments in certain EU countries: as much as 50 percent in Switzerland, 25 percent in Holland, 20 percent in Belgium, and between 6 and 8 percent in Scandinavia and the United Kingdom; there is also growing interest in the market in France. Yet some Fair Trade-certified producers pay little attention to labor rights and "buy bananas from cooperatives that pay other workers below minimum and violate rights" (G. Bermúdez, interview by author, 2004).

when they leave, things often go back to "normal" (Frundt 2004a). Since the snapshot does not present the whole picture, someone has to fill out the details. Unions have a basis for claiming a key role in the certification process because they represent those involved in daily production. Some certifiers, such as Social Accountability International (SAI) program director Judy Gearhart, acknowledge the need "for more union input into the auditing process and increasing return visits" (2005). To put it more theoretically, the right of association at the local level retains preeminence among other socioeconomic rights.

The importance of this point was illustrated in Honduras in early 2005. The banana unions had persuaded Chiquita to use plastic bags without the Durisban (Chlorpyriphos) insecticide coating. However, Ameribi, a locally owned plantation supplying Chiquita, refused. In April, forty-eight members of the Ameribi union SITRAAMERIBI went on strike to demand the use of insecticide-free bags. The company attempted to declare the strike illegal and fired the forty-eight workers. Because unions invoked the global framework agreement, Chiquita reinstated the workers, and the independent producer promised to use untreated bags. Yet a process that automatically involved worker input could have prevented such a case from getting so out of hand.

The Dole Opportunity

To meet market demand, in 2003 FLO approved distribution of certain bananas through Dole. Unfortunately, as indicated above, Dole currently has a poorer labor rights record than Chiquita, notwithstanding its recognition of a UFW strawberry workers' union and several unions in Honduras. Indeed, despite its membership on the SAI board, Dole has consistently quashed attempts to organize unions and has often withdrawn from unionized locations without an adequate transfer agreement. In 2001 Dole did nothing when its independent producer in Ecuador fired the general secretary of one of the country's few banana unions when he demanded contract enforcement. In 2005 Dole denied illegal violations and union firings by its supplier Josepha and gained decertification of another agricultural union (US/LEAP 2005, 5). The company is now expanding banana production in nonunionized Cameroon and Brazil. It is the marketing agent for independent FLO producers in Peru and Ecuador, where it has signed a memorandum of understanding but has not recognized any union.[8] In northern Peru, Dole harvests, packages, certifies, and ships Fair Trade bananas grown by tiny farmer groups represented by the Organic Banana Producers (CEPIBO). Yet EUROBAN members

---

[8] FLO does not demand that "traders" like Dole recognize unions, but following FLO criteria, they must respect ILO conventions 89 and 98.

charge Dole with severely exploiting these farmers and causing those seeking to strengthen CEPIBO to be fired (see Drewes 2005). The FENACLE union in Ecuador has repeatedly informed Dole of its difficulties at the Prieto and Josepha plantations. While the transnational has listened to FENACLE's complaints, no changes have resulted. "Workers [in Ecuador and Peru] fear to speak about unions" states German Zepeda of COLSIBA. "There is suspicion, not freedom of association for bargaining and striking" (2005). Unions were also angered by Dole's environmental violations (use of the fungicide DBCP, pesticide spills), its advocacy of a tariff-only system, and the treatment of its pineapple and flower workers.[9]

In March 2006, COLSIBA gave the company a five-month ultimatumto demonstrate its openness to union organizing, especially in Ecuador and Costa Rica. The union notified EUROBAN, US/LEAP and others that unless there were major changes, it would begin taking tough actions to convince Dole and its national suppliers to end union repression overall. US/LEAP and EUROBAN affiliates began contacting supermarkets in anticipation. Seventeen organizations notified Dole by letter in May 2006, charging it with failing to respect basic worker rights. Simultaneously, US/LEAP, COLSIBA, and six other organizations released a special report entitled *Dole, Behind the Smokescreen*, documenting the violations (see Dole, www.usleap.org). In September, they unanimously agreed that Dole had failed to take any meaningful steps to improve respect for worker rights at its operations or those of its suppliers. The unions and NGOs therefore escalated pressure on Dole. EUROBAN and the Confédération Générale du Travail (CGT) in France (where Dole-Europe is based) inaugurated a full-scale campaign. US/LEAP stepped up support work in the United States. By early 2007, Dole reluctantly began a dialogue with COLSIBA affiliates in Ecuador and Costa Rica, hoping for an agreement.

The Test of Fair Trade Itself

Because most certification schemes, including those of FLO, have failed to fully address freedom of association, workers and consumers have confronted the issue head on. Following a COLSIBA request, FLO is considering adding union representatives to its board, risking a potential membership split among European and some Latin participants. COLSIBA persists in demanding that FLO hold its distribution agents as well as its direct producers accountable on labor rights. In 2004, COLSIBA discovered that FLO's official certifier for the U.S. market, TransFair USA, was promoting nonunion and solidarista

---

[9] In October 2005, US/LEAP demonstrated at the SAI meeting in New York. Despite making promises, Dole did not negotiate with SintrasSplendor, the union representing flower workers at Dole's Splendor plant in Colombia. A year later it announced the plant would close (www. usleap.org).

bananas. As a result, COLSIBA publicized its opposition to the Fair Trade program. Seeking to resolve the conflict, US/LEAP encouraged TransFair to negotiate with COLSIBA. When traditional supporters of Fair Trade (the Fair Trade Federation, Equal Exchange, Oxfam America, Lutheran Social Concerns, Coop America, and the Latin American Campesino movement) learned about potential transnational and union involvement, they voiced major concerns about the possible displacement of traditional peasant production, insisting that any agreement truly protect small holders.

In 2005 the confluence of these forces brought COLSIBA and TransFair USA to jointly announce their collaboration for "the development and growth of the market of Fair Trade union bananas" for the United States. The agreement signified the potential alliance of three very important banana constituencies: unionized banana workers, small farmers, and trade-conscious consumers (COLSIBA/TransFair 2005). It also marked a major step in the long effort to implement freedom of association as an essential certification principle, in this case of "quality bananas." In the signed accord with COLSIBA, TransFair pledged that it would ship only union-approved (not necessarily union) bananas. The two organizations "share a common vision to organize, empower and raise the standard of living of farm workers ... to collaborate further with the union movement ... bearing in mind the interests of banana farm workers as well as those of small-scale producers" (COLSIBA/TransFair 2005). To do this, the two organizations agreed to coordinate banana plantation inspections that included local union representatives, to work together on marketing Fair Trade union bananas, and to create a coordinating committee that would evaluate progress biannually.

The COLSIBA/TransFair agreement temporarily united both small-holder and union interests with a transnational struggling to regain its foothold in the U.S. retail market.[10] In the months that followed, however, various forces impeded the plan: guidelines and time frames were not always clear. TransFair and COLSIBA had to debate the extent to which certifying producers understood trade union fundamentals and truly negotiated collective bargaining agreements. In addition, mechanisms had to be solidified to handle marketing and labeling questions and to avoid potential corruption in the allocation of FLO premiums within fledgling unions. In November 2005 Hurricane Gamma left many of Chiquita's Honduran plantations under water, putting on hold any potential Fair Trade shipments. Despite strenuous union objections, Dole became TransFair's new suitor. Nevertheless, the TransFair/COLSIBA accord represents the kind of fresh thinking indicative of vibrant unionism and an

---

[10]   Meanwhile, other groups advocate Fair Trade towns. In Italy, CTM has petitioned more than one hundred communities, hospitals, and schools to purchase Fair Trade bananas and recognize worker rights.

alliance that addresses consumers directly in a way that benefits small producers and workers.

New kinds of organizing are happening in the banana sector. After briefly summarizing the historical rise of banana unions, this chapter has examined three organizing approaches pursued by current unions that to some degree reflect the campaign leverage approach articulated by others in this book. The first is the unions' work with NGO supporters (EUROBAN, US/LEAP) to gain direct negotiation with transnational banana firms. This has resulted in unions' winning several local accords with Del Monte and a global framework agreement among Chiquita, COLSIBA, and the IUF. The second is their collaboration with NGO networks and small-farmer organizations like WINFA to develop a unified position on trade policy, and especially to resist or modify the tariff-only system of the EU. On the ground, COLSIBA affiliate members like Florintino Chavez and Auria Vargas Castañeda have participated in workshops and organized delegations to lobby government officials about trade. The unions have also formed broader global alliances that can assist their public campaigns. The third approach is labor's increasing sophistication in its use of certification programs and Fair Trade to reduce union repression and open space for organizing workers. Leaders like Honduras's German Zepeda and Iris Murgia, Costa Rica's Gilberth Bermúdez, and Ecuador's Guillermo Touma and their fellow unionists have marshaled certification standards to gain greater freedom to bargain. The result has also brought increasing consumer attention to labor conditions in the banana sector. Each strategy has its limitations: companies like Chiquita can backtrack on their global framework agreements and redirect union organizing energies toward monitoring accountability. Relationships with small-farm groups also require constant vigilance due to the varied interests involved. Finally, companies are continually revamping their marketing approaches to exploit contradictions (e.g., selling Fair Trade-certified fruit at WalMart!). Nevertheless, by skillfully developing an adaptive, alliance-based approach to different corporations, by collaborating with farmer associations to confront trade policies, and by strategically cooperating with certification programs and Fair Trade marketing, banana unions have created a notable counterforce against the global race to the bottom that deserves emulation.

6. DOCKERS VERSUS THE DIRECTIVES

Battling Port Policy on the European Waterfront

PETER TURNBULL

Global companies now dominate the maritime industry. By the turn of the millennium, the six leading shipping alliances accounted for around 60 percent of world container traffic, and the five largest container terminal operators handled well over a third of all container boxes to pass through the world's ports. More important, these companies no longer confine their activities to port-to-port movements or within-port handling but now provide door-to-door services from the manufacturer to the distributor or final customer. With operations in all the different transport modes, these transnational transport and logistics companies not only benefit from globalization and the ever-expanding volume of world trade, but they also "act as a catalyst for reduced restrictions on international trade, promote new technologies and market them on a global basis, seek both national and international policy measures to support expanded transport investments, and often discourage regulatory measures to internalize the negative social and environmental costs associated with transport activities" (Janelle and Beuthe 1997, 200). Put differently, international developments in the transport sector are both a cause and an object of globalization.

The major concern for port labor in the global era is that by redefining the scale and scope of their operations, global transport companies have effectively reconstituted the geography of social relations among capital, labor, and the state, considerably strengthening their own power and control while disempowering others. This is not to suggest that trade unions in the transport sector are now powerless in the face of globalization. On the contrary, a combination of associational power, arising from well-established collective organizations, and structural power, arising from the strategic location of transport workers in the economic system (Wright 2000, 962), has led to a robust defense of transport workers' interests (Silver 2003, 99; Turnbull 2000, 2006). Moreover, the immobility of infrastructure capital and the strategic localization of global companies (Mair 1997) mean that capital must be sufficiently embedded to exploit labor as a factor of location and not just a factor of production. As a result, transport companies are less likely to use relocation as a strategy to reduce cost in response to declining profitability. For transport workers, however, this can lead to a defense of their local place over the defense of wider, international, class interests. Transport unions, for example, have often cooperated with, or conceded to, the demands of capital and the nation state to restructure their port in order to make it more competitive in the international market for port services, which has typically involved a combination of job losses, greater flexibility, and a deterioration in dockworkers' terms and conditions of employment (Turnbull and Wass 1997; forthcoming). Even if transport unions think globally, they invariably act locally.

Within Europe, this tendency is exacerbated by the nature of economic integration and the political opportunity structure of the European Union (EU). Supranational institutions within the EU are primarily dedicated to implementing and maintaining a single market, with industrial relations and social policy left principally in the hands of EU member states (Scharpf 1999; 2002, 665–66). The result is "a *multi-level political economy*, where politics is decentralized in national institutions located in and constrained by integrated competitive markets extending far beyond their territorial reach" (Streeck 1998, 431, original emphasis). The problem for organized labor is not simply the fact that markets are no longer coterminous with national borders but that any pressures for the political defense of social cohesion—the desire to prevent the market economy from becoming a market society—tend to be deflected to national systems of politics and/or employment regulation where cross-border competition and xenophobia, rather than international solidarity, might then prevail (1998, 432).

With its roots firmly embedded in the nation state, the European labor movement is particularly disadvantaged by the developing economic and institutional structure of the EU (della Porta and Kriesi 1999, 19). European trade unions face a double dilemma. First, while there may be strong incentives to operate at the European level and ample opportunities to do so via a range of supranational institutions (Stevis 2002), as long as industrial relations and social policy are left primarily in the hands of member states, "unions still have to act in national arenas, *relying on familiar national resources and practices*" (Martin and Ross 2000, 122, emphasis added). Thus, "the limits on market regulation at the EU level built into its political institutions give unions strong disincentives to invest resources in the Europeanization of their structures and strategy"

(122). Second, if and when trade unions do engage with the process of European integration and the political opportunity structure of the EU, they can easily "succumb to an elitist embrace," characterized by "a suppression of both political alternatives and mobilization capacity" (Hyman 2005, 24, 27). Here the dilemma is between the "logic of membership" and the "logic of influence," where the former "requires unions to maintain their representative credentials by articulating the wishes and interests of their constituents" and the latter "requires them to adapt their aims and methods to the actual decision-making processes on which they exert an impact" (24). As della Porta and Kriesi (1999) point out, the EU's technocratic process of formulating, analyzing, revising, debating, amending, and reformulating policy within an elaborate network of interacting committees leaves little room for grassroots mobilization:

> It is as far removed from the capacities and inclinations of the local movement constituencies as are the seats of these supranational organizations. The "transnationalization" of political mobilization poses, in other words, a problem for the development of the *action repertoire* of social movements. (20, original emphasis).

For Europe's dockworkers, these dilemmas were thrown into very sharp relief when the European Commission published a proposed directive, *On Market Access to Port Services,* in February 2001 (CEC 2001), which included, among other things, the right of port users such as shipping lines to employ their own labor instead of recognized dockers. While traditional repertoires of collective action had been sufficient to defend workers' interests in the context of national port reforms during the 1980s and 1990s,[1] national unions and global union federations (GUFs) now recognized that they needed to engage their members in a new politics of scale at the European level (Turnbull 2006). In the ensuing "war on Europe's waterfront" the dockers secured a remarkable victory when the European Parliament rejected the directive in November 2003. Their success can be attributed to a strategy of labor internationalization, defined as sustained and routine cooperation with actors from other countries against the actions of one or another state or international organization (Tarrow 1999), and a new unconventional repertoire of collective action, most notably the Euro-demonstration and Euro-strike but also stop-work meetings to educate dockworkers on the threats posed by the directive and coordinated action against international shipping lines (Turnbull 2006). Less than a year later, however, battle lines were redrawn when the Commission proposed a revised directive, *On Market Access to Port Services* (CEC 2004). On this occasion, trade unions played the "information-gathering report-writing

---

[1] A notable exception was the United Kingdom (Turnbull, Woolfson, and Kelly 1992).

lobby resolution-passing game" (della Porta and Kriesi 1999, 20) while not abandoning, or seemingly jeopardizing, their ability to mobilize grassroots support and participation in direct forms of action. Europe's port workers, it seems, have navigated a new course for organized labor through the dilemmas of European integration and the political opportunity structure of the EU.

Following the social movement model of strategic union choice developed by Frege and Kelly (2003), the next section explores the evolution of European port policy by focusing on the four independent variables depicted in figure 7—namely, the strategies of transnational employers and the supranational state, the process of social and economic change, the institutional context of industrial relations, and trade unions' own organizational structures. Union strategies could be interpreted as nothing more than the outcome of changes to these independent variables in a national context, or the result of differences between place in an international comparative context. Frege and Kelly, however, caution against such simplistic interpretations by introducing a process variable to capture the internal dynamics of union revitalization. Thus, framing processes refer to the ways in which unionists perceive and think about changes in their external context as threats or opportunities. In particular, when, and why, do unions develop new strategies based on a very different repertoire of contention rather than repeat well-worn behavioral patterns in responding to new challenges? These questions are examined in a subsequent section through a comparison of port workers' response to the first (2001–3) and second (2004–6) "ports packages" proposed by the European Commission and championed by global capital.

The Evolution of European Ports Policy

Although it is often difficult to disentangle state policies and employer strategies on the one hand from broader social and economic changes on the other, there is little doubt that all these variables have exerted a profound effect on the strategic choices of European port unions. Traditionally, port employers and member states sought to defend national port interests against any encroachment by the Commission, but in more recent years they have increasingly accepted the central tenets of a European common transport policy and the progressive liberalization of the port transport industry following the Treaty of the European Union (TEU) signed at Maastricht in 1992.[2] These developments were both a response to, and a vehicle for, closer European economic integration and marked a significant departure from past practice. Prior to the TEU, the political decoupling of economic integration and social protection issues enabled transport unions to defend port workers' interests through two different means.

[2] The treaty marked a significant advancement in the EU's competencies in the fields of economic and monetary policy, industrial policy, trans-European networks, and transport policy.

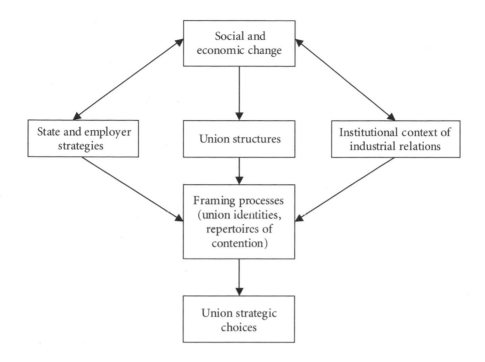

Fig. 7 A social movement model of union strategic choice. *Source:* Frege and Kelly 2003, 13.

First, this was accomplished by using traditional repertoires to defend local and national interests against any incursion by international capital, a process that Tarrow (1999) describes as "domestication." Second, it was achieved through occasional "resource borrowing," where the focus was still on domestic action but with the assistance of external allies (1999). Post-TEU, these strategies have proven far less effective, and are arguably untenable in the longer term, as the tide of supranational liberalization rises over national dock labor schemes and port-level industrial relations. While dockworkers may be well organized at the local and national levels, union structures have been slow to adapt to the increasingly international orientation of the industry, the business strategies of global employers, and the new priorities of the national and supranational state.

Socioeconomic Change and the Strategies of the Supranational State and Transnational Employers

In most European countries, ports are an integral component of the nation's transport infrastructure and are typically developed as maritime, industrial, and distribution areas that not only provide services to users but generate employment and economic growth for the local, regional, and even national economy (Barton and Turnbull 1999; Turnbull and Weston 1992). Nation-states fiercely defended their particular port systems and related transport polices from any incursion by the European Commission, principally on the grounds of subsidiarity.[3] For many years, the Commission accepted the desire of member states to retain autonomy with respect to seaports (Carossino 1982, 11–12). However, under the TEU 1992, transport policy was placed "in the forefront of the moves towards the completion of the internal market" (CEC 1992, 4). With over 90 percent of European external trade and over 40 percent of intra-EU trade transported by sea, ports were clearly central to closer economic integration. As the political priorities of member states shifted, the Commission was given a mandate to integrate Europe's ports into the common transport policy.

In a *Green Paper on Sea Ports and Maritime Infrastructure*, the Commission sought to create a "level playing field of competition" for European ports (CEC 1997), which challenged the autonomy of public port authorities and the interests of many private port operators. Speaking on behalf of the public port authorities, the European Sea Ports Organisation (ESPO)[4] expressed support for systematic liberalization but argued that "[i]mproving ports' performance is not … achieved by pan-European co-ordination of port development… . [It] is a responsibility of the ports and will come about through free and fair competition" (ESPO 1998, 4; 1996, 8). However, while both ESPO and the Federation of Private Port Operators (FEPORT 1998, 9)[5] expressed concerns about pan-European rules on port investment and pricing, they were favorably disposed toward the Commission's proposals for "developing a regulatory framework aiming at the more systematic liberalization of the port services market" (CEC 1997, 4). Global container terminal operators, in particular, were keen to exploit pent-up demand in the Mediterranean but argued that open access to the port services market was a prerequisite for any major investment on their part. Like ESPO and FEPORT, the shipping lines were content to settle questions of infrastructure investment and port charging in

---

[3] Within a federal system of governance, the principle of subsidiarity ensures that policy issues are handled by the lowest competent authority. Thus, the central European authority should have a subsidiary function, performing only those tasks that cannot be performed effectively at a more immediate or local level by member states. This means that the EU may act and make laws only where member states agree that the action of individual countries is insufficient.

[4] ESPO was formed in 1993 and currently represents over 98 percent of all European seaports.

[5] FEPORT was also established in 1993 and currently represents around eight hundred private terminal operators and stevedores who collectively handle almost 90 percent of all EU cargo.

the medium to longer term but regarded the liberalization of port services as "the area where more real progress within a short timeframe may be expected" (Carlier 1998).[6]

For the shipping lines, this was a question of economics and opportunity as well as political practicalities. Charges levied by the public port authority for the use of port facilities are typically around 5 percent of the total door-to-door cost of transporting goods, whereas cargo handling changes represent 10 to 25 percent. For short-sea shipping, which the Commission has been very keen to promote as a more sustainable form of transport, these costs can be as high as 40 to 60 percent (CEC 1997, 14). Labor costs typically account for 60 to 70 percent of these cargo handling charges, and any delays to shipping caused by labor (e.g., shortages or strikes) can be very costly. Conversely, any improvement in labor productivity and the utilization of equipment in port has a particularly beneficial effect for shipping lines in terms of reducing the vessel's waiting time *for* a berth as well as reducing the time a vessel spends *at* the berth (UNCTAD 1987). This means that any improvement in port efficiency will have a disproportionate effect on the economics of onward cargo movement in terms of cost and transit time to market (Goss 1990, 214–15). Put differently, improving labor productivity and the efficiency of port services can significantly extend the market, providing new trading opportunities with new trading partners. In fact, opening up the European port services market to greater competition would not only reduce costs and drive up productivity but also redefine the geographic scale of the market.

While the reform of public port authorities in respect to operational autonomy and commercial freedom, transparency of accounts, public limited liability, and the introduction of new executive management structures was commonplace throughout the EU during the 1990s (Barton and Turnbull 1999; ESPO 1996), the reform of port labor arrangements, or dock labor schemes, proved far more problematic. Port unions proved adept at exploiting national industrial relations systems to defend their members' interests, and union organization proved highly resilient in the face of concerted attempts by the state and national port employers to reform dock labor schemes (Barton and Turnbull 2002; Saundry and Turnbull 1999; Turnbull 2000). The Commission's proposed directive, *On Market Access to Port Services*, however, threatened to impose a new form of cross-border competition on national dock labor schemes while simultaneously exposing the geographical limitations and internal fissures in union organization at the international level. As Stevis (2002, 48) points out, "regulatory competition at the level of sectors and firms will be a disaster for union politics."

---

[6] Manual Carlier was the chairman of the Port Working Group of the European Community Shipowners' Association (ECSA).

The Institutional Context of Industrial Relations and Union Structures

Across Europe, the institutions associated with corporatism still remain, but the purpose and functioning of these institutions have changed, especially in the Eurozone, where the focus of wage negotiations is now directed toward cost control and international competitiveness (Grahl and Teague 2003). In general, industrial relations in Europe have become more voluntaristic and less obligational. For example, collective bargaining, as Marginson and Sisson (2002a, 333, and 2002b, 678–80) point out, often looks more like social dialogue than agreement making under the pincer of cross-border competition at the macro level and coercive comparisons at the micro level. The port transport industry is by no means immune from these pressures, but the balance between worker protection and international competitiveness is very different.

With the notable exceptions of the United Kingdom and Ireland, the dockland labor market in most European countries is highly regulated, and microcorporatist patterns of industrial relations are commonplace. For example, dockworkers are usually afforded professional status, and preferential employment rights are granted to recognized dockers. Thus, there are still extensive regulations controlling the supply of port labor, ranging from statutory registration schemes in Belgium to "cooperative companies" (a form of workers' cooperative) in Italy. In addition, national dock-labor schemes typically involve port-based and/or industry-wide regulations on the daily allocation of dockworkers to the operative companies and the mandatory provision of training and various benefits, such as attendance money when dockers are available for employment but no work is on offer. Industrial relations are characterized by multiemployer collective agreements at the industry level and codetermination at the workplace level, leading to standardized terms and conditions of employment for many dockworkers and a strong collective voice (Barton and Turnbull 1999; Turnbull and Wass 2007).

In some European countries—for example, Belgium and Germany—such extensive forms of regulation and "rich bargaining" are only to be expected given the prevailing national system of industrial relations. In countries such as the Netherlands, however, dockworkers have been able to fill the vacuum created at the workplace level under the centralized national industrial relations system (Schilstra and Smit 1994). Dutch port workers, like their contemporaries in many other European countries, are renowned for their militancy and workplace organization (Smit 1992; Turnbull and Sapsford 2001). In Spain, for example, where most unions typically rely on votes in the quadrennial works council elections to exert influence rather than invoke rank-and-file activism, the Coordinadora, the principal dockers' union, is one of only a handful of strong occupational unions (Rigby and Lawlor 1994, 262) with membership density in most ports in the region of 80 to 90 percent.[7] Attempts to reform Spanish ports have met with concerted opposition and often prolonged strike action (Saundry and Turnbull 1999; Waterman 1990). Whether dockworkers are universally strike-prone is questionable (Turnbull and Sapsford 2001), but in Europe at least they are certainly militant and well organized.

The reliance of European port unions on the "logic of membership" in their domestic arena has not precluded major reforms to national dock-labor schemes in several member states. In recent years, many European transport unions in countries such as Belgium, Germany, Ireland, Italy, the Netherlands, and Portugal have worked in concert with employers and the nation-state to reform work practices and thereby improve labor utilization and port performance. In other European countries, such as Denmark, Finland, Spain, and Sweden, however, transport unions have mobilized their traditional repertoire to defend workers' interests and resist more extensive port labor reforms.[8] In all these countries, unions have still reported some deterioration in their members' terms and conditions of employment, but in a wider international context European dockers have fared much better than port workers in other continents in the age of globalization (Turnbull and Wass 2007). As a result, many public port authorities, and certainly global terminal operators and international shipping lines, have become increasingly frustrated by what they regard as a slow and costly process of national port labor reform.

It was in this context that several member states, most notably Spain, determined to upload their domestic liberalization policies to the European level and open up another front in the ongoing assault on port workers' monopoly position (Börzel 2002, 193–94). In fact, the Transport and Energy commissioner, Loyola de Palacio, who initiated both port directives, was a former minister in the Spanish conservative government, so it was no surprise when the Spanish state subsequently announced that it would liberalize its own port laws in accordance with, and in anticipation of, the proposed 2001 directive. Moreover, the Spanish government used its presidency of the EU in 2001 to broker a political agreement between member states on the first ports package during the initial Council of European Ministers' deliberations (Turnbull 2006). As the impetus for liberalization shifted from the national to the international arena, port unions quickly realized that they could no longer rely on domestic organization and traditional repertoires

---

[7] Other unions are also recognized in Spanish ports, bringing the total combined union density figure closer to 100 percent in the major ports.

[8] Port unions in the United Kingdom, in contrast, were "marginalized" by the abolition of the National Dock Labour Scheme in 1989 and the subsequent privatization of trust ports (Saundry and Turnbull 1999; Turnbull and Wass forthcoming; Turnbull, Woolfson, and Kelly 1992).

to defend their members' interests. But shifting scale to the European level would be no easy task.

It is hardly surprising that most European employers have been reluctant to engage in pan-European collective bargaining with organized labor, in the ports or any other industrial sector (Martin and Ross 2000, 131). Indeed, the prospects for supranational collective bargaining in the port transport industry are distinctly poor. Both ESPO and FEPORT, for example, have steadfastly refused to enter into negotiations or even social dialogue with port unions on the grounds that they are business organizations rather than employers' associations. Thus, whereas European joint committees and sectoral social dialogue committees are well established in other transport sectors such as civil aviation, inland waterways, railways, road transport, and sea transport, there are no similar bodies for European ports (CEC 2003). This situation reflects deficiencies in workers' own organizations at the European level as well as the hostility of both national and global capital to any international regulation of industrial relations or wider social issues.

Most European transport unions are affiliated with the International Transport Workers' Federation (ITF), but there are some notable omissions, including major port unions in France, Spain, and Sweden. There is also an uneasy relationship between the ITF and the European Transport Workers' Federation (ETF), the ITF's regional European organization. The latter dates back to jurisdictional disputes between the ITF and the Federation of Transport Workers' Unions in the European Union (FST, the forerunner of the ETF),[9] which was only partially resolved by an agreement reached in 1994 recognizing the ITF's responsibility for the coordination of international solidarity and relations with non-EU institutions and the primary role of the FST with respect to the institutions of the EU. The differences between these two international organizations were mirrored in the approach of individual transport unions. While some unions adopted a "fortress Europe" approach to any international action, which they sought to effect via the ETF rather than the ITF, others regarded the ETF as a wasteful duplication and preferred all international activities to be coordinated by the ITF (ITF 2002). These fissures were opened wider by the emergence of the International Dockworkers' Council (IDC), a rival grassroots federation born out of the long-running dispute in the port of Liverpool at the end of the 1990s.[10] As a result, port workers' organizations at the European level fail to satisfy two of the most important conditions for effective international trade unionism: organizational comprehensiveness, in

---

[9]   In 1999, the FST was dissolved, and its members joined with the ITF's European affiliates to create the ETF.

[10]   In several member states (e.g., Spain and Sweden) rival national port unions are affiliated with different international federations (ITF/ETF or IDC), which has exacerbated domestic union rivalries and transposed these differences to the international arena.

the form of extensive affiliation with the global union federation, and internal authority, as demonstrated by affiliates' willingness to follow a central strategy (Ramsay 1997, 526–27).

The dilemma of reconciling the logic of influence with the logic of membership further undermines the internal authority of the ITF/ETF. Given their reliance on traditional repertoires of collective action in domestic space and the past success of domestication, with occasional resource borrowing, it is perhaps not surprising that dockworkers were the last transport group to join the political structures of the FST (in October 1993). However, the new dockers' section of the FST quickly determined to establish social dialogue with the Commission and European port employers (FST 1993). It is not surprising that the logic of influence proved largely fruitless, given the employers' reluctance to engage in social dialogue, and this logic was far removed from the interests of rank-and-file dockworkers. While dockers favored direct action, certainly in domestic space, the goal of the FST, in the words of Hughes de Villele, the FST's general secretary at the time, was to be "very proficient ... We have to be right. We have to fight on the basis of facts, not conflict" (interview by author, 1995). The IDC, in contrast, as a grassroots organization initially denied access to European institutions, has followed the logic of membership from the outset.

In light of our four independent variables—social and economic change, supranational state and global employer strategies, the institutional context of industrial relations, and union structures—it would appear that the odds were stacked against Europe's port workers when the Commission proposed its first ports package. But framing processes led to the emergence of an internationalization strategy that dockworkers deployed with great effect within the political opportunity structure of the EU. When the second ports package was announced in October 2004, union strategy changed tack as the complex and contested dynamics of European politics created new opportunities for labor internationalization.

Framing an Internationalization Strategy

Framing processes often express elements of a union's identity and typically draw on familiar ideas about trade union action (Frege and Kelly 2003, 14).[11]

---

[11] The account that follows is based on secondary sources (e.g., newspaper reports, internal union documents, and correspondence between dockers' unions/federations) and primary data (e.g., participant observation at several union meetings and semistructured interviews with numerous union officials, dockworkers, employer representatives, and Commission officials). The research began in the summer of 2000 when the ETF/ITF was presented with a list of questions from the Commission related to port policy and market access. The request was debated at an

As a result, these processes can be subject to a debilitating "drag of the past" as workers cling to accustomed modes of action, especially when they have been previously successful (Piven and Cloward 2000, 415). In a domestic context, initiatives led by union officials and a changing institutional context or crisis can provide the impetus for a reframing of union identities and the emergence of a new repertoire of contention (Frege and Kelly 2003, 19–21). In an international context, a "scale shift" is also required. This is not simply a question of reproducing, at a different level, the claims, targets, and constituencies where contention begins: it involves new targets, new alliances, and changes in the focus of claims and perhaps even identities (Tarrow 2005). The institutions of the EU offer a variety of venues in which local, national, and international union organizations can mobilize, and these supranational institutions are not only a primary target of international actors but also a potential fulcrum around which these actors may turn their attention and activities (Haworth and Hughes 2002, 66; Tarrow 2005). But to reiterate, the particular form of Europeanization, to date, has failed to equip unions to cope with the challenges posed by economic integration (Martin and Ross 2000, 123), and while it is self-evident that unions need to extend coordinated action to incorporate the international level if the distance between their members and European integration is not to increase (Waddington 2005, 527), too one-sided an engagement with the Brussels machine can be a recipe for bureaucratic inertia and the estrangement of rank-and-file workers (Hyman 2005, 24–27; Stevis 2002, 148–49). What, then, are the political opportunities for organized labor to press their claims at the European level, and how can workers redefine their interests in ways that will help them to overcome their collective action, coordination, and coalition problems?

According to Marks and McAdam (1999), the structure of political opportunities available to challenging groups provides incentives for collective action by affecting people's expectations of success or failure. Consequently, these opportunities do more than shape the timing and fate of collective action:

> Organizers are also very likely to tailor their efforts to the specific kinds of changes they see taking place in the political systems they seek to challenge.

ITF Dockers' section meeting, and the author agreed to write a response to the Commission's questions as an internal discussion document for the unions. This continued a close working relationship with the ITF that has previously involved major research projects (e.g., Turnbull and Wass 1995), instruction at ITF educational schools, and research presentations at the quadrennial ITF congress in New Delhi (1998) and Vancouver (2000). The secretary of the ITF dockers' section included the author on the internal mailing list for all e-mail correspondence, campaign updates, committee reports, and the like. In return, the author made available the research findings from a recently completed study of labor relations and port performance in eight member states (Barton and Turnbull 1999). Thus, the research process approximated to the model of strategic corporate research presented by Tom Juravich in chapter 1 of this book.

In particular, *where* and *how* they seek to press their claims will reflect their view of where the system is newly vulnerable or receptive to their efforts. (102, original emphasis)

When considering where organized labor will seek to press its claims, compare the Council of Ministers and the European Commission. The former is an intergovernmental body, so the path to exerting pressure on its decision making runs through domestic action within individual member states, whereas the latter is a permanent supranational body that is open to representative groups at the European level. When considering *how* organized labor will seek to press its claims, compare the Commission and the European Parliament. The Commission values expertise above representation (Tarrow 2005), making it open to a logic of influence and conventional activities including institutionalized, elite lobbying taking place within established political channels. The European Parliament, in contrast, as the only democratically elected decision-making body in the EU, is more open to the logic of membership and unconventional pressures, such as noninstitutionalized, symbolic, or mass protests outside established political channels (Marks and McAdam 1999, 103–5).

Historically, the European Parliament has been the most reliable supporter of an effective social dimension to European integration (Hyman 2005, 16), and over the past decade it has come to exercise real power over significant areas of policymaking. The majority in the European Parliament is not tied to supporting the European Commission or the Council of Ministers, and while there is a high level of voting cohesion within party groups, with members of the European Parliament (MEPs) voting more along party lines than national lines, these groups remain relatively loose organizations. Moreover, voting for MEPs in European elections is mainly oriented to domestic rather than EU issues (Marks and McAdam 1999, 106; Hix, Raunio, and Scully 2003: 192–95). This created significant opportunities for reframing union strategies during the war on Europe's waterfront (2001–3) waged against the Commission's first ports package.

In the absence of any prior consultation with the Commission or any social dialogue with employers, organized labor was ill prepared when the first proposed directive, *On Market Access to Port Services,* was published in February 2001. The initial task for union leaders at the local, national, and international levels was to convince rank-and-file dockers of the threat posed by "self-handling," defined as "a situation in which a port user provides for itself one or more categories of port services" which thereby conferred "the right to employ personnel *of his own choice* to carry out the service" (CEC, 2001, 28–29, emphasis added), especially as the directive contained provisions for such activities to be approved by a competent national authority (article 11) and subject to established safety standards (article 14) and social protection (article 15). Several European transport unions were confident that, with minor amendments to the text of the directive, their national dock-labor scheme and industrial relations system would continue to offer protection. Thus, their initial response was to target the Commission and pursue the logic of influence through the ETF (Turnbull 2006).

The ITF, in contrast, was convinced that the directive would create "ports of convenience," leading to a deterioration in training, health and safety standards, and a race to the bottom akin to that in the shipping industry, where vessels sail under a "flag of convenience" (FOC) and employ "crews of convenience" (Lillie 2004). For example, if costs were driven down significantly in Mediterranean ports, this could open up new transshipment routes for international shipping lines and shippers on east-west trade routes (Asia-Europe-North America) via the Suez Canal, with integrated (door-to-door) services offered throughout Europe from a southern hub instead of direct port calls in northern Europe. Subsidiarity would then count for nothing in these member states. The ITF determined to oppose the directive on principle, not textual detail, and "to mobilize big actions against specific issues" (Kees Marges, ITF Dockers' secretary, interview by author, 2003), most notably against the right to self-handling.

The framing process, which was intended to create a stronger European identity among rank-and-file dockworkers and to develop a new unconventional repertoire of collective action, began with a process of education, or what the ITF described as the "learning phase" (Kees Marges, ITF Dockers' secretary, interview by author, 2003). This took place at all levels of union organization, with the explicit intention of building more effective union articulation—stronger interrelationships among workplace, national, and international levels of organization. For example, the ITF produced leaflets and other educational materials that were distributed to all European affiliates and then coordinated educational stop-work meetings to coincide with the federation's Week of Action on FOC shipping in September 2001. At the other end of the union hierarchy, new labor networks emerged within specific port ranges in northern Europe, Scandinavia, and the Mediterranean, which strengthened and extended existing social relations of trust, reciprocity, and cultural learning among different port communities, as well as providing a forum, via electronic networks, for debate at the grassroots level.[12] These activities laid the foundations for a more detached identity that would travel across borders and a greater willingness to act in support of union claims. Indeed, as the campaign shifted from conventional to unconventional action, from the logic of influence to the logic of membership, the union hierarchy became increasingly dependent on these new labor networks to mobilize rank-and-file support (Turnbull 2006).

Port workers soon realized that they shared a "community of fate" as *European* dockers, whereby any local or national employment protection they enjoyed was now dependent on collective action at the international level, and

---

[12] See www.havenarbeiders.be and www.havenforum.nl.

they actively participated in a succession of coordinated strikes against international shipping lines and mass demonstrations against the supranational institutions of the EU. The former were mainly organized across particular clusters of ports and were an immediate response to attempts by shipping lines to preempt the directive by employing seafarers to undertake dock work on short-sea routes. Action against the supranational state was targeted principally at the European Parliament and was timed to coincide with various stages of the legislative process. Initially, the ITF/ETF and IDC staged separate strikes and mass protests, but the actions of the Spanish state in seeking to preempt the directive by reforming its own national port laws prompted the Coordinadora, the leading member of the IDC's European Zone, to contemplate rapprochement and coordinated action with the ITF/ETF (Turnbull 2006). Concerted action culminated in the first ever pan-European dock strike in January 2003, involving twenty thousand dockers. This was followed by mass demonstrations outside the parliament in Strasbourg in March 2003. In September 2003 the ITF/ETF organized street demonstrations involving nine thousand dockers in Rotterdam in protest against the final text to be debated in the European Parliament, and the IDC did the same in Barcelona with six thousand dockers.

When the vote on the third reading of the directive finally came in November 2003, the Christian Democrats and Liberal MEPs voted in favor (with the exception of the Belgians, whose national government ultimately opposed the directive) while, with the notable exception of the Italians, virtually all the Socialists and Greens voted against. The final vote—229 against, 209 in favor, and 19 abstentions—was therefore the outcome of both party political and national/local concerns, but there was little doubt that the deciding factor was organized opposition to self-handling (Turnbull 2006; Van Hooydonk 2005, 198).

In general, the European Parliament is more likely to veto Council positions when the vote splits between left and right (Hix, Raunio, and Scully 2003, 195–96). Following European elections in 2004 and the accession of ten new member states, the political composition of the European Parliament has swung significantly to the right and thereby decidedly in favor of port transport liberalization. This, in turn, forced the labor movement to consider alliances as well as opposition to the second ports package. Fortunately, several prominent member states, as well as employer and wider business interests, were openly opposed to the directive announced in October 2004. In fact, the headline in *Lloyd's List* on January 25, 2005, declared: "Everyone hates it."[13]

Although the basic principles, underlying doctrine, and key objectives of the second ports package were the same as those of the first (CEC 2004, 2),

---

[13]   Only forwarders and shippers were openly in favor of the directive. The latter group includes the big manufacturers, retailers, and third-party logistics companies, as well as major shipping lines such as Mærsk.

there were important differences that raised the ire of virtually all stakeholders. Several member states—most notably Germany, the Netherlands, and the
United Kingdom—while expressing support for the broad principle of market
liberalization, expressed disappointment at the early retabling of the directive
on several counts of policy and process.[14] The former concerned technical and
operational issues, such as authorizations for new port service providers and
compensation for outgoing service providers, while the latter highlighted a
democratic deficit at the heart of EU policymaking. Not only had the Commission "failed [once again] to present a convincing justification for implementing
a Port Services Directive" (Van Hooydonk 2005, 205), but it had seemingly ignored the views of the industry and the decision of parliament. For the labor
movement, "the reintroduction of the ports directive was a real offense to the
dockers; it represented a total disregard, a total disrespect of the democratic
process" (Swedish Transport Union official, interview by author, 2006).

Not surprisingly, the Commission was called to task for insufficient prior
consultation with stakeholders and the failure to undertake a proper impact assessment. Such criticisms highlighted a sharp disjuncture between the
views of the Commission and those of the major players in the industry.
While the Commission regarded port liberalization as a matter of urgency
and likened the ports sector to the "wild west" (Karamitsos 2005) simply
because it is one of the few remaining service sectors in the EU without a
European regulatory framework, the industry itself was more conservative
and yet confident because European ports are among the most competitive
and cost-efficient in the world.[15] At key stages of the legislative process, the
Committee of the Regions[16] (CoR 2005) and the European Economic and
Social Committee[17] (EESC 2005) agreed with the industry rather than the
Commission.

ESPO and FEPORT were particularly strident in their condemnation of
the second ports package. Port employers did not dispute the basic principles
underlying the proposed directive—most notably the overall aims of ensuring
free and nondiscriminatory access to the market for port services, introducing
principles of good governance and transparency, and ensuring the neutrality

---

[14]   Germany's state secretary for transport declared that "the proposed Directive is not a suit-
able instrument for achieving [its] objectives" (Ralf Nagal, quoted in *Lloyd's List*, November 18,
2005). See Deloitte (2005) on objections raised in the Netherlands and Department of Transport
(2005) for the views of the U.K. government.

[15]   European container-handling charges, for example, amount to half of Asian prices and
one-third of American charges (FEPORT 2005, 5).

[16]   The Committee of the Regions consists of representatives of regional and local government proposed by member states and appointed by the Council of Ministers.

[17]   Members of the European Economic and Social Committee, who are appointed by the
Council of Ministers, represent the various interest groups that collectively make up "organized
civil society."

of the managing body of the port towards port users—but in their view the Commission had "not demonstrated or justified why such interventionist and potentially negative measures are necessary for a sector which is well-performing and internationally competitive" (ESPO press release, September 8, 2005; see also ESPO 2004, 2005b; FEPORT 2005). In a significant shift in policy, both ESPO and FEPORT no longer insisted on the inclusion of self-handling in the proposed directive, and both organizations, for "reasons of proportionality and subsidiarity," determined that these issues were best set out at the local or national level (ESPO 2005a, 2005b, 5; FEPORT 2005, 8–9). More telling, both organizations expressed their desire "to avoid unnecessary social unrest" (FEPORT 2005, 9), which "could create an unstable climate for potential investors" (ESPO 2004, 2) and impose direct costs on service providers and users that "seem to go unnoticed by the European legislative authorities" (FEPORT 2005, 9). Even the European Community Shipowners' Association (ECSA 2005, 6) was prepared to see self-handling excluded from the second ports package, despite championing this issue during the war on Europe's waterfront (Turnbull 2006).

Less than a week before the publication of the second ports package, Bill Milligan, chief executive of the Strike Club (the mutual insurer of ship owners, charterers, and vessel operators against strikes and other causes of delay), acknowledged that the pan-European dock strikes and mass demonstrations that accompanied the first ports package had "opened a new chapter in labour activism" (Brewer 2004). Armed with a new repertoire, port unions were able to frame their response to the second ports package in a very different fashion. Thus, whereas most unions engaging with the EU have largely abandoned contentious politics in favor of industrial legality (Hyman 2005, 35), port unions have developed their capacity and demonstrated their willingness to engage in unconventional action, and in the process inflict significant costs on both global capital and the supranational state. As Hyman (2005, 27) demonstrates, because most European unions lack the nerve to say no, this in turn dilutes the logic of influence. On the other hand, by adding the argument of force to the force of argument, port unions have been able to play the information-gathering, report-writing, lobby resolution-passing game to much greater effect.

Despite assurances that the second ports package was more "socially minded" (Karamitsos 2005; de Palacio 2004), port unions once again rejected the directive *On Market Access to Port Services* because of the threat it posed to dockworkers' livelihood (ITF/ETF 2004). The dockers' section of the ETF declared the directive to be "unnecessary, unbalanced and provocative" (press statement, October 10, 2004) and the federation made an early commitment to "take all necessary legal measures to firmly oppose this manoeuvre and to ensure that this new text is not adopted by the European Parliament" (ITF/ETF

2004). The condemnation of the IDC went a step further: "The sole objective of this Directive is the elimination of European dockworkers' unions" (IDC *News*, November 3, 2004). Once more, the IDC called for official cooperation and coordinated action with the ETF. Joint action was still problematic[18] but, in the event, unnecessary.

Although strikes and demonstrations once more accompanied the key legislative stages of the directive, these actions were more symbolic and more clearly targeted at the supranational state rather than (global) capital.[19] Instead, the ITF was keen "to keep the support of our allies" (Frank Leys, current ITF Dockers' secretary, interview by author, 2005), including, on this occasion, port employers as this was more likely to sway the legislative process in the unions' favor. As a result, the emphasis shifted from unconventional to more conventional activities, with far greater importance attached to securing amendments to the proposed directive. This is not to suggest that the logic of membership was abandoned—quite the contrary—as strike action and mass demonstrations were deployed to great effect at key stages of the legislative process. Moreover, port unions were under no illusion that their new allies and more persuasive voice were the result of their continued capacity and previous resort to unconventional action.

This time around, labor's voice—the force of their argument—was clearly heard. The Committee of the Regions, for example, in rejecting the second ports package, highlighted fears that self-handling would lead to a deterioration in social conditions in Europe's ports (CoR 2005, para. 1.22). Likewise, the European Economic and Social Committee added further legitimacy to labor's objections (EESC 2005, para. 3.15). Subsequently, opponents of the Commission's proposals secured two important votes against the directive in September 2005, in the European Parliament's Committee on Employment and Social Affairs and the Committee on the Internal Market and Consumer Protection. When the Transport Committee of the parliament met in November 2005, over three hundred amendments had been tabled by MEPs. Voting at this crucial committee stage "descended into farce" (Stares 2005) when MEPs first voted narrowly against rejecting the directive outright by twenty-six votes to twenty-two, with one abstention, then adopted various compromise amendments, but finally rejected the directive as amended by twenty-four votes to twenty-three. To confuse the issue still further, in the

---

[18]   In the words of one ITF official, "This is a big problem for many affiliates, their faces turn red at the very mention of the IDC" (anonymous, interview by author, 2005). The ITF's official position, adopted at the congress in Vancouver (2002), is that individual affiliates are at liberty to make contact and cooperate with the IDC.

[19]   For example, "symbolic demonstrations," such as that staged on November 21, 2005, numbered several hundred rather than several thousand dock workers, and strikes tended to be shorter than stoppages during the 2001–3 campaign.

final vote of the day MEPs passed a motion to send the directive to the plenary of the European Parliament in January 2006 without any amendments. Consequently, several "allies" of organized labor, most notably ESPO, joined them in calling for the directive to be rejected outright by the parliament.

When the directive was debated in the European Parliament in January 2006, more than six thousand port workers from sixteen countries took to the streets of Strasbourg, and many ports across Europe stopped work in protest. As missiles broke windows in the parliament building and riot police fought running battles with demonstrators in the surrounding streets, the second ports package was rejected by a resounding 532 votes to 120 (with 25 abstentions). Only two other directives, out of a running total of more than a thousand put forward by the Commission since 1999, have been rejected by the European Parliament. The ports directive has now been rejected twice. In February 2006, ports were formally removed from the scope of the Commission's equally controversial proposal for a directive on services in the internal market. In March 2006, the Commission finally withdrew its proposal for a port services directive.

During the 2004–6 campaign against the Commission's second ports package, organized labor faced a very different political opportunity structure than it had during the war on Europe's waterfront from 2001 to 2003. Nonetheless, port unions were successfully able to navigate a course through the powerful currents of European economic integration while simultaneously steering clear of the "elite embrace." Armed with an internationally based repertoire of contention from their previous battles with global capital and the supranational state, and sharing a common identity and stronger sense of interdependence, port unions were able to pursue the "logic of influence" and more conventional activities to much greater effect in their latest campaign to scupper the directive *On Market Access to Port Services*. In particular, transport unions found that port employers, member states, and important supranational institutions of the EU were now persuaded of labor's arguments against the inclusion of self-handling in the second ports package. Even the ECSA was no longer spoiling for a fight over this issue. Clearly, the choice unions face between the logics of membership and influence is not an either/or decision but a question of balance (Hyman 2005, 24). In their campaigns against the proposed port directives, organized labor has demonstrated the importance of being able to tilt the balance in response to the changing strategies of transnational capital and the supranational state, the process of social and economic change, the institutional context of industrial relations, and the unions' own organizational structures, extending from the local to the national and international.

For this reason, Europe's port workers are well placed to respond to the Commission's latest strategy to develop a pan-European ports policy. Instead of announcing a third ports package, the Commission has decided to hold a series of "consultation workshops" at different European ports, attended by all the major stakeholders, to debate the principal policy issues facing the industry. Discussion documents will be prepared prior to each workshop, and reports on the proceedings, including potential policy proposals, will be issued at the end of each consultation process. When Commission officials attended a meeting of the ETF dockers' section in October 2006 to announce their new strategy, they were left with no doubt that Europe's port unions could, and would, mobilize actions against the Commission and any other stakeholders who side with the Commission on any policy proposals deemed to be detrimental to dockworkers' interests. In particular, organized labor will continue to oppose self-handling and any tendering proposals that obviate well-established job security provisions in Europe's ports. The ETF has agreed to participate in the consultation process but is well aware that the Commission's new approach will draw organized labor into the logic of influence. The ETF has urged affiliates to keep rank-and-file dockworkers informed on the consultation process. If dockers remain primed for action, the global unions will still have recourse to the logic of membership and a repertoire of contention that can impose significant costs on global capital and the supranational state.

7. GOING NATIONAL OR EUROPEAN?

Local Trade Union Politics within Transnational Business Contexts in Europe

VALERIA PULIGNANO

Following from Levinson's (1972) argument about the need for labor to develop a countervailing power to global capital, the research literature has drawn attention to the dynamics in trade unions that leads them both to cooperation with capital to secure jobs and employment through business success on one hand, and to confrontation with capital over the distribution of the rewards on the other hand. In particular, it has been argued that this is a complex, dynamic, and changing relationship shaped and constrained by a context in which the labor movement itself is a significant actor. But what sort of actor is it?

It is clear that European trade unions have been tenacious supporters of a wide range of projects delivered by the European Commission (EC) on the establishment of employees' information and consultation and, more broadly, participation rights within Europe. National trade unions have also been supporters of such European initiatives as a good in themselves. However, to date the evidence on national unions emerging as a European institution by means of building up organizational capacity, social cohesion, and alliances in Europe seems limited. Numerous commentators have observed that cross-national differences in union contexts create constraints on the development of social cohesion and international solidarity among European trade unions. This is reflected in the fact that trade unions across and within countries have evolved quite differently with respect to strategic orientations and identities (Hyman 1999; Gordon and Turner 2000). As a result, organizational priorities, structures, governance and control, and policies and customs across unions are often markedly different, even within the same industry or sector.

Additionally, cultural and linguistic barriers are thought to create problems of communication across and within the trade union movement and to increase the transaction costs concerning the formation and the sustaining of possible transnational alliances (Stirling and Tully 2004). Because of these differences and the political democratic nature of the tradition of independent unionism, unions typically have deep-rooted desires for maintaining autonomy and national identity. The question is how these pressures to maintain autonomy and national identity will impact the labor movement's capability to coordinate activity and establish organizational patterns for union action across borders in Europe.

Some literature suggests that union difficulties in establishing coordination are a product of the differences in national industrial relations systems and social welfare policies, as well as significant imbalances in union penetration and the relative power of trade unions across borders (Cooke 2005). In brief, working successfully with such cross-national diversity and overcoming barriers of difference seem to be critical for national unions. However, the internationalization of production within transnational companies detaches unions from the regulatory frameworks of national industrial relations agendas. The result is either direct policies of union exclusion or the pressure for "concession bargaining." This is much more evident during periods of company restructuring where jobs in different local plants are threatened and companies use "coercive comparisons" (Coller 1996). Under coercive comparisons, individual sites are under continuous pressure to improve performance, with the risk of otherwise being starved of investment and ultimately run down and closed. These methods are used by management to place pressure on local workforces and trade unions. More specifically, the ability of trade unions to respond to the process of transnational corporate restructuring is weakened because transnational capital plays plants and local unions against one another (Katz 1985; Kochan, Katz, and McKersie 1986). This means that workers within more regulated labor market economies, with traditionally high labor costs and rigid working conditions, are often jeopardized by those in less regulated labor markets with more flexible working conditions.

In Europe, this practice became more frequent starting in 1992 with the program of European integration and the implementation of the European Economic and Monetary Union (EMU). Numerous commentators have tried to examine the extent to which European integration has given European trade unions strong reasons to elaborate new strategic directions within the pathway of cross-national coordination and cooperation. However, the initial experiences of interunion coordination within the European Union (EU) have been disillusioning. According to Hyman (1999), the coordination of European unions does not seem to be moving in any particular direction. Why?

In this chapter I argue that one of the factors limiting the capacity of the labor movement in Europe to coordinate across borders is the difficulty in creating links between the European, the national, and the local levels of union structures. I will discuss these aspects in depth by examining how they reflect the necessity by trade unions in Europe to strongly engage in the development of an effective new political agenda. Specifically, a new understanding of cross-national unions' coordination and cooperation has to address the need for new organizational and structural forms to cover the diverse categories of workers both horizontally and vertically. In practice, this means trade unions should ask themselves whether they are willing and able to make a choice regarding where and how to organize their action strategically and consequently create the structural condition to support and implement that choice. This does not imply eliminating the cross-national differences among union organizations, structures, and identities, but it means coordinating those differences in pursuit of developing a unique, democratic, and cooperative voice. In this light, the chapter highlights the crucial view that national, local, and European levels of the labor movement should be seen as reinforcing one another in a mutually inclusive and articulated relationship. This means that a strong integration between the different levels of the diverse unions' structure and organization is necessary to guarantee cross-national union coordination and solidarity. For unions this requires considering themselves active participants in the redefinition and reinvention both of their movement across Europe and of Europe itself.

The chapter assesses this argument by referring to the case of transnational restructuring in General Motors (GM) in Europe in 2004. The analysis of the GM case suffers from the methodological difficulty of generalization because it involves a particular organization. However, it can shed light on various interactive processes that in this case contributed to solving problems created by cross-border union activity. It emphasizes the crucial role of a bottom-up approach in the supranational (European) trade unions process to coordinate across borders. Hence, the aim of the chapter is to critically evaluate this case of GM in the light of the national trade unions' attempt to establish cross-border coordination in response to the management challenge of industrial change in Europe. I start by presenting the experience of coordination developed by the metalworkers' trade union federation in Europe (European Metalworkers' Federation). I illustrate how in the metal working sector, trade unions' ability to use European institutions (such as the European works councils, or EWCs) to coordinate activity across borders for cross-border bargaining purposes was material in reducing, but not eliminating, management's attempt to force local and regional unions to compete against each other to save their jobs—what in the United States is called "whipsawing" and in some European countries is called "social dumping." I argue that this reflects differences in national trade union structures and strategies as well as local union interests. Hence, international solidarity has been controversial in GM Europe, since it has contributed to shaping a bargaining framework where local union interests and national policies prevailed over European orientations and purposes.[1]

The research design benefited from semistructured interviews with local trade unions and works councilors in the different GM local plants, as well as with members of the EWC in GM. Interviews were conducted during visits to the different production units, as well by telephone. Primary and secondary sources, particularly local plants' and trade unions' internal documents and bargaining agreements, were also collected during the interviews and used for the purpose of the research.

Cross-Border Coordination: The European Metalworkers' Federation Experience

It is generally acknowledged that the emergence of transnational capital is associated with the process of the internationalization of product markets resulting from transnational political and economic integration and the deregulation of national economies. The last three decades have been characterized by a major debate on the capacity of employees within transnational companies to challenge transnational management (Levinson 1972; Ulman 1975; Northrup and Rowan 1979; Ramsay 1999). A coherent framework has been provided to discuss the extent to which organized labor can elaborate effective strategies to deal with transnational management. One argument is that for unions to have any countervailing influence in the internationalization of global trade and investment capital, they need to match the scope and the level of transnational power in order to develop international structures for coordinated collective bargaining with transnational firms. In this view, effective international coordination can take place at the level of bargaining activities. This means extending collective bargaining relations to deal directly with the decision makers responsible for the priorities and policies of transnational firms (Levinson 1972). Under this model, the process of international bargaining should follow different stages. The first stage requires company-wide union support for national action in one country against one transnational subsidiary. The following stages include multiple negotiations

[1]   The chapter draws from a European Trade Union Institute for Research Education and Health and Safety research project on "Trade Unions Anticipating and Managing Change in Europe" funded by Article Six-Innovative Measures-European Social Fund.

with a company in several or many countries, followed in turn by integrated, comprehensive international negotiations. Gordon and Turner (2000) illustrate how efforts for cross-border bargaining activities need to be accompanied by a structured coordinated action among trade unions if they aim to be efficient. This implies that unions need closer relations among key union leaders and national and local activists in order to shift resources into transnational activities, such as collective bargaining. Thus these different stages for international bargaining represent a crucial aspect of the broad framework for strategic corporate research and campaigns, as outlined in chapter 1 by Tom Juravich.

Since the mid-1990s, the European Metalworkers' Federation has been issuing policy papers on procedures for the coordination of trade union activity in Europe and which cover bargaining and representation matters. These argue that "information, consultation and negotiation need to be rooted within coordinated structures of employee representation and bargaining" (European Metalworkers' Federation 2000, 1). According to this perspective, cross-national coordination corresponds to a strategic design, which is necessary in order to set up a transnational dimension in Europe, given the diversity that characterizes national contexts. The European Metalworkers' Federation is to achieve coordination by introducing common guidelines and minimum standards at the European level that national unions should follow. Concrete proposals and guidelines will then be established for a joint position regarding collective bargaining and employees' rights to representation within the EWCs. Specifically, in accordance with the European Metalworkers' Federation, national trade unions should be committed to negotiating wage agreements that conform to coordinated collective bargaining guidelines. Accordingly, wage agreements should equal the inflation rate and the development of productivity.

Additionally, in the mid-1990s the European Metalworkers' Federation elaborated common rules regarding the content of the EWCs' agreements. In particular, agreements are to establish procedures and the content of the negotiation; involve union experts in the negotiation; indicate frequency and number of meetings and premeetings per year among union representatives and with management; identify the select committee's tasks and role within EWCs; and establish a coordinator within the EWCs, responsible for strengthening the position of the union. The coordinator is the point of contact between the employee representatives within EWCs and the European Metalworkers' Federation and is tasked with guaranteeing that the interests of European workers are safeguarded. In both cases, the European unions' strategy is to ensure that the structures of bargaining and employee representation and works councils work in accordance with the content of the policy developed at the European level (Pulignano 2005).

The most recent initiatives for coordination illustrate the elaboration of "socially responsible company restructuring."[2] This approach underlines the European Metalworkers' Federation goal to restrict opportunities for management to instigate international labor movement competition. The result is to consider coordination as a precondition for the use of EWCs as a forum to negotiate over the economic and social implications of restructuring. The aim is to oppose the downward spiral of working conditions generated by management pressure on local unions for concession bargaining. However, the autonomous negotiating activity at the local level is not bound by any rules relating to bargaining scope or content, nor is it ultimately controlled at the EU level.

Transnational Restructuring in Europe: The Case of GM

American automobile companies such as GM have had a strong presence in Europe for a very long time. GM opened its first assembly plant in Europe in Denmark in 1923, followed a couple of years later by plants in Antwerp (Belgium) and in Luton (Britain), where the company acquired Vauxhall Motors. Soon after, it also acquired the Adam Opel AG in Russelsheim, Germany. In 2000, GM Europe took full ownership of the Saab Company in Trollhattan, Sweden, following a joint venture agreement between Saab-Scania AB and GM. This accompanied the setting up of the new European GM group headquarters in Zurich in 1986.

The approach followed by GM management in Europe emphasized organizational change, with a focus on increased flexibility coupled with cost cutting as the way to increase competitiveness under a regime of lower production costs and lower-priced goods. Accordingly, manufacturing in Europe has been organized in platforms for different car models as the way to increase management flexibility by exchanging models and production volumes within the same platform from one plant to another.

This organizational change triggered a shift toward cross-national and cross-company alliances and cooperation with other potential competitors, such as the one with Fiat in Italy in the mid-1990s. Accordingly, the American car manufacturer was driven to develop transnational restructuring along regional lines in Europe, America, and Asia. Restructuring in Europe, in particular, was most effective when it involved relocating production units and new models to reduce costs, including making cuts in suppliers, energy use, taxes, capital expenditures, and, most important, labor costs. This in turn

[2]   See European Metalworkers' Federation 2005b.

reinforced competition across different plants and increased the level of job cuts overall.[3]

Despite these drastic labor force reductions, GM has faced financial difficulties since the late 1990s (*European Industrial Relations Review* 2005a). In GM's European operations this resulted in a series of further restructuring efforts. GM cut approximately twenty-one thousand jobs in Europe from 1998 to 2001. Then, in early September 2004, it announced that it would cut another twelve thousand jobs involving the three main brands GM owns in Europe— Opel, Saab, and Vauxhall. According to GM management, this would have led to the closure of one entire plant, with Germany or Sweden as the countries in Europe left carrying the heaviest burden of cuts (European Metal Workers' Federation 2005a). The announcement of job losses led initially to an unofficial strike at the Bochum, Germany, plant, which halted production in other plants in Europe because the German site is a supplier to Belgian and British GM plants (Bartmann 2005). At first it was not clear from the GM announcement which site would have been primarily affected by the closure. A great deal of pressure was put on the employee representatives at the GM Saab plant in Trollhattan, Sweden, with around six thousand employees, and Opel plants in Russelsheim and Bochum, Germany, with nearly seventeen thousand workers in total. This pressure is aptly captured by the description of Hakan Scott, a union official at the Swedish plant, of GM's threat "to shift production of the Swedish plant's main model, which at that time made up almost two-thirds of the 115,000 cars built annually" (George and Mackintosh 2004, 22).

The strategy of "regime competition," promoting international competition between unions and plants based on the diverse systems of labor market regulation in Europe, is nothing new for GM. For example, Hancké (2000) describes the coercive comparisons deployed by GM management on its European operations in the late 1990s. The aim was to place pressure on local workforces, works councils, and local unions and through local negotiations to leverage cost reduction and flexibility as the result of a round of concessions bargaining. At that time, the European Employee Forum (EEF), established in 1996 as one of the most active EWCs coordinating the negotiation on issues relating to cross-border restructuring, decided that there must be a European framework agreement that would be the basis for the coordination of the different plant-level agreements in Europe. The first European agreements at GM were signed in July 2000 and in March 2001. They were organized as the European trade unions' response to the announced restructuring program, which involved a workforce reduction of six thousand jobs

---

[3]   Between 2000 and 2002 employment in GM went down 1.90 percent in Europe, 12.34 percent in the Unites States, and 5.42 percent in Japan.

at Opel in Europe in 2000 and in 2001 another two thousand workers in Luton, Britain, and approximately ten thousand workers at plants in Zaragoza, Spain, and Antwerp, Belgium. At that time the intention of the EEF was to prevent any plant closures and redundancies by creating "safety fences" through the coordination of the local negotiations by the European framework agreement (EIRO 2001). So the EEF had some experience in negotiating European agreements in a context of restructuring, and this experience was of help when the big announcement of cross-national restructuring at GM Europe followed in 2004.

Coordinating Union Responses to Transnational Restructuring at GM Europe: The 2004 European Framework Agreement

The GM announcement in September 2004 of the company's intention to close a production plant because of overcapacity in Europe and losses in European markets was made through the media without proper notice or consultation with the workers' representatives from the EWCs. A European trade union coordination group was established with participants from the European Metalworkers' Industry Federation, representatives of all concerned national trade unions, and EWC members, in order to develop a bargaining role for EWCs that could feed into developing alternative strategies to deal with the employment effects of restructuring. The trade union presence in the coordination group was crucial to support the EEF in the negotiation process with management and to ensure integrity and social cohesion to the group as well as strengthening cross-border connections among workers. This was particularly true in Sweden and Germany, where some of the European protagonists remembered the GME management's 2004 attempt to "pit the headquarters of its loss-making German and Swedish units against each other in a competition to build the next generation of its mid-sized Opel and Saab cars" (George and Mackintosh 2004, 22).

The European trade union coordination group agreed on common basic demands for "no closure and no forced redundancy" as the result of a coordinated platform. One basic aim was to avoid the risk of cross-national competition based on different employment and working conditions across countries, which reflects a defensive approach to coordination. In practice, the main objective was to develop a clear commitment by local trade unions of no negotiations at the national level concerning the GM restructuring plan. The obligation was on national unions and local works councils to engage in bargaining cross-nationally by establishing a European framework agreement where common rules regarding no forced redundancies could be adopted for all the sites affected by restructuring. Central to the approach was the European

Metalworkers' Federation's acceptance of economic and industrial restructuring as a driving force for change. "Restructuring is not simply ignored or opposed as such but managed in accordance to correct criteria, which envisage negotiated solutions acceptable for both employees and management" (European Metalworkers' Federation 2005c, 4).

The Copenhagen declaration, which was signed by the German (IG Metall) and the Swedish (Svenska Metall, SIF, and CF) trade unions on October 1, 2004, manifested the joint unions' rejection of any management attempt to use the national-level industrial relations system to negotiate the outcomes of restructuring. In contrast, the German and the Swedish unions viewed the EWCs as a critical instrument in this process. The union leaders made clear that "plant closure, mass redundancies and violation of collective bargaining agreements do not contribute to regaining success" (European Metal Workers 2004a). Trade union leaders examined the devastating effects on employment of the local negotiations over employment guarantees in return for flexible working time that were undertaken in 1997 in Germany and by mid-1998 in other plant-level bargaining rounds in Spain, Belgium, and Britain where GM car plants were located. These cases were used to illustrate how the agreements in one country or plant affected the others, thus forcing all to negotiate similar concessions, and ultimately destroyed the initial advantages that individual unions had secured without ensuring long-term job protection. In an interview, the chair of the GM EEF commented that "it was a big mistake what German unions did in 1997 when they hit with concession bargaining on wages and working time flexibility legislation at the car plants in Antwerp and in Luton. At that time we were blind and we were not aware of the fact that that road would not have brought us anywhere" (IG Metall union official, interview by author, 2005).

On October 14, 2004, the European trade union coordination group organized a European day of action against the GM plant closure decision, which involved the participation of over fifty thousand employees in strikes and solidarity demonstrations from all GM plants across Europe. As a result of the day of action and the involvement of the European trade union coordination group with the EEF in its negotiations with management, and of discussions on the steps to be taken to accompany the restructuring process, in December 2004 management representatives of GM and the GM EEF signed a European framework agreement on restructuring and costcutting. The agreement provided for twelve thousand jobs to be cut, including ninety-five hundred in Germany (including Russelsheim, Bochum, and Kaiserslautern). This agreement provided for the cuts in Germany to be secured by means of voluntary severance, partial or early retirement for older workers, outsourcing, and so-called transfer agency, a government-subsidized scheme to offer workers retraining and wage guarantees rather than compulsory redundancies. The aim of the agreement was to put into place a framework within which the restructuring at GM European facilities could be managed according to the European Metalworkers' Federation social principles for coordination.

The goal was to minimize the economic consequences of restructuring for employees and the wider community. In keeping with this, the framework agreement was seen as representing the trade unions' common attempt to manage the downward pressure on wages and prices by using the EWCs as a strategic tool to help maintain job security while soliciting cross-border trade union solidarity. The main point of the agreement, indeed, was seen as resisting "forced redundancies and plant closure." Reinhard Kuhlmann—at that time general secretary of the European Metalworkers' Federation—described the outcomes of the negotiation as the "victory of reason" (European Metalworkers' Federation 2004b).

As indicated, the effect of the European framework agreement at the European level was to lead GM management to agree on the common principle of no forced redundancies and no closures of European plants. However, the outcomes illustrate a certain cross-national diversity concerning the content of the local negotiations that followed the European agreement. For example, in Germany, the Opel Russelsheim plant will be kept open through 2010. It was also agreed that GM management would make redundancies compulsory in return for German workers' accepting lower Christmas bonuses, further measures to make working time more flexible, and a one-year wage freeze. Conversely, at the Saab Trollhattan plant, management initially gave a vague guarantee to keep the Swedish site open until 2008. This followed a management decision to base production of the new mid-range models, such as Vectra and Saab model cars, at the German site of Russelsheim as a result of the so-called future agreement of March 4, 2005. However, in both the German and the Swedish plants job security was guaranteed in return for early and partial retirement schemes, which covered 4,500 employees at the German plants and nearly 540 employees at the Swedish plants. Other measures contained in the agreement included the use of outsourcing, asking employees to go to work for future joint ventures with Opel suppliers, and voluntary transfers.

One can argue that the European agreement created a framework that guaranteed no plant closures and allowed local negotiations in both Germany and Sweden. Nevertheless, although guarantees against plant closures were agreed upon for each site, it was indicated that a total of ninety-five hundred jobs were to be progressively cut through voluntary severance in Germany and a further two thousand employees to be made voluntarily redundant among the other GM facilities in Belgian, Spain, Sweden, and Britain in the near future. An article from the *Financial Times* noted that as a result of this operation, the management of GM in Europe was able to cut twelve thousand employees across Europe and save 500 million euros (Bergstrom, Mackintosh, and Milne 2005). This occurred not only because of the program for the direct workforce reduction mentioned above but also because in some locations, such as Germany, the transfer of production coincided with a new local wage-moderation deal with GM employees. This had the countereffect of gradually cutting the company's premium pay rates and increasing working time flexibility in other GM German plants. Likewise, the reduction in job security in Sweden was negotiated between unions and local management according to national legislation in return for employers' granting extra premiums to voluntarily redundant employees.

European and Local Interests in Transnational Workplaces in Europe

Though Opel Russelsheim in Germany and Saab Trollhattan in Sweden are the only plants where formal agreements securing employment and production location have been explicitly negotiated under the 2004 European framework agreement, similar deals have been concluded in other plants in Germany (Bochum and Kaiserslautern) as well as in other countries in Europe as a response to the German and the Swedish initiatives. These special agreements have addressed concessions in wages and work hours that coincide with the labor force reductions with the goal of minimizing the employment costs of the change. Table 7.1 presents some features of these agreements, including a description of the employment arrangements in the five main GM car-producing countries in Europe: Germany, Sweden, Britain, Spain, and Belgium. In particular, in Germany the agreements were negotiated by the local works councils covering the plants in Russelsheim, Bochum, Kaiserslautern, and Eisenach (*European Industrial Relations Review* 2005a). Of these four plants, Eisenach was the only facility not affected by the restructuring.

By establishing the "no forced redundancy and no closure" policy, the framework agreement followed a top-down approach, acting as an umbrella under which these basic rules and provisions become binding for all the follow-up agreements at the plant level. On the other hand, the local negotiations that followed the framework agreement took place outside this umbrella, resulting in content differences in the areas of wages and working conditions. Specifically, the content of local negotiations reflects the contextual conditions, such as employment security policies and employee representation structures and strategies, of the country where the local agreement was negotiated. Consequently, the local bargaining agreements are the expression of the local union interests in the process of negotiation with local management. Thus, it may be argued that under the European framework agreement the entire picture of European unions turns out to be a blend of "Euro-realism"—simultaneously engaging in Europeanization while sustaining local interests (Schroeder and

TABLE 7.1.
Local agreements on production and employment at five GM car plants in Europe

Sites	Germany	Sweden	Spain	Britain	Belgium
Employment arrangements	*Russelsheim, Bochum, Kaiserslautern* 9,500 job losses by 2007 through voluntary redundancy, early retirement, outsourcing, transfer of employees (1,500 job losses in Bochum) Job security until 2010 Investment commitment: new Saab 9-3 model to be produced in Russelsheim Reduction of production capacity at the stamping operations in Bochum	*Trollhatan* 540 job losses by 2005 through voluntary redundancy and early retirement Vague promise of job security until 2008 and "open competition" with Russelsheim	*Zaragoza* 610 job losses by 2006 through early retirement, early retirement, voluntary redundancy, disability Job security with early retirement and voluntary redundancy starting from September 2006	*Ellsemere Port* 300 job losses by 2005 through outsourcing, transfer of employees No job security	*Antwerp* 524 job losses by 2005 through increase in productivity, extension of working time, transfer of employees, outsourcing, and insourcing Extension of production capacity: new press shop at Antwerp
Working conditions Pay	*Russelsheim* 2005: 0% wage increase 2005–2010: 1% wage increase below the national collective agreement *Bochum, Kaiserslautern, Eisenach* 0% wage increase No Christmas bonus	75% pay increase for early retirement	Company's bonus on early retirement and voluntary redundancy Employment guarantees	No company bonus on early retirement and voluntary redundancy to be negotiated at the local level because of budget restrictions	No company bonus for absenteeism Reduction of social guarantees for employees (i.e., family social activity)
Working time	*Russelsheim, Bochum, Kaiserslautern* 40 hours a week and extension of 15 days production time (including Saturday) to adjust to fluctuating demand				Extension of the night shift from 7 to 8 working hours.
Organization of production					Reduction of the speed of the production line. Productivity increase through new continuous improvement; reduction to two team meetings per week.

Weinert 2004). The result is to reduce, but not to exclude, the possible future threat of relocation by management.

The diversity across the national-based union representative structures as well as differences in the degree of integration between national and local bargaining in each country determines the nature and extent of locally specific agreements that result from European negotiations. For example, in Germany, in accordance with the "dual" system of representation, the local works councils deal with a surplus payment at the plant level on top of the base amount already negotiated by the trade unions at the branch level. Thus the German agreement was a clear attempt to maintain local control and protect local interests while negotiating concessions on wages and work-time flexibility in return for promises by management to maintain employment security by transferring the new Vectra and Saab model cars to Germany. As indicated, the "future agreement" (*Zukunftsvertrag*) was negotiated between management and local works councils, and it covered all the plants of the company in the country. It discussed employees' mobility as well as outsourcing and retraining for employees who were transferred to outsourced joint ventures. It also included several significant wage and hour concessions for the ninety-five hundred employees in Russelsheim, Bochum, and Kaiserslautern, who were covered by voluntary redundancies.[4] The agreement mandated a wage freeze in 2005, which covered the workers at Russelsheim (extendable to 2010 for the employees at Bochum and Kaiserslautern). After 2005 there will be a cut of 1 percent of the company's premium pay negotiated in the national collective agreement. Moreover, the agreement allows a greater number of workers at Bochum and Kaiserslautern plants to work up to forty hours a week and fifteen extra days per year (including Saturday) to adjust to fluctuating demand, maintaining normal hourly rates without pay increases until 2010.

The Swedish, Spanish, and British agreements are ad hoc responses to specific crises, such as the threat of closing the Trollhattan and the Ellsemere Port plants in 2004 or laying off 618 employees at the Zaragoza plant in Spain. In addition, these agreements reflect the different functions of the employee representative structures, their level of involvement in local negotiations, and the strategies and power of the local actors. In Spain, for example, the "single" system of representation allows the works councils to formally negotiate at the local level under the minimum standards indicated at the branch level. As a result, local works councils in Zaragoza negotiated job security with the company through September 2006. More specifically, that local agreement—which was negotiated with management on December 14, 2004—deviated from the preexisting rules on flexibility under which the employer could uni-

---

[4]   By 2007 fifteen hundred employees in Bochum will be made redundant on a voluntary basis, and thirty-five hundred workers among the Russelsheim, Bochum, and Kaiserslautern sites will be involved in early retirement and work-time reduction.

laterally decide on employees' dismissals. The rule change led to a situation where almost a quarter of the employees at the Spanish plant were allowed to reach the legal requirement of sixty as the age for retirement in 2006. In an interview, a member of the works council considers the Spanish local agreement a "local success." It helped to manage the local crisis by protecting working conditions without further concessions on work-time flexibility and job cuts (Confederación Sindical de Comisiones Obreras union official, interview by author, 2005).

Likewise, in Sweden unions did not negotiate concessions (under the form of the German employment security contracts). They accepted the redundancies as the outcome of market problems. Although the Swedish structure of employee representation allows the local works councils to bargain locally for wages under the requirements of the national collective agreement, Swedish trade unions had as their goal bargaining to protect the jobs of those workers affected by company restructuring without lowering their working conditions in return for employment security. The moderate incidence of bargaining concessions in working conditions by Swedish local works councils is explained by referring to the active labor market policy in the country. Accordingly, in Sweden there is a strong macroeconomic strategy, which aims at securing employment opportunities for members versus any threat of company relocation. This is relevant to explain why the Swedish union did not lower its bargaining conditions as the result of whipsawing by GM management. This implies that workers' representatives in Sweden are more likely than, for example, their German counterparts to accept job cuts where there is a surplus capacity (Bartmann 2005). In an interview, the chairman of the works council in the Trollhattan plant stated that "the aim of the local negotiation in GM restructuring at the Trollhattan plant was to save people and not jobs." He pointed out that "under the umbrella of the framework agreement we were able to negotiate higher social benefits for the people of the plant involved in the early retirement and the voluntary redundancy plans" (Svenske Metall union official, interview by author, 2005).

The British agreement was characterized by the ability of the employer to cut around three hundred employees in Ellsemere Port without negotiating any form of voluntary redundancy and early or partial retirement, as had been done in the Spanish, Swedish, and German cases. This partly reflects the fact that British shop stewards need employers' recognition in order to formally negotiate with management. In this context, the European framework agreement was advantageous for British local representatives. As a Transport and General Workers (T&G) union official argues,

> Despite losing the argument with management to ask for voluntary redundancy and early or partial retirement because of management asking for cost

savings, I must admit the framework agreement gave us the scope to explore alternatives in case of company restructuring. This implies the use of out-sourcing and the transfer of employees to other GM plants in Britain as an alternative to the drastic solution to laying off people. Without a framework agreement we would have expected restructuring taking place much quicker without informing us—perhaps we would have heard about it on the radio as happened in the case of the Luton plant in 1998—and involving much more forced redundancy. (Interview by author 2005)

Finally, the agreement in Belgium, in marked contrast to the other countries, was concluded under the management promise of expansion of production capacity to the Belgian site. Specifically, the plan would have meant the future establishment of a stamping operation in Antwerp. In Belgium, the employee representative structure is organized in accordance with a single system of representation, and local works councils negotiated locally with management. Hence, local works councils in Antwerp negotiated increases in productivity and cost savings (for an equivalent of 30 million euros) in return for the guarantee of the company to invest in the local Belgian plant. The chair of the works councils in Antwerp stated that "we have paid for the stamping operation" (Algemen Belgisch Vakverbond union official, interview by author, 2005). The agreement included concessions on the level of flexibility of the plant, such as the extension of the night shift from seven to eight hours and the development of the continuous improvement program. The agreement also guarantees job security for 226 out of a total of 524 employees (60 of them below age twenty-six). The remaining 298 employees will be covered by early retirement and a program granting them transfer rights to other plants in the same auto manufacturer. Additionally, the establishment of the new stamping operation in Antwerp will coincide with the transfer to Belgium of part of the production capacity of the stamping operation in Bochum, Germany.

The diversity of the national-based representative structures and their different functions in local negotiations increased the fragmented nature of the local agreements concluded in the GM European plants under the umbrella of the European framework agreement and created the conditions for potential future whipsawing by management while lowering local working conditions in exchange for guaranteed job security. This is illustrated, for example, by the German local works councils' conceding reductions in wage increases as well as measures for work-time flexibility in return for short-term job protection. Likewise, the Belgian example shows how cost savings were negotiated by local unions in return for the company's promise to expand capacity at the Antwerp plant.

Hence, although the European trade union coordination body was crucial to encouraging international union solidarity in GM in Europe, it was not enough to restrain management from using the threat of whipsawing unions while increasing interunion competition. One explanation is the lack of structural links between the European and the national (and local) union levels of representation, a weakness that currently characterizes the European trade union movement. The lack of vertical links exacerbates the cross-national differences in structures of representation, their functions, and the nature and content of the local negotiations. Thus, strengthening the vertical links between European and local structures of representation by means of delegating competencies to the higher level in order to negotiate on the social effects of transnational restructuring would certainly help to coordinate cross-national structural and institutional differences while promoting international cooperation. This requires a strong political willingness by the national and local unions to delegate resources and power to the European level. In the concrete case of GM, this would have served to grant legitimacy, in the guise of a formal mandate from local unions to the trade union coordination body. One possibility for overcoming this problem might have been the requirement that all trade unions and European works councils must be represented in this body and the information passed on to the national trade unions and the employees in the plant. Some trade unionists also recommend that the framework agreement should contain a clear commitment by the company regarding future investments in the plants that are threatened by management. If the company agrees to take responsibility for covering the above matters, trade unions will more easily work jointly toward results without the risk of being engaged in a competitive struggle.

European coordination on restructuring matters is used by trade unions more to pursue their existing goals than to develop an alternative and strategic approach to European industrial relations. It reflects the insularity of national unions and the lack of a strategy relevant to interfirm competition (Anner et al. 2006). According to the case study presented in this chapter, the agreed-on rules to manage transnational restructuring under the European framework that have resulted from cross-border coordination activity by the European Metalworkers' Federation in the auto sector have produced partial effects on management's attempt to whipsaw unions across borders. They have, however, not eliminated the employer's effort to play workers off against each other in local negotiations. As the result of weak structural links between supranational, national, and plant-union levels, local works councils in GM performed the dominant role in managing restructuring while emphasizing local rather than European interests. Within this context, the European Metalworkers' Federation's approach has not enabled the coordination initiative to accommodate the cross-national differences in union representative structures and their different bargaining roles while producing alternative and strategic effects in local negotiations. Therefore, these common coordinated rules have acted more like sideshows to predominantly national and local developments.

What can be detected as a critical issue by this study is the lack of motivation and commitment among both national and local unions to make the shift in strategy necessary in order to discuss and manage the broader employment implications of restructuring from the national to the European level. This leads to a weak capacity for the trade unions to coordinate local negotiations transnationally. In brief, the lack of vertical integration between the European, national, and local structures of employee representation leads to benchmarking rather than coordinating the trade unions' respective local agreements across borders. It should be clear that "no negotiations are a national issue alone, but that all have implications beyond national borders" (European Metalworkers' Federation 2001) and that therefore it is crucial to strengthen the cross-national coordination in bargaining issues by making more explicit reference to European rules and sectoral policies.

As indicated, linking the European to the national level is difficult because of the lack of political will as well as the fear by national trade unions of losing their influence at the local level. The result overall is to narrow the scope for trade unions to develop strategies to take the offensive at the transnational level. I believe that, on the whole, the significance and effectiveness of union cooperation across borders in Europe consist of the changes in attitudes among the trade union actors, who are increasingly open to European support on regulatory matters by the European level. At the same time, this implies the creation of vertically and horizontally integrated structures of trade union organization. It may make sense for the trade unions to reinforce the vertical links between supranational and national levels—that is, for example, to create structures for European company-based bargaining while horizontally introducing coordination rules in order to regulate cross-border restructuring. This may help the trade unions to gain power in challenging management prerogatives in the context of transnational change.

Overall, this means that unions in Europe need to find European rather than national solutions in the case of cross-border restructuring. To be more specific, trade unions need to move away from a national and provincial focus when they are seeking international solidarity, which, as Hyman (2004) would argue, expresses commonalities at the same time as it accommodates diversity. In practice, this would require the integration between the different regulatory levels of the trade union structures. The GME restructuring case illustrates that the weakest link of the trade union chain is the national level. Therefore, more linkages between European and national union leaders, structures, and strategies are needed as well. This can be created by maintaining a productive and constant exchange of information between all actors involved in the process (worker representatives in the different locations, the EWC, the European Metalworkers' Federation's coordinator, the national trade unions, and the European Metalworkers' Federation). The failure of any one of these actors to actively engage jeopardizes each of the other trade unions affected by GME restructuring. Moreover, the GM case shows that this is vital not only from the very beginning and during the whole negotiation process but also after the signing of the European framework agreement. Indeed, as the GM case demonstrates, reaching a European agreement does not completely protect the trade unions from new management attempts at whipsawing. Trade unions and workers therefore need to accompany this process with an intensive and continuous exchange of information through meetings, worker exchanges between plants (and across borders), and newsletters. This would help in setting up a common ground of shared issues and actions before going into local negotiations, while also helping to develop linkages between the different levels of the trade union structure. It can also be recommended that the European Metalworkers' Federation take clear responsibility in advance when cross-border restructuring occurs.

This is a serious assessment since it sheds light on the balance of power between the national and European levels. Therefore, it is my view that integration between the different levels of trade union structures is also, formally, a political process. Unions cannot establish effective structures to link the European and the national union levels without a protracted effort to educate the national unions, officials, and employee representatives about the importance of establishing a European view, where national interests and orientations in the case of restructuring need to be coordinated rather than simply aligned as autonomous national and local trade union policies. This requires new ideas on both the unions' and the institutions' side, especially from those governing the future trajectory of the European social model. On the other hand, it also requires clear rules and principles for the creation of a trusted and binding form of cross-border union cooperation—for example, the December 2005 signing by GM, the EWC, and the union of the "European Solidarity Pledge" on the Opel Delta plants in Europe in order to prevent the implementation by GM of another round of cost cutting and the playing of workers against each other in the site-selection-process strategy (*European Works Council Bulletin* 2006). In this way it may be possible to increase capacity and interunion trust to challenge the dominant position of transnational firms while supporting the development of new models of cross-border campaigns and other strategic initiatives for trade unions and their allies across Europe.

8. LABOR-COMMUNITY COALITIONS, GLOBAL UNION ALLIANCES, AND THE POTENTIAL OF SEIU'S GLOBAL PARTNERSHIPS

AMANDA TATTERSALL

The idea that the workers of the world should unite is deeply rooted in union rhetoric, yet the means by which global union alliances can be effectively sustained is less apparent. This chapter uses lessons from labor-community coalition practices to help explore the elements of effective long-term global union alliances. In doing so, it suggests there are generalizable lessons about coalitions, whether between unions or between unions and community organizations, that can inform our understanding of union collaboration. It considers the possibilities for creating powerful global union alliances in the service sector through a case study of the Service Employees International Union's (SEIU) new global partnerships unit.

The chapter first outlines the key elements of labor-community coalitions, identifying five significant indicators of coalitions, including common concern, structure, organizational commitment, organizational capacity and culture, and campaign scale. These are then explored through the global partnerships unit established by SEIU in 2004. The core organizational elements of the unit are identified, and then its campaign practices are examined using examples from the Driving Up Standards campaign between SEIU and the United Kingdom's Transport and General Workers Union (T&G or TGWU) between 2004 and 2005.

Union collaboration lies at the heart of strategies for enhancing union power. Union movements exhibit tendencies toward both unity and fragmentation, with collaboration representing an ascendancy of the forces of solidarity over fragmentation at a particular historical period (Hyman 1975; Ellem and Shields 2004). Global union alliances are just one manifestation of this broader form of union practice.

While international collaboration has been used in the maritime, logistics, telecommunications, and manufacturing sectors for decades (Banks and Russo 1999; Hickey 2004; Juravich and Bronfenbrenner 2003; Cohen and Early 2000; Meyer 2001), until recently the service sector had rarely been a site of deep global collaboration. However, rapid decline in union density has promoted new forms of union campaigning to rebuild union power. Furthermore, as firms in all industries have increasingly merged, successful organizing campaigns have required more than just nationally organized movements (Harrod and O'Brien 2002; Lillie and Martinez-Lucio 2004; SEIU 2005). Service unions have now joined these other sectors in making global organizing a priority to establish union recognition and bargaining power.

This chapter suggests that global union collaboration, as one form of union collaboration, may be able to draw insights from another form of collaboration—between labor unions and community organizations. Over the last fifteen years, since the publication of seminal books such as *Building Bridges*, coalitions between unions and community organizations have become a key part of union renewal (Brecher and Costello 1990; Reynolds 2004). This surge of coalition practice in the industrialized world was preceded by the practice of social movement unionism in the Global South, which connected unions and movements for democracy (Moody 1997; von Holdt 2002). Labor-community coalitions have, in particular, been used to resist global corporations, and depending on the industrial scale of those corporations, have had varying success (Herod 2001). However, as capital has globalized, it has been necessary to revisit traditional definitions of the community as "local" (Ellem 2005). While the term "community" in labor-community coalitions implies notions of local place, employers and government operate at multiple scales, which requires that unions be capable of resistance and confrontation at multiple scales of power (Tattersall 2006). This may mean including a broader range of multi-scaled coalition stakeholders, such as global unions. Thus, this chapter adapts scholarship on labor-community coalitions to enhance our understanding of a different form of coalition, the global union alliance, in order to explore when those alliances are likely to be powerful.

Lessons from Labor-Community Coalitions

Labor-community coalitions vary, and whether they can build powerful sustainable campaigns depends on the degree of reciprocal, interdependent connection between coalition partners (Tattersall 2005). This section explores five features of coalitions—common concern, structure, organizational commitment, organizational culture, and a coalition's scale—as a framework for understanding the potential of global union alliances.

The common concern at the heart of a coalition affects the degree of organizational participation and reciprocity. Ad hoc coalitions have a distant form of common interest, where the subject of the coalitional relationships is in the interest only of the party seeking solidarity. For global alliances, an example is a one-time picket against a firm's corporate headquarters in solidarity with a strike in another country. For labor-community coalitions, interconnection deepens when the common concern is in the mutual interest of each of the participating parties. Organizational self-interest for a coalition's core issues makes an organization more likely to deepen its commitment to the campaign. The depth of a coalition's purpose also effects organizational interconnection and support. As a coalition moves from planning tactics to longer-term strategy, it creates a deeper, more powerfully negotiated collaboration (Reynolds 1999). Thus the sustainability and depth of global alliances is likely to increase, depending on the degree to which the coalition's goals reflect the direct interest of each of the union partners, and the extent to which the global alliances build a joint strategy for power.

The structure of the coalition relationship also affects the power of a coalition. Lasting relationships require formal interconnection though decision-making structures. Indicators of organizational interconnection include groups having equal decision-making power, the participation of senior organizational leaders, and the space for open negotiation of campaign planning (Tuffs 1998; Nissen 1999). Formal decision making is also assisted by informal support, such as through brokers or bridge builders between organizations (Rose 2000; McAdam, Tarrow, and Tilly 2001; Obach 2004). Coalition brokers are dedicated union officials working for the union who act as the regular contact points for external organizations and are responsible for executing coalition decisions within the union (McAdam, Tarrow, and Tilly 2001). Bridge builders are people with experience in both community organizations and unions who translate cultural differences between organizations and help to build trust (Rose 2000). As the trust between organizations deepens, the types of organizations participating can also narrow. Instead of being formed on a come-one-come-all basis, coalitions are self-selecting—members are hand-picked because they have a particular kind of interest or capacity (Tattersall 2005). Global union alliances can increase trust by complementing formal decision making with informal bridge builders and brokers to assist with cultural exchange across national boundaries. An example occurred during the United Parcel Service (UPS) 1997 strike, when the International Transport Federation's (ITF) World Council of UPS Unions coordinated a series of European strikes and actions to coincide with the U.S. strike. These activities were coordinated by and linked to the International Brotherhood of Teamsters (IBT) by a dedicated IBT staff working in the IFT World Council's head office in London. These IBT staff members, who had previous experience in working with international union federations, acted as European bridge builders for the IBT with the ITF (Banks and Russo 1999).

A coalition's power is enhanced by the degree of organizational commitment because such commitment increases the resources an alliance can deploy. Commitment is enhanced by leadership support and demonstrated through the mobilization of a union's or community organization's resources for a coalition, including financial commitment, activating organizational members in coalition events or activating a union or community organization's external political and organizational relationships to support the coalition's agenda, and willingness to activate member involvement in coalition events.

The power of a coalition is conditioned by the organizational capacity of its participants and its ability to negotiate differences in organizational culture. Union and community organization capacity varies—some unions have powerful allies or the capacity to mobilize their members; others may have expertise in forms of campaigning (Frege, Heery, and Turner 2004). The capacity of a coalition's participants shapes the potential power of the coalition. Furthermore, a coalition can experience conflict and tension due to contradictions in organizational culture, which can reduce common understanding and trust (Dreiling 1998).

Finally, coalitions can be distinguished by the scale(s) or level at which they operate. Scale is a concept used by labor geographers to understand the spatial aspect of power (Sadler and Fagan 2004). For instance, corporate power, while often categorized by the mobility of capital, can also be constrained by the local, such as in human service work or resource extraction where capital is restricted from moving from specific local places; this creates a capital fix, such as with a mine or property services (Walsh 2000; Ellem 2003). The local scale can be a powerful site for union resistance because it is where people live, work, and can directly participate in decision making and action (Wills 2002). A coalition deepens its power if it is able to sustain organized activity at multiple scales because the power of decision makers, such as government or a firm, is rarely focused at only one scale. While a transnational firm may have the capacity to shift its capital globally, human service industries, such as cleaning or school bus driving, are fixed in specific localities. While firms have a choice about where to invest, the work of janitors or school bus drivers remains tied to where its consumer base is located (Herod 2001; Ellem 2005). Organizing power at that local scale may enhance the power of the union (Savage 1998; Walsh 2000). Furthermore, because a coalition's power comes from the people that it mobilizes, having the capacity to operate at multiple scales, particularly the local, increases the degree of rank-and-file participation.

These indicators—common concern, structure, organizational commitment, organizational capacity and culture, and scale—are indicators of coalition power. Table 8.1 displays these indicators across a framework of

TABLE 8.1.
A framework of union-community coalitions

	Ad hoc coalition	Support coalition	Mutual-support coalition	Deep coalition
Common concern	Solidarity from one group to another Initiated by one group (union or community)	Coalition activities focused on one organization's interest	Issue of coalition in the mutual direct interest of participating organization	Issue in mutual direct interest of participating organization's members Long-term plan to build power
Structure	Episodic, temporary engagement Tactical, event-based No formal coalition formed	Short-term coalition Some formal shared decision making Informal dominance by initiating party Hasty, reactive engagement	Joint decision-making structure Midterm focus and planning Brokers and bridge builders Union leaders participate in coalition	Decentralized structure, connections between organizations at membership level A separate formal coalition office
Organizational commitment	Instrumental engagement Campaign distant from organization member	Organization leaders dominate decision making; campaign distant from union members Commitment mainly from organization whose interests are served	Some mobilization of union members Partner organizations mobilizing their relationships (politicians, media) to support coalition	Union actively engaging rank and file Local structures and local activity happens autonomously
Organizational capacity and culture	Participant organizations require only limited capacity Participant organizations may have very different cultures	Participant organizations have varied capacity and culture; variations may cause relationship to break down	Similar culture/political practice or bridge builders to assist Organizations working toward building similar capacity	Organizations have similar capacity and similar culture
Scale	Can operate at any scale, from local to global	Coalition operates at same scale as decision makers (e.g., the state or the city)	Effective strategy for power at scale of decision maker(s)	Mobilizing capacity at several scales, including local

increasingly powerful coalition forms, ranging from ad hoc coalitions to deep coalitions. This table shows how each indicator contributes to increasingly powerful labor-community coalitions.

This framework of variations among labor-community coalitions is useful for understanding powerful union alliances more generally, including international union alliances. For the second half of the twentieth century, when many unions, particularly in the service sector, constrained themselves to the national scale and were closely tied to national regulation, international union relationships were in most cases episodic and distant—such as ad hoc coalitions (Ramsay 1997; Gallin 2002; Castree et al. 2004). There were some notable exceptions, particularly in mining, manufacturing, logistics, and telecommunications, where unions developed global councils and cross-border campaigns to take on corporate giants such as GE (Meyer 2001), Bridgestone Firestone (Juravich and Bronfenbrenner 2003), UPS (Banks and Russo 1999), Crown Petroleum (Hickey 2004), and Cable and Wireless Communications (Cohen and Early 2000). The pressure for experimentation with global union alliances, which arises from the challenges that globalization poses to union power, has moved into the service sector.

The service sector has historically been a site of labor-community coalitions, particularly given the common interests between public-sector workers and consumers for quality services (Johnston 1994; Tattersall 2006). Yet privatization has increased the need for service unions to exercise employer pressure, now at an international scale, in addition to more local consumer-based coalitions. In particular, the creation of global partnerships by the SEIU is an innovative form of global alliance in the services sector. Below, I examine the establishment of the global partnerships unit and outline its structure. I then use the framework for coalition power to analyze the global alliance's key elements in relation to the Driving Up Standards campaign. This case study included interviews with nine key SEIU international staff members, unstructured interviews with four regional SEIU organizers, unstructured interviews with three T&G officers, and three anonymous interviews with U.K. union officials between November 2005 and May 2006; analysis of SEIU's conference minutes and internal documents; a T&G leadership speech on the alliance with the SEIU in March 2006; and participant observation of an International Transport Organizing Committee (ITOC) and two union trainings, one involving the SEIU organizers in December 2005 and the second involving SEIU and the T&G in March 2006. My data focused on the SEIU staff in order to understand the background and day-to-day operations of the partnerships unit; however, I also undertook interviews with the T&G and other U.K. union officials in order to understand how the SEIU's organizational changes have been evaluated in the United Kingdom.

Global Partnerships: SEIU's Global Union Alliances

In 2006, the SEIU International represented over 1.8 million U.S. and Canadian workers across four industries: hospital services, long-term care, the public sector, and business and property services (SEIU 2006). It has an international office in Washington, D.C., and over three hundred locals operating through twenty-five state councils. Over the last ten years it has led the debate in the United States on experimenting with growth strategies to organize nonunion workers (SEIU 2004c).

SEIU's global partnerships unit had its inception at the June 2004 convention, aiming to build "global strength," one arm of a seven-point platform of collaborative union strengths (SEIU 2004a). The need for global strength came from the increasing challenges of winning for workers in a national context, struggling to build local leverage against transnational firms. Tom Woodruff, executive vice president of SEIU, describes the situation: "The world has changed a lot. Companies that used to be in your home town are no longer located in your city. By 2004 many members worked for companies that were multinational. To win members' contracts, we had to campaign at a multinational level." (interview by author, 2005). The desire for global strength aimed to "move the union global as capital had done" (2005).

The need for global capacity was reinforced by SEIU's industry strategies and its program of comprehensive campaigning. SEIU's organizing strategies are hinged on the plans of the industries it organizes, mapping the patterns of growth in the industry, the major firms, and their relationships and role in setting workplace conditions, in order to identify firms and regions to target in organizing drives (SEIU 2004c).[1] Woodruff argues that long-term organizing plans compelled the union to take on global organizing; with the "increasing consolidation of the world's economy … in ten to twenty years each industry sector will be dominated by three to four global companies" (interview by author, 2005). Building global strength was a logical next step for building power in industries that are not confined by national boundaries.

While the idea of global strength is daunting, SEIU argues that the contradictions of centralizing capital expose opportunities for unions to organize against it (Herod 2001). The trend toward "the concentration of economic power into fewer hands creates the advantage" of fewer corporate targets for organizing large numbers of workers (Tom Woodruff, interview by author, 2005). In addition, SEIU's global organizing strategy is targeting industries that are tied to place. SEIU and the newly formed Change to Win federation's primary aim is to unionize "the more than 50 million American workers who work in industries that cannot be outsourced or shipped overseas" (CTW

---

[1]   These include building services, public sector, health care, and long-term care.

2006). SEIU is targeting forms of work where capital has less mobility, such as in distribution, retail, and human services, to try to overcome the difficulties faced by U.S. unions in industries such as manufacturing and information technology when attempting to organize in the context of the offshoring of hundreds of thousands of jobs each year (CTW 2006).

The impetus for global strength came from experiences in several core industries, where the union was unable to build sufficient leverage within the national borders of the United States (SEIU 2005). But previous global work tended to involve one-sided requests, asking for short-term favors from local unions (Debbie Schneider, interview by author, 2005; Emily Stewart, interview by author, 2005). The global partnerships unit sought to shift away from ad hoc solidarity requests to create a systematic capacity for international work.

The global partnerships unit, which was founded in November 2004 and is responsible for the global strength program,[2] has a reflexive and evolving structure. In 2004, the convention resolution stated that the unit's aim was "to build global strength to win for workers," placing an emphasis on outcomes (SEIU 2004b). This strategy has developed, with the unit now more focused on partnerships that build union capacity internationally across the SEIU's core industries (Debbie Schneider, interview by author, 2005).

The global partnerships unit has a multipronged structure. First, it coordinates specific campaigns with a global scope. These campaigns are organized out of particular industrial divisions within the union—for instance, the school bus campaign is coordinated by the public-sector division. The global partnerships unit manages these campaigns, "coordinating and exchanging strategy, lessons and best practice" and provides support staff (Debbie Schneider, interview by author, 2005).

Second, the global partnerships unit fosters dedicated partnerships to build union capacity globally for all partner unions. Schneider notes two key examples, a regional partnership in Australia with the Liquor Hospitality and Miscellaneous Workers Union (LHMU) and a partnership in the United Kingdom with the T&G (Debbie Schneider, interview by author, 2005). The LHMU is a low-wage service union in Australia that has shifted to organizing since the late 1990s in order to grow in industries such as hospitality, hotels, and cleaning (janitorial services). Similarly, the T&G is a transport and general union that is exploring organizing opportunities in cleaning services. These relationships grew out of long-standing exchanges, initially based on sharing strategies for growth, and are now focused on building global capacity in the building services industry. In Australia and New Zealand SEIU is

---

[2]   While I refer to the global partnerships *unit*, it doesn't have a formal name inside the union—"it's somewhere between a division and a department" (Debbie Schneider, interview by author, 2005).

assisting the LHMU and the Service and Food Workers Union (SFWU) to coordinate the "Clean Start" campaign, and in the United Kingdom it is supporting "Justice for Cleaners" in London (LHMU 2006; T&G 2006a). These partnerships involve the SEIU's employing former local union organizers as SEIU officials in each country. They are also long-term, where the goal is to build global union capacity across the cleaning industry (Debbie Schneider, interview by author, 2005).

Third, the global partnerships unit works with targeted global union federations (GUFs) to build their organizing capacity. GUFs are international, industry-specific union groupings. SEIU has attempted to create two organizing projects within these federations. Inside the Union Network International (UNI), the GUF for skills and services, SEIU has helped establish an organizing committee and global organizing plan for property services by providing an organizing director at the international office, and staff and support in several countries including Poland, South Africa, India, the Netherlands, and Germany. A similar project is planned with the International Union of Food, Agricultural, Hotel, Restaurant, Catering, Tobacco and Allied Workers' Associations (IUF).

Within this multipronged structure, campaigns are selected according to industry organizing priorities and the availability of union relationships. The goal is "to not pick campaigns because of global input but by asking where are the important players in the industry—and choosing to go after those players" (Debbie Schneider, interview by author, 2005). While that is the intention, it has not always been the case in practice. For instance, the Driving Up Standards campaign was selected as a test run for global organizing, given the opportunity of a strong relationship with a U.K. union (Emily Stewart, interview by author, 2005). Campaign choice has been a product of the intersection between industry priorities and available union relationships and their organizational capacity.

Driving Up Standards: Global Union Coalitions

The global partnerships unit entwines selected unions, committed leadership, cultural bridge builders, formal decision-making structures, and exchanges to interconnect unions in strategic alliances. Using the coalitions framework outlined above, SEIU's global partnerships unit demonstrates an attempt to intensify the SEIU's global alliances by moving away from traditional ad hoc international solidarity:

> There is a long history of international solidarity, conferences, meetings, a lot of labor tourism; at best it was holding on to what you had…. [W]orkers here were on strike and unions in other parts of the world would take some

solidarity actions…. [W]hat we are driving at is that's not good enough, the solidarity is certainly a good thing but that it's not enough. We have to organize globally. We have to figure out ways to organize workers in these companies in a number of different countries at the same time. (Tom Woodruff, interview by author, 2005)

This section examines the possibilities and lessons from the SEIU's global partnerships unit using the five elements outlined above and in table 8.1, drawing on examples from the Driving Up Standards campaign. This campaign responded to the shortcomings of SEIU's attempt to organize private school bus contractors for U.S. FirstStudent, a major contractor and standard setter in the industry that operated with a low wage, nonunion business model in the United States. Previous organizing drives were resisted and often failed through the National Labor Relations Board processes. Yet FirstStudent was owned by FirstGroup, a U.K. company that has a working relationship with the T&G. The relationship included rights for union stewards on the job, access to management to settle grievances, and strong workplace contracts.

In 2006, the T&G was the United Kingdom's largest general union, representing over eight hundred thousand workers. While representing all kinds of workers, it represents four main industrial sectors: food and agriculture, manufacturing, services, and transport. The union has a decentralized structure, with shop stewards, workplace branches, and regional offices (T&G 2006b). Under the leadership of Tony Woodley, the union's general secretary, the T&G has shifted to an "organizing agenda," prioritizing strategies for growth and member development in industries such as building services, airlines, and logistics (T&G 2006c).

The formation of a global union campaign between the SEIU and the T&G was seen as the only way to build sufficient power to create an environment where SEIU could unionize U.S. bus workers. This campaign was SEIU's first long-term initiative within the global partnerships unit.

Common Concerns

The global partnerships unit is built on the overarching interest that unions have in "growth" rather than on an "abstract" concern for solidarity (Tom Woodruff, interview by author, 2005). From SEIU's perspective, a mutual interest in growth is relatively easily cultivated; union density is linked to power, and "if the unions internationally are not strong enough to check the companies' profits then the companies are just going to drive standards down" (Emily Stewart, interview by author, 2005). Tom Woodruff contrasts alliances over density with alliances with community groups, noting: "When aligning with community groups a mutual objective is hard to figure out, but in global union work, a mutual objective is not difficult. The goal is to organize company A, inside industry A.... [I]t is easier to establish common interest where the mutual objective is measured and growing" (interview by author, 2005).

A common interest in growth is the basis for the long-term mutual interest alliance between the SEIU and the T&G. Indeed, beyond the Driving Up Standards campaign, SEIU and the T&G are supporting each other in local growth strategies; the T&G is supporting the SEIU by taking action in the United Kingdom to improve working standards in the United States, and the SEIU is supporting the T&G's growth by providing experienced staff to help it organize cleaners (janitors) in London (Emily Stewart, interview by author, 2005; participant observation, T&G speech to Change to Win Organizing Conference, 2005).

Underpinning the alliance is not only a mutual commitment to growth but also a desire to learn and develop similar strategies to achieve that growth. These include a desire to research industries with growth potential, to understand industry power, and to expand and develop strategies for organizing nonunion workers. The T&G's relationship with the SEIU derives in part from its desire to strategically enhance its own internal shift to organizing (T&G union official 2, interview by author, 2006).

However, difficulties can still surface when negotiating specific campaign issues. This again requires the negotiation of a specific common interest, which SEIU has found to be a difficult process. Real, mutual self-interest must be engaged in the specific campaign. Organizers in SEIU talk of searching for campaign issues and strategies "where everyone is participating and gets a share of the outcome" (Emily Stewart, interview by author, 2005). There is an acknowledgment that this is difficult and is often preceded by learning about how other unions work and what their direct interests and goals are (2005).

Negotiating a specific common interest also requires the individual unions to have a clear understanding of their own self-interest and to be capable of calculating the risks and opportunities from alliance work; strong coalitions develop from strong individual organizations. Thus the organizing focus of a global coalition needs to connect to local union priorities; the more specific the connection between the local interest and the global priorities, the deeper the interest, engagement, and organizational connection to the coalition.

The complexities of common interest are evident in the Driving Up Standards alliance between SEIU and the T&G. This alliance is a campaign for improving the conduct of FirstGroup, which is a large operator of school buses in the United States and trains and buses in the United Kingdom. Both unions have members and potential members in FirstGroup and its American subsidiary, FirstStudents, and in the long run each has a mutual interest in improving the standards of employment and regulation in the bus industry. However, there is a disconnection in the "mutuality of interest." SEIU's interest in raising standards directly connects to a wide-scale organizing drive in the United States—creating a deep self-interest. In contrast, the T&G already has very high union density. SEIU officials acknowledge that the campaign has limitations due to the "lack of mutuality" because the T&G has limited "growth potential" (Debbie Schneider, interview by author, 2005). Similarly, T&G union officials noted that union member engagement in the campaign has sometimes been difficult; while there has been support for SEIU members in solidarity with poor working conditions in the United States, U.K. member participation has been motivated more by altruism than by self-interest (T&G union official 3, interview by author, 2006). While there is a common interest in growing unionism across the industry, there is less of a fit between self-interest in the two national contexts and the campaign's goals (Emily Stewart, interview by author, 2005).

That said, the organizational relationships have allowed the T&G to expand and learn new campaign techniques. In the United Kingdom, the Driving Up Standards campaign has featured a public community campaign, research of the transport industry, and a corporate campaign targeting the First Group's Annual General Meeting (AGM) that has supported the campaign capacity and organizing agenda of the T&G (T&G union official 1, 2006).

Achieving common interest requires permanent ongoing negotiation and open communication, and tensions over bargaining outcomes may prove to be hurdles for global union alliances. This is magnified when, despite union intentions, firms often divide and conquer employees by offering different contracts and terms across borders (Martinez-Lucio and Weston 1995). Given that building trust takes time and given the centrality of wage outcomes to members' interests, it may be a significant challenge to sustain joint action over contract bargaining, as withholding on a contract could amount to a type of permanent solidarity rather than mutual self-interest. Yet the relationship between the unions provides a framework for creating a mutual interest around driving standards up. For the T&G that meant preventing the "creeping Americanization" of working conditions, and for the SEIU that meant acting with transnational support to raise U.S. standards (Emily Stewart, interview by author, 2005). This was supported by joint activity and exchanges between U.K. and U.S. workers linking their common experiences that proactively guarded against corporate attempts to divide these workers by nation.

Additionally, labor-community coalition practices may provide useful lessons. A public-sector coalition by unions and community organizations in Chicago included demands for a union contract for workers and community demands for improved public services. Early on in the relationship, key organizers agreed on a set process. The community organization stated up front that it did not expect the union to refuse to sign a contract if one was offered (Community organizer, interview by author, 2005). To build trust, the organization instead requested that the union be open about its negotiating tactics and the content of its contract to allow the community organization to adjust its strategy according to the changing patterns of the dispute. The coalition recognized that wages and conditions, as core self-interest, had to be managed within the context of the coalition. So the community organization agreed to the union's negotiating its contract with the public service separately from the community organization's campaign while continuing a process of open and transparent dialogue with the organization. This private relationship allowed the community organization to demonstrate that it respected the needs and limitations of the unions involved while trust between the organizations developed. Simultaneously, the union ensured that its public-sector employment contract did not prevent its taking further political action over the broader public-service concerns that the community organization was campaigning for.

Openly negotiating and respecting the self-interest of coalition partners is an important mechanism for enhancing trust in global union alliances. Holding out contractual agreements across borders will sometimes be a useful tactic but cannot be the basis for developing international bargaining agreements. As relationships build, agreed processes for dealing with conflicts of interest may provide a stepping-stone for ensuring that mutual self-interest and reciprocity are sustained as alliances develop and strengthen.

Organizational Structure

The SEIU global partnerships unit aims to move beyond "ad hoc attempts to use existing relationships and instead provide a permanent base for union relationships" (Steve Edwards, interview by author, 2005). The partnerships unit is a group of handpicked unions who share a common interest in growth. As Debbie Schneider notes, "if there is no interest about organizing," an alliance will be difficult (interview by author, 2005). Indeed, relationships are cultivated through long-standing informal relationships (such as with the LHMU or T&G), or through "exploratory visits to other countries"—including Australia, the United Kingdom, the Netherlands, and Germany—to find instances where there is "a commitment between unions to try and reinforce organizing with each other" (Emily Stewart, interview by author, 2005). Union leaders play a critical role in creating stable global alliances. In the Driving Up Standards campaign, strong leaders "generated the will" that could withstand tensions and negotiation and ensured that the relationships lasted (Emily Stewart, interview by author, 2005). For instance, when debates around campaign styles became heated early on in the relationship, leadership intervention by the T&G in the United Kingdom helped keep the relationship on track (T&G union official 1, interview by author, 2006).

In individual campaigns, organizational relationships are formally connected through governance structures. In the Driving Up Standards campaign, the International Transport Organizing Committee, established in
April 2004, evolved out of a year of one-time exchanges between the unions.
The committee included equal numbers of SEIU and T&G members, including the senior leadership of both unions and rank-and-file representatives
from the T&G (participant observation of ITOC meeting, March 2006). SEIU
organizers repeatedly stated that global unionism requires artful diplomacy
to negotiate campaign strategy, and it was in this committee that diplomatic
disputes would be negotiated (Debbie Schneider, interview by author, 2005;
Emily Stewart, interview by author, 2005). As Stewart observes: "This was to
be the forum for critical decisions. If we were going to push one union or another beyond their comfort zone, this would be the governing body to make
that decision, hear the problems and deal with issues around that" (interview
by author, 2005).

The campaign had a dual structure, between operation and strategic management. Day-to-day decision making was left to union officials through
teleconferences and local meetings, while this formal structure bound the
unions through an open safe space for dispute resolution and strategy
development.

Interconnection between the two unions is also facilitated through membership and leadership exchanges. The Driving Up Standards campaigns used
exchanges at union meetings and conventions to personalize and connect the
campaign to the rank and file of each union. These visits "built up support
for the campaign ... sparking outrage" and a willingness to act amongst the
union as a whole, in addition to the leadership (Steve Edwards, interview by
author, 2005). Exchanges were used when union commitment was escalated.
T&G rank-and-file bus drivers came to the first bus meeting in Chicago in
September 2004 to launch the international exchange. Then U.S. workers attended the T&G AGM in early 2005 before the T&G lobbied for U.K. politicians to undertake a tour of FirstStudent work sites in the United States (Emily
Stewart, interview by author 2005).

Organizational Commitment

To enhance ongoing organizational commitment, the global partnerships unit
created formal brokers and bridge builders between unions to resource global
interaction. SEIU provides significant resources for regional offices and organizers in Australia, the United Kingdom, South Africa, India, and Poland.
Dedicated staff is vital for building local commitment to the global coalition.
As Tom Woodruff argues: "Everyone is so busy ... we have found that to have
effective partnerships with sufficient energy and resources to foster those

partnerships and make them happen that we need people focused entirely on this ... through dedicated staff" (interview by author, 2005). A dedicated staff moves a coalition from good intentions to creating a sustainable capacity to act. Thus the Clean Start for Cleaners campaign in Australia, which is a joint SEIU-LHMU-SFWU campaign, followed from the SEIU's employment of a dedicated staff person, Michael Crosby, and his establishment of a research and organizing team.

Organizational Culture and Capacity

Union brokers also act as cultural bridge builders between different national contexts and union cultures. SEIU officials argue that the most significant obstacle to international exchange is "learning the language of union and industry practice" in other countries (Emily Stewart, interview by author, 2005). These include anything from legal and regulatory differences to understanding the accepted codes of local union practice. Having a cultural translator helps prevent cultural mismatches from creating conflict between the parties. In the Driving Up Standards campaign, Steve Edwards was hired as a bridge builder to help build more formal relationships between the unions. Steve was employed by SEIU in March 2004 to be based in Washington, D.C., but his background was as head of the transport division at the T&G in the United Kingdom. His relationships with the T&G and his knowledge of local U.K. union practice enabled him to act as a full-time "bridge between SEIU and campaign with the T&G in the UK" (Steve Edwards, interview by author, 2005). Later on, this bridge-builder model was reproduced in the United Kingdom—in September 2004 a U.K. union official was hired as an SEIU organizer to work with the T&G in London.

A key cultural difference in the Driving Up Standards campaign is between acceptable types of campaign practice (Steve Edwards, interview by author, 2005). SEIU has traditionally used a very "in your face" style of direct action, particularly in its Justice for Janitors campaigns (Emily Stewart, interview by author, 2005). SEIU also relies on comprehensive campaigns, including alliances with community organizations, corporate campaigning, and aggressive media as usual practice, because it does not have strong preexisting relationships with government or corporations.

This is unlike union practice in other countries. For instance, in the United Kingdom, unions have traditionally relied on strong, informal relations with government, and unions have a weaker tradition of corporate or community campaigning (Frege and Kelly 2004). The common mode of union action is industrial disputation (Steve Edwards, interview by author, 2005). In the United Kingdom, the T&G has a strong tradition of rank-and-file involvement in campaign planning, which is different from SEIU practice in the First Student campaign. The T&G includes rank-and-file representatives in the cross-union decision-making structures, while the SEIU relies on paid staff (participant observation, ITOC meeting, March 2006).

In the Driving Up Standards campaign, campaign style is a diplomatic issue. At one level, there has been a desire among the T&G to learn new tactics, such as corporate and community campaigning (Steve Edwards, interview by author, 2005; T&G union official 2, interview by author, 2006). This exposure to SEIU's expertise in this more aggressive form of campaign has been welcomed by the T&G because it has added to the T&G's internal capacity and supported its own shift to organizing. However, concerns have been raised locally within the United Kingdom that the learning process between SEIU and the T&G is less than mutual, and even among some of the key supporters of organizing, some U.K. union officials have argued that SEIU's engagement is sometimes seen as a one-way street where SEIU is the teacher and the U.K. unions are the students. In particular, there is some concern that SEIU does not sufficiently respect the strengths of the U.K. unions, such as their strong rank-and-file steward structures (anonymous U.K. union official, interview by author, 2006).

While there is a broad recognition inside the T&G staff that the union benefits in its relationship with the SEIU by expanding the T&G's capacity to organize nonunion workers, there have been debates about the merits of adopting SEIU organizing strategies or adapting those strategies by connecting them to local union strengths, such as strong stewards networks (T&G union official 2, interview by author, 2006; T&G union official 3, interview by author, 2006). This tension in the United Kingdom is not surprising given the magnitude of the global alliances and the fact that these alliances are new for service-based unions like SEIU. It is also a possible consequence of the problems over mutuality of interest in the Driving Up Standards campaign, rather than an inherent obstacle in the alliance. It should also be acknowledged that some of the detractors of the SEIU alliance are motivated by other reasons, such as being resistant to the prospects of change or recognizing that the change process is risky and keeping the option available of blaming SEIU if things don't go well.

However, criticisms have also come from strong supporters of change, and thus this tension around reciprocity and mutual learning is a current weakness to be overcome through negotiation, experience, and relationship building. Differences in campaign modes also complicate global alliances because they can potentially threaten other traditionally important relationships, such as with the government or employers. In the Driving Up Standards campaign SEIU has no corporate relationship with FirstStudent and therefore has nothing to lose from an aggressive campaign against the employer (anonymous U.K. union official, interview by author, 2006). In contrast, the T&G has strong union density and through this has achieved a "consent-based relationship" with the company that provides union benefits including strong safety standards, good pay and conditions, and organizing rights for union stewards (anonymous SEIU organizer 1, interview by author, 2005; T&G union official 1, interview by author, 2006). In these circumstances, collaborative relationships with another union can threaten employer collaboration. Indeed, in attacking FirstStudent, the T&G potentially threatens the benefits of its consent-based relationship. Consequently, the Driving Up Standards organizing campaign has to delicately manage the desire for global solidarity alongside the potentially conflicting interests deriving from the contrasting status of the employer, FirstStudent.

The degree of organizational capacity and commitment in the Driving Up Standards campaign ensures that the coalition is well resourced. SEIU's commitment is demonstrated financially. The T&G's commitment is evident in its willingness to mobilize its powerful union relationships for SEIU. The T&G has repeatedly lobbied FirstGroup, including tendering public submissions critical of FirstGroup's labor practices and mobilizing its parliamentary supporters to tour the United States and support a parliamentary motion critical of antiunion practice (Steve Edwards, interview by author, 2005). The mutual commitment of each union produces a powerful, interdependent coalition capable of action in the United States and United Kingdom.

Scale

While global union alliances represent an innovation at the global scale, their effectiveness relies on the capacity to mobilize and engage at other scales. For all the technical expertise of a global corporate campaign, as SEIU's Debbie Schneider says, "you can't campaign well without workers, bosses notice if you don't have them, it's a matter of doing both"(interview, 2005). As Herod (1997) argues, the local remains important even with the globalization of capital. Engaging workers and harnessing union capacity across countries require the global partnerships unit to work inside the countries at multiple scales.

Yet while multiscaled action is vital, it is extremely difficult to sustain and has been a significant challenge in the Driving Up Standards campaign. The campaign has two key arms: first, a political and corporate leverage campaign around FirstGroup's attempt to expand into British Transport, and second, an industry-wide campaign around the standards of yellow bus operators in the United States. The U.K. campaign is a political leverage campaign, using studies, customer awareness, media, and political influence to demonstrate that FirstGroup's antiunion behavior in the United States should not be rewarded with expansions in its U.K. transport operations. The second arm of the campaign in the United States is a labor-community coalition campaign to improve the regulation of standards for yellow bus contracts, where workers, with parents and the local community, lobby school boards to demand that the board contract only with companies that meet basic levels of maintenance, monitoring, and labor conditions to protect quality bus services for schoolchildren.

The difficulty for the Driving Up Standards campaign is that the immense breadth of this activity makes it "hard to go deep" (anonymous SEIU organizer 2, interview by author, 2005). This was particularly the case early on, when the campaign was focused on mobilizing "U.K. leverage" to the exclusion of deep worker participation in either country (anonymous SEIU organizer 1, 2005). However, the worker-community school board campaign and the activity focused on the 2006 AGM have engaged union members in both countries in more meaningful activities that have a direct impact on union leverage, which has assisted the campaign's multiscaled capacity.

As one SEIU official said, reflecting on the Driving Up Standards campaign, "[T]he will has been good, the execution has been difficult" (Emily Stewart, interview by author, 2005). This chapter has attempted to introduce a framework for understanding how the execution of global alliances works, drawing from the work of labor-community coalitions.

This chapter has identified five key indicators of labor-community coalitions and then explored those indicators by focusing on a very new global union alliance, SEIU's global partnerships unit. Studying this unit and the Driving Up Standards campaign reveals similarities between the operations of effective global alliances and effective coalitions. There was a close correlation between the emphasis on common concern and effective global partnerships. The mutual interest in growth and achieving a campaign fit was an important but challenging feature of the campaign. Mutual interest remains a goal of the global partnerships unit, but it is a constant test to renegotiate this during campaign practice. Similarly, organizational interaction was an important and variable feature of the global union alliance. The formal and informal interconnection between the unions created bonds of increasing trust as well as providing a space for negotiating tensions and cultural differences. Yet cultural tensions remained a feature of those relationships. Finally, the role of scale is equally important. Without engaging workers at a local scale, the union can easily be "third-partied" in campaigns. Multiscalar campaigning is the great challenge for global alliances, as stretching from the local to the global thins resources, and meaningful local engagement requires meaningful local action, which can also be a challenge.

Despite these successes, the Driving Up Standards campaign has not proceeded without complications, which signal potential challenges for future global alliances more broadly. Like labor-community coalitions, the effectiveness of union exchanges relies on reciprocity and mutual interest to be effective, and it is on these questions that the global union experiment has some detractors. The global partnerships unit has proceeded quickly, often attempting to initiate campaigns and activity despite tensions within or between unions and the local union movement. SEIU has sometimes been perceived as trying to "pick winners" in this local context, exacerbating local tensions, and has been criticized for being insensitive to local union practices, capacity, and differences. For this, the global partnerships experiment has been criticized outside the United States. Yet the global partnerships unit has the potential to create powerful internationalisms in the fast-growing service sector, and international union organizing in this sector presents an opportunity to shift worker conditions internationally. The SEIU has refined and led comprehensive union campaigns in the United States, and spreading these lessons to partner unions globally is a very welcome step.

Heeding the experience of labor-community coalitions, this chapter emphasizes that future global union structures and strategies should proceed as alliances that join distinct, differently interested organizations, requiring space for open negotiation. I suggest the goal is not single global unions but global union coalitions capable of negotiating different interests and cultural practices at multiple scales of organization and power. Sensitivity to reciprocity, respect for difference, and mutual learning will be critical if these alliances are to have longevity within different national contexts.

As capital centralizes into smaller numbers of global firms, unions such as SEIU are seeking to engage at the global scale. Global union alliances are just one example of a possible source of powerful collaboration that can support a renewal of union power. This examination of SEIU's global partnerships unit suggests that global union alliances can learn from the practice of labor-community coalitions to help create powerful global union collaboration.

9. INTERNATIONAL FRAMEWORK AGREEMENTS

Opportunities and Challenges for Global Unionism

DIMITRIS STEVIS AND TERRY BOSWELL

In 1966 the United Auto Workers (UAW) spearheaded the creation of World Company Councils (WCC) in order to promote union collaboration with respect to particular companies. By 1974 there were more than thirty of them, but none had been able to engage a transnational firm in substantive dialogue, let alone any form of bargaining. Fourteen years later the International Union of Food, Agricultural, Hotel, Restaurant, Catering, Tobacco and Allied Workers' Associations (IUF), one of the international trade secretariats (pre-2002 name for global union federations [GUFs]) that had pursued the WCC strategy, signed the first in a series of agreements with the French company Danone. Seven years later it signed its second agreement with another French company, Accor. On January 22, 2007, Building Workers' International (BWI) signed the fifty-fifth international framework agreement (IFA), while European works councils (EWC) and European industry federations (EIF) have signed at least nine agreements with extra-European implications, which we call extraterritorial agreements.[1]

---

[1]   As of March 6, 2007, the *Hazards Magazine* website included fifty agreements because it excluded UNI's agreement with Falck and was not updated to include the Nampak, Turner, and National Australia Group agreements (*Hazards Magazine* 2007). It also does not include the ICEM's agreement with the German company RAG that was signed in 2003 but not posted in the ICEM website until late 2006. We include the Falck agreement because it satisfies our criteria. We do not include the Metro unilateral statement that UNI lists as an agreement or UNI's agreement with the Universal Postal Union. The second group of nine agreements is often included in lists of global agreements because of their extra-European impacts (*European Industrial Relations Review* 2005b). Our list includes the agreements with Vivendi, Suez, Air France, Club Mediter-ranèe, GM Europe, Triumph International, Ford-Europe, CSA Czech Airlines, and GeoPost. This number is probably conservative.

What makes IFAs different from other statements that involve unions and corporations at the global level is that they are negotiated between unions and transnational corporations and are not unilateral codes of conduct promulgated by corporations. While IFAs aim to establish certain rules that regulate the corporation's labor practices at the global level, they are not collective bargaining agreements that can be enforced in national or international law. Their value depends on the regulatory provisions that unions have managed to negotiate and, of course, on the ability of unions to exert pressure on the corporation through organizing and campaigns.

Many GUFs and national unions consider these global agreements as their major accomplishments and priorities, even though they recognize their limitations. During 2006, for instance, both the IUF (2006) and the International Metalworkers' Federation (IMF) (2006) completed reviews of the strategy, while BWI had done so a few years earlier (IFBWW 2004). What explains the attention that many GUFs are paying to IFAs? More important, what significance do IFAs have for union efforts to organize and bargain with the world's largest transnational companies? Can they actually enable GUFs to act more like real global unions, or are they simply one more tool that employers use to undermine union cross-border challenges to global capital?

So far the research on global agreements is limited, but interest in them is strong (see, for example, Bourque 2005; Hammer 2005; Gibb 2005; Müller, Platzer, and Rüb 2005; Rudikoff 2005; Tørres and Gunnes 2003). What becomes apparent is that like all policies, global agreements can be examined from at least two angles. One is to focus on their regulatory provisions; another, and the one examined in this chapter, is to focus on whether they are helping advance global union collaboration. This dimension is important because the regulatory provisions and practical accomplishments of these agreements have been modest so far and can easily lead to their premature dismissal. Yet historically, they are the first instance of formal and negotiated agreements between unions and corporations at the global level. Since they are a relatively recent phenomenon, most having been negotiated since 2001, there has not been enough time to come up with reliable evaluations of their record and potential. As we will show in the discussion that follows, their chances for empowering the organized and organizing the unorganized will depend largely on whether they become

Specific information on global agreements was provided by: Jim Baker and Dwight Justice (ICF-TU); Jim Catterson and Dick Blin (ICEM); Ron Blum, Robert Steiert, Rob Johnston, Jenny Holdcroft, and Peter Unterweger (IMF); Marion Hellmann (BWI); Paul Garver (IUF); Philip Bowyer (UNI); and Klaus Franz (European Employee Forum—GM). Jorge Campos Miranda (regional director of the IMF for Latin America and the Caribbean) graciously provided us with important information on IMF agreements in the Americas. We have also benefited from comments by Ron Blum, Philip Bowyer, Kate Bronfenbrenner, Paul Garver, Marion Hellmann, Christy Hoffman (UNI), Jenny Holdcroft, Dwight Justice, and Dan Gallin.

integrated in global cross-border strategies, such as comprehensive campaigns, that link workers, unions, and labor-related nongovernmental organizations (NGOs) from all affected countries in the Global North as well as the Global South in dealing with the largest transnational firms around the world.

We start by reviewing the main explanations for the emergence of global agreements, because we think that an understanding of their European origins is necessary for the fuller understanding of the opportunities and challenges they present for global unionism. We then examine whether, and in what ways, they contribute to a stronger global unionism. We close the chapter by identifying and discussing whether and how the strategy of global agreements and the strategy of global campaigns can be brought together to advance a stronger global unionism. Central to our discussion throughout the chapter is the belief that in order to create global solidarity, national unions must commit to more supranational global union organizations, not replacing them (something that is neither possible nor desirable) but complementing them within a multitiered system of global unionism (Boswell and Stevis 1997; Stevis 1998; Fairbrother and Hammer 2005). In the absence of such organizations, these agreements, as well as campaigns, will not achieve their fullest potential and are likely to provide the basis for division rather than unity.

Our information comes largely from primary sources. These include background discussions with a host of global unionists over the last seven years, many of whom also provided us with additional information as well as comments on our work (see acknowledgments note). We have also benefited a great deal from the comments and presentations of various unionists in a number of meetings, particularly the Global Unions Conference that took place in February of 2006 and the IMF's World Conference on global agreements (September 26–27, 2006). We have also analyzed the texts of all IFAs. These are available on the websites of the GUFs or were provided to us upon request. The texts of the nine extraterritorial agreements that we have identified are available in the EWC database of the Social Development Agency.

We have also taken full advantage of various electronic sources of information on labor, such as the web pages of GUFs, the European Trade Union Confederation's Social Development Agency, and Eironline, the electronic news and analysis source of the European Foundation for the Improvement of Living and Working Conditions, which is also the source of extensive research on related subjects. Finally, the *European Works Councils Bulletin*, and the *European Industrial Relations Review* are invaluable sources of information on the subject.

What Explains Global Agreements?

The main factors that have been offered as explanations for global agreements include globalization, the failure of global governance, corporate social responsibility, global union federation strategies, and national and regional industrial relations. All of these have something to offer in terms of explaining some or many of these agreements. After addressing each one of them, we will suggest the most plausible explanations and their implications.

In the most general sense, global agreements are responses to globalization. General causal evocations of globalization, however, hide more than they reveal and can very well lead to mechanistic explanations. What we need are historically situated analyses that recognize that globalization is uneven, both synchronically and diachronically (Steger 2005). Unions are affected differentially by globalization, depending on their sector and the country in which they are located (Müller, Platzer, and Rüb 2005). Thus, a northern union in a labor-intensive industry, such as textiles, is likely to be more vulnerable to globalization, while a southern union may see it as an opportunity. That was certainly the case between U.S. and official Mexican unions during the North American Free Trade Agreement (NAFTA) debates (Stevis 2002; Stevis and Boswell 2001), and it is the case now between Mexican and Chinese unions.

Global public governance received a major impetus with the formation of the World Trade Organization (WTO) and the strengthening of financial institutions such as the International Monetary Fund and the World Bank. The unwillingness of the WTO to place labor rights on its agenda has been considered a failure of public governance from the point of view of most of the global labor movement. The slow response by international financial institutions to address concerns raised by unions and NGOs has only exacerbated these tensions. The reasons given by the governing bodies to explain their unwillingness to include labor rights on the agenda provoked more demonstrations and considerable debate (see van Roozendaal 2002; Alston 2005; Langille 2005). It is worth noting, however, that the move toward global agreements had started delivering some results even before the demonstrations in Seattle, Quebec, Genoa, and Miami. The question more pertinent to this discussion is why companies would want to sign global agreements once it became apparent that public policy changes were unlikely.

This brings us to the role of corporate social responsibility (CSR) as an explanation for global agreements. Instances of CSR have existed for many decades. Since the late 1980s, however, CSR has become more prominent as a response to corporate and/or comprehensive campaigns by unions and other groups (for a discussion of the evolution of comprehensive campaigns see chapter 1 by Tom Juravich) As of March 2006 more than 2,300 corporations had signed on to the United Nations' global compact. Yet almost all codes are unilateral, and even those that are multistakeholder often remain voluntary (OECD 2000; Wick 2005). Judging from the web pages of many of the corporations that have signed agreements, these are corporations that do wish to promote their social responsibility. Moreover, many of the global agreements that have been signed have titles that refer to CSR, yet corporate social responsibility is also not a complete answer. If it were, we would expect U.S. companies to be at the forefront, given that they account for most CSR instruments.

Global union organizations, in collaboration with national unions, have played a very important role in channeling CSR toward global agreements (Justice 2001; *European Works Councils Bulletin* 2004a and 2004b; *European Industrial Relations Review* 2005b). The IUF provides the bridge between the WCCs of the 1970s and the global agreements strategy that other GUFs have also adopted in order to both engage the corporation and strengthen their role in global union politics. While national and regional unions and workers' organizations have played a central role, this has been a strategy shaped at the global level with the promulgation of the International Confederation of Free Trade Unions (ICFTU)/International Trade Secretariats (ITS) Basic Code of Labor Practice (ICFTU 1997), the goal of which was to take advantage of CSR to engage the corporation with an eye toward some form of global industrial relations. Yet the initiative of global unions does not tell us why some corporations chose to negotiate rather than promulgate additional unilateral codes.

This brings us to the last explanation. As described in chapters 6 and 7, the same changes in corporate structure and ownership that led U.S. unions to begin to move toward strategic corporate research and comprehensive campaigns in the last two decades have now begun to move some unions in Europe to make a similar shift toward strategic research and cross-border strategies, including comprehensive campaigns. This shift owes a great deal to the increasing transnationalization of important European companies and their efforts to abandon their commitment to historical forms of collaborative industrial relations (Rudikoff 2005). Yet continental industrial relations make it more difficult for companies to do away with unions or prevent their formation (for example, in Scandinavia and Germany) or dismiss diminishing unions, as is the case in France.[2] The Europeanization of industrial relations has also proven to be of increasing assistance to unions, even though the labor provisions at the European Union (EU) level are well below what unions have and are seeking (EESC 2006; European Trade Union Confederation 2006). The formation of European works councils, in particular, has played an important role, and this is likely to be the case with the 2001 European Company Statute (*European Industrial Relations Review* 2002; Kluge and Stolit 2006). While EWCs are limited to consultation and information, they are embedded in EU policy (Stevis and Boswell 2001; Weiler 2004). Moreover, as many as fifty EWCs have signed joint texts that move beyond consultation and information, with about one third of

---

[2]   For a broader view on globalization and the social welfare state see Rieger and Leibfried 2003.

them having global implications (*European Industrial Relations Review* 2005b, 16; also Beirnaert 2006). In short, then, while a wide variety of factors have led to global agreements, the ones that more directly explain their emergence are the strategies of GUFs along with the Europeanization of industrial relations.

The political geography of global agreements clearly demonstrates the influence of continental European industrial relations, a fact recognized by most of the GUFs (see IMF 2005, 41). All but seven of the fifty-five IFAs are with continental and northern European countries, with fifteen German companies taking the lead in the last two years, followed by nine French, six Swedish, five Dutch, and three Italian companies. All other countries on the list of IFAs have two or fewer companies. There are no Canadian, British, Asian, or Latin American companies involved, and, until October 2006, the only U.S. company (Chiquita) was one that produced mostly outside the country. The signing of an agreement with the Turner company, a subsidiary of the German-owned Hochtief and a collaborator of the Swedish-owned Skanska (both of which have signed agreements), can be considered an important development and one that we explore further. Our background discussions and observations, however, indicate pessimism with respect to agreements with companies from the United States, Japan, and South Korea. One important reason why some corporations do not want to sign agreements is their objection to having GUFs as signatories. In short, they do not want global social dialogue and, even less so, global industrial relations. The nine extraterritorial agreements naturally focus on European companies, mostly French (five), with several important and hopeful exceptions. Two of these agreements are with Ford-Europe and GM-Europe, while there is also a strong EWC joint text with General Electric (*European Works Councils Bulletin* 2005a). We will return to the potential significance of these extraterrestrial agreements in the last part of the chapter.

The continental European origin of most of the transnational firms that have signed agreements accentuates certain sectoral imbalances, but these are not simply due to the geography of the agreements. In some instances, the leading companies in various industrial sectors are from the United States, the United Kingdom, and Japan (e.g., oil, rubber, information technology, electronics). In other instances, unions involved with the public sector have centered their attention on opposing privatization, outsourcing, and the range of measures involved in state restructuring, although these developments in turn may provide an occasion for global agreements in due course. Even so, there remain important sectoral gaps among EU-based transnational firms in areas such as financial services, information technology (particularly computer-related companies), and transportation services in general. On the other hand, an early concern about attracting lead companies has been put to rest as global giants such as Carrefour, DaimlerChrysler, Bosch, and the European Aeronautic Defense and Space Company (EADS) have joined.

Finally, why are these corporations joining? While global agreements are superior to codes of conduct, they are not binding. Yet they are negotiated with unions, something that transnational companies refused to do from the 1960s until the late 1990s, and set a precedent that may well legitimate the role of unions in global industrial relations. Increasingly, employer associations are paying attention to global agreements (IOE 2005). The 2003 report of the International Organization of Employers (IOE 2003, 7) notes that at a high-level meeting of executives of companies that have signed IFAs, "perhaps the key observation was that companies that have signed IFAs principally see them as a vehicle for deepening dialogue, first and foremost, and *not* as an industrial relations exercise. The difficulty however is that International Trade Unions [GUFs] see them very much so as the latter" (italics in original) (for an incisive analysis see Rudikoff 2005).

In light of the above, we offer three plausible explanations why corporations choose to sign global agreements (see also Müller, Platzer, and Rüb 2005; Collectif de l'ethique sur l'etiquette 2005). In some cases, corporations are deeply anchored in collaborative national industrial relations and are either not willing or not yet able to break away from them. With very few exceptions, transnational corporations remain dependent on national alliances and markets. Some of those corporations may well choose to abide by these commitments for the sake of industrial peace and as a result of enlightened human resource policies. Important insights and comparisons about how transnational firms that have signed agreements view their relations with their workers can be garnered from their web pages and from their reports to the Global Reporting Initiative (2006). Others are already looking for opportunities to break away from the national model when operating outside their countries.

A second plausible explanation, not necessarily at odds with the previous one, is that, while global agreements are not typical CSR instruments, they may very well be of a more profound and sophisticated kind, with their own dynamics and implications. In some parts of the world, such as Europe, using a unilateral code of conduct to avoid more consequential social regulation may not do; offering an IFA, however, may provide evidence of commitment to social dialogue, an important element of EU-level industrial relations (Stevis and Boswell 2001). Even though mandated by EU law, social dialogue between European unions and business has moved glacially toward the adoption of policies. From the point of view of transnational firms, global agreements that are not mandated by any law are likely to move even more slowly unless unions can force them in that direction.

Finally, a third reason why European firms may be signing these agreements largely in the context of the continental European industrial relations environment is that, until now, that environment has not served to test the agreements to any great degree. Within Europe, most are with firms in sectors and countries that are already highly organized and where global corporate restructuring has yet to take place. While there have been some attempts by the GUFs to push the corporate signatories to the agreements to uphold them in the Global South or North America where their subsidiaries actively oppose unionization, this frontier has not yet been adequately tested (Oswald 2006; for examples that may test this frontier see IMF 2006; ICEM 2006). Quite possibly, this more positive attitude towards IFAs by European-based transnational companies may change as these same firms begin to face more hostile relations with their unions within Europe (see chapters 6 and 7) and as GUFs strengthen their demands that agreements cover the companies' operations in more contested union terrain in North America or the Global South. The IUF, for instance, is concerned both about the regulatory weakness of IFAs and their utility outside of the relatively sheltered institutional space of the European Union, particularly in countries with weak labor laws. Non-European firms have refused to consider IFAs, and most GUFs have been unwilling or unable for organizational reasons to fight for them in environments where they are most needed (such as those discussed by Darryn Snell in chapter 10).

Global Agreements and Global Unionism

The major factor making global agreements attractive to GUFs is the fact that they are negotiated between unions and corporations. Yet all IFAs are nonbinding, although some include provisions that make them less voluntary than others, and a few even reach toward the beginnings of formal global industrial relations, such as those with Danone, Chiquita, and Volkswagen. European extraterritorial agreements are stronger in regulatory terms, some approaching collective bargaining. In terms of regulatory provisions, GUFs have three key goals for IFAs. First, the agreement must cover all core labor standards (CLS), thus further legitimating them. In this they have been quite successful, and there is a clear difference between them and corporate codes of conduct in terms of covering freedom of association and the right to organize (OECD 2000, 13; ILO 2003; Wick 2005). Second, the agreement must not be limited to the permanent workers of the company but should cover all workers who have any employment relationship with the company, including suppliers. If only "official employees" are covered, only a small portion of Coca-Cola or IBM workers would be subject to an IFA. While global agreements are successful in covering a company's formal employees, they are much less so with suppliers (IFBWW 2004; IMF 2006; USW 2006). Third, the IFA must institutionalize the relationship in the sense that there are permanent arrangements for interactions, monitoring, and implementation. Here there is a great deal of variation, ranging from high institutionalization to ad hoc arrangements. We comment extensively on institutionalization below.

One of the early, often incorrect, criticisms of cross-border campaigns was that they were primarily initiatives by U.S. unions seeking to protect their own interests. As this book has shown, they are now a global phenomenon, originating in unions in the Global South as well as the Global North and involving extensive mutual support by unions and NGOs from the Global North for cross-border campaigns originating in the Global South. However, the same kinds of criticisms formerly raised about U.S. comprehensive campaigns are now being lodged against European-based global agreements. In what follows we examine whether global agreements facilitate global union collaboration. We do so at three levels. First, do GUFs or other global entities play a central role in the negotiation, signing, and implementation of these agreements? Second, do these agreements allow for the meaningful participation of unions beyond the original participants, which are often from the country of origin? If not, do they provide for the eventual inclusion and meaningful participation of host-country unions from across the corporation's deployment? Third, is there any evidence that unions other than the original participants have become involved in the pursuit of new agreements or the implementation of existing ones? While we base our accounts on the signatories, we modify them, as relevant, to reflect patterns in the negotiation and implementation of agreements. Focusing only on signatories can very well obscure who the major players are. It is only by looking at union participation in all three stages that we can get an accurate picture. Even then, the formal provisions of the agreements cannot tell us exactly what happens on the ground.

It is our view that global unionism is best served by organizations and other arrangements that are long-term and inclusive. While we recognize that important criticisms have been launched against GUFs now and in the past, initiatives that strengthen GUFs are necessary lest individual campaigns, global agreements, and autonomous workers' organizations end up fragmenting global union politics. We also recognize that giving more responsibilities to GUFs without giving them more resources and authority is a sure path to failure.

As we have noted, GUFs played a central role in the conception and pursuit of the global agreement strategy. This is evident by the fact that they are signatories of all IFAs, often against stiff resistance from corporations. Yet there are important variations in their roles, reflecting the influence of various national unions. The IMF has signed the largest number of IFAs (fifteen, ten of which are in Germany). It is the only one among the federations that have signed multiple agreements that has not been the sole signatory of any of them, choosing to cosign with European works councils (EWCs; nine) and world works councils (WWCs; three),[3] or national unions; this is not surprising given the dominance of the auto and metals sector and auto-industry unions (all affiliates of the IMF) in the EU, particularly in Germany. The more recent agreements with Renault, EADS, Peugeot-Citroën, and Arcelor are encouraging in broadening the national origin of the federation's agreements as well as in terms of the role of the IMF itself.

The BWI follows with twelve agreements, mostly with German, Swedish, and Dutch companies. Its agreements vary more than those of any other GUF. In some cases it is the only union representative, in others it has collaborated with national unions, and in still others it has acted along with workers' organizations. On balance, a number of the global agreements that the BWI has signed very much enhance its organizational standing. Equally significant is the fact that the BWI has signed the first global agreement that applies within the United States.

The International Federation of Chemical, Energy, Mine and General Workers' Unions (ICEM) follows with eleven agreements (one cosigned with BWI). It usually signs agreements with national unions (eight) and has the broadest distribution in terms of the nationality of companies.[4] While it plays a leading role in a number of agreements—and seeks that role—the major challenge facing the ICEM is how to translate what may seem to be nationally inspired agreements into long-term, global agreements.

The Union Network International (UNI) follows with ten from various European countries as well as one from South Africa, tending to sign with national unions. Most of UNI's earlier agreements were very short and informal, but more recent ones have become more detailed in both their goals and the federation's role.

All four of these federations continue to place strong emphasis on negotiating additional IFAs. The historical leader, the IUF, has fallen behind, partly because of corporate resistance and partly because of its review of the strategy (IUF 2006). There is good reason to argue, however, that the IUF's agreements greatly enhance the autonomous standing of the organization and that its restructuring agreement with Danone may be as close to collective bargaining as agreements have gotten.

---

[3]   We are using the term "world works councils" (WWCs) broadly to cover organizations that use different names. Their commonality is that they set up an organization consisting of workers from across the whole corporation that is recognized by the corporation. WWCs are not union entities, but unions play a dominant role. We are not including here arrangements that have been set up by GUFs but are not recognized by corporations, as was the case with the WCCs of the 1960s and 1970s. For the sake of simplicity we will subsequently use "world councils" to refer to WWCs.

[4]   ICEM has signed agreements with two non-European companies (Anglogold and Lukoil), IUF with another two (Chiquita and Fonterra), UNI with Nampak and the National Australia Group, and BWI with Turner.

Among federations that have adopted the global agreement strategy, only the International Textile, Garment and Leather Workers' Federation has not signed any agreements. The remaining federations have so far not prioritized the strategy. However, Public Services International (PSI) has cosigned the Electricité de France (EDF) agreement, and an alliance led by the International Transport Workers' Federation has signed an extraterritorial agreement with the Czech Airlines. The latter is also the only GUF that has negotiated a global collective agreement (Lillie 2004). Education International (EI) and the International Federation of Journalists have not shown any interest. Both the PSI and the EI have focused on the prevention of privatization, as they represent sectors that are less globalized and privatized.

This brings us to participation through workers' organizations. World councils have played a dominant role in the Volkswagen and DaimlerChrysler agreements and a very important role in all stages of the Renault and Falck agreements. The SKF world council is the sole implementer of the agreement, while the Peugeot-Citroën agreement includes provisions that are likely to result in a world council.

Some analysts have argued that global unionism can be served well by permanent and well-financed organizations, such as world councils and EWCs (Steiert 2001; also see Müller, Platzer, and Rüb 2005). Their advantage is that they are permanent, recognized, and funded by the corporations. The amount of money necessary to bring workers from various countries together on a regular basis is beyond the resources of all GUFs as well as most national unions. While we also think that permanent and well-funded organizations are desirable, we share the concerns expressed by various critics. First, these organizations are based on a collaborative system of industrial relations and may co-opt as much as they empower workers (Greven and Russo 2003; Müller, Platzer, and Rüb 2005). Second, they are corporation-based and can very well segment the labor force. For that reason, we think that permanent world councils organizations in which GUFs play a central role are preferable to totally autonomous councils, or even councils that are coordinated by a major national union.

The concerns about world councils apply to EWCs as well. Moreover, the regionalism of European councils makes them even less appropriate unless they morph into a global arrangement. EWCs were involved in the early IUF agreements but did not sign an IFA until 2003. Since then they have signed ten of them. This pattern coincides with the activation of the IMF, which in most cases has cosigned agreements with world or European councils. EWCs have played a prominent role in negotiating the agreements they have signed and have an implementation role in a larger number. Often collaborating with them, the European Metalworkers' Federation (EMF) has also been involved in four agreements. While increasingly important players in IFAs, EWCs and

European industry federations, such as the EMF, are the primary labor participants in the extraterritorial agreements. EWCs have signed seven of the nine
and European industry federations five. What is worth noting is that when a
world council is in place, it is considered the more appropriate instrument by
the participating unions, such as DaimlerChrysler (European Foundation for
the Improvement of Living and Working Conditions 2003). Moreover, some
agreements, such as those with Falck, EDF, Arcelor, and Peugeot-Citroën, envision the transcendence of EWCs by world councils. This move from regional
to global worker organizations is a positive development, in our view.

Finally, in most cases national unions play the central role in the negotiation and implementation of agreements and have signed twenty-five of the
IFAs. It is not surprising that the national unions most involved would be from
the countries of origin of the transnational firms that have signed agreements.
What is worth noting, however, is that only in exceptional cases, such as those
of EDF and the National Australia Group, have national unions from host
countries directly cosigned agreements. With these comments in mind we
move on to the examination of the institutional arrangements of the agreements pertaining to unions.

In light of the preponderance of European companies and the leading role
of European unions, is there any evidence of participation or potential for participation for unions from other venues within the transnational company?
This is a particularly important issue because unions outside the country of
origin have often felt neglected or excluded (IMF 2006, 6–7). We can identify
three ways through which "outsiders" have formally participated or can formally participate in global agreements. The first consists of agreements where
GUFs play a dominant or important role. By virtue of the fact that they are
global, unions in other parts of the world can express their views through these
organizations. While this is an important, if variable, route to participation, we
think that agreements that have more explicit arrangements that broaden participation are desirable. There are ten agreements that allow participation by
unions from throughout the corporation's deployment, including Telefonica,
EDF, and Lukoil. Finally, in at least six cases—Volkswagen, DaimlerChrysler, SKF,
Falck, Renault, and Peugeot-Citroën—participation can take place through an
existing or envisioned world council.

As of March 6, 2007, Asian workers participated only through the EDF
"Consultation Committee" and through the SKF world council. There were no
Japanese or South Korean unions involved in the negotiation, signing, or imple-
mentation of global agreements. In light of the significance of Japanese trans-
national firms this is a major gap. The Japanese trade union federation REN-
GO (2006) suggests, however, that the federation is considering the possibility,
and sectoral unions have broached the possibility with Japanese corporations.
While some Japanese companies would accept a global agreement, they are not

willing to sign one if a GUF is also a signatory. As a result, the efforts at covering Nissan under the Renault agreement are very important. The only instances of formal British union participation are in the EDF agreement and National Australia Group agreements, but there is strong evidence that some important British unions, such as Amicus, are supportive of the strategy and of global union organizations' playing a more central role. Other than the Turner agreement, which involves five U.S. unions, including the Teamsters and the International Association of Machinists (IAM), the participation by U.S. unions is limited to the DaimlerChrysler and SKF world councils. Quite possibly, they could also end up participating through the arrangements envisioned in the Telefonica, Lukoil, and Arcelor agreements. Finally, Latin American unions already participate directly in the Chiquita, Telefonica, and EDF agreements and through the world councils of Volkswagen, DaimlerChrysler, and SKF. In the future they are likely to also participate through the institutional arrangements envisioned by the Peugeot-Citroën, Arcelor, and Endesa agreements. There is strong evidence that both Latin American and South African unions are exploring the potential of the strategy. For instance, South African unions have signed two global agreements; the IUF's Chiquita agreements have been signed by a regional labor organization (see chapter 5); South American unions of the Spanish companies Endesa and Telefonica have been active participants in the efforts to get results out of the agreements; and, finally, IMF affiliates are actively involved in these agreements, particular those of Volkswagen and DaimlerChrysler. Southern unions are concerned not only about the utility of these agreements but also that they be treated as the equals of northern unions. For these reasons, the November 2006 decision of a number of South and North American unions to establish a Global Workers Council in the Brazilian-owned steelmaker Gerdau, a major aim of which is to persuade the company to sign a framework agreement, is a positive development because southern unions played a leading role.

On balance, then, the majority of the agreements provide for some formal global participation through GUFs, and some agreements also do so through their world councils or other institutional arrangements. However, the formal participation of unions outside Europe or the few other countries represented on the list is rather limited. This is a challenge that GUFs and European unions have to face because the slow response of unions from various parts of the world may reflect not simply an inability to join but also an unwillingness to do so (Franz 2002; Anner et al. 2006). While the major problem is the limited role of U.S. unions and the absence of Japanese unions, it is essential to involve unions from the south, particularly those countries receiving the largest amount of investment, lest the agreements be seen as another northern initiative. This makes the third angle from which we look at union involvement all the more important. Is there any evidence that unions from countries that are formally underrepresented in IFAs are participating in efforts toward global agreements or in the implementation of those agreements?

A review of the web pages, observation, and background discussions show some signs that there has been an increased participation in IFAs by unions in countries where they had previously been underutilized, but there are some significant differences in how they are being used in those newer companies. As we noted, the British union Amicus is positively predisposed, as are other British unions (Amicus 2006). A number of U.S. unions, such as the United Steelworkers of America (USW) and the Services Employees International Union (SEIU), are supportive of the strategy in principle but only in the context of a comprehensive cross-border campaign (Hickey 2004; Quan 2006). The most prominent development in that direction is the Turner agreement signed in October 2006. According to a report by the International Federation of Building and Wood Workers (IFBWW) (now BWI), the Hochtief agreement had helped U.S. unions even before 2004 in their disputes with Turner, a Hochtief subsidiary. The 2006 agreement, in fact, is the result of long-term efforts between BWI and U.S. unions, five of which have signed it. The Communications Workers of America (CWA) is participating in the campaign and negotiations with Deutsche Telecom and are involved in efforts to unionize Telefonica workers in Puerto Rico. SEIU has been involved in the Securitas and Group 4 campaigns (SEIU 2005; Quan 2006), Securitas being one of the more recent signatories of an agreement. The IKEA agreement was used as leverage in the Graphic Communications International Union's (GCIU) campaign against Quebecor (on the Quebecor campaign see International Brotherhood of Teamsters 2006), because Quebecor had the contract to print IKEA's catalog in one of its U.S. plants. Ultimately the IKEA connection turned out to be a key component in GCIU's (now merged with the Teamsters) eventual victory at Quebecor. Finally, the Statoil agreement is considered one of the important factors contributing to the positive resolution of the Crown Petroleum lockout (Hickey 2004).

While we have not seen any evidence of collaborations between major Asian unions and unions from other parts of the world in actions relating to global agreements, we have noted that the Japanese RENGO has formally expressed its interest in global agreements (RENGO 2006), as have some South Korean unions. The Carrefour agreement was successfully used to help unionize South Korean workers as well as ensure that the buyer of the corporation's assets in South Korea was one that respected the union. The DaimlerChrysler agreement was successfully used to help workers in Ditas, one of its Turkish suppliers (Gibb 2005).

There is also evidence that additional Latin American unions have been involved in campaigns around the implementation of global agreements, particularly with respect to Telefonica and Chiquita (Riisgaard 2004; IMF 2006; Frundt chapter 5). We cannot conclude from this limited evidence that global agreements have managed to bridge the gaps that we have noted nor that they have been successful in solving disputes in the corporations covered, although there are some concrete examples of that (see IMF 2006; IFBWW 2004). We do think, however, there is some evidence that the strategy can become truly global and that, at the very least, it is far too early to abandon it.

From Campaigns to Agreements and Agreements to Campaigns

In line with our focus on the implications of global agreements on global unionism, we turn now to ways in which the campaign and agreements strategies can be fused into cohesive global strategies. We start with what we think is the major issue among unions who are otherwise interested in the global agreement strategy. In a recent white paper the USW (2006) expressed its support of global agreements, provided that they became stronger and more enforceable. The German union IG-Metall has also made it clear that "it is far better to have no international framework agreement at all than a weak one" (Rüb 2004, 8). Nonetheless, the evidence shows that continental European unions are more likely to be involved in global agreements while U.S. unions are more likely to use global campaigns (see Hickey 2004; Quan 2006; Juravich chapter 1). Underlying this pattern are differences in industrial relations and the uneven impacts of globalization on national unions.

European unions and global agreements have been justifiably criticized for being too constrained by the collaborative nature of industrial relations common, in particular, in the Netherlands, Germany, and Scandinavia (Greven and Russo 2003; Tørres and Gunnes 2003). Thus it is imperative that European unions recognize that the rest of the world is not accustomed to the same industrial relations and may not be able or willing to adopt them. This, however, does not automatically make all militant tactics and strategies more politically radical. Rather, it is very possible that politically conservative unions are forced to adopt militant tactics because they are faced with recalcitrant companies, while more politically progressive unions may use global agreements as just one element of an aggressive multifaceted global campaign.

At the same time, many unions in North America and the Global South, as well as European unions and various GUFs, are critical of existing global agreements because they have not adequately addressed workers and unions in the Global South and in doing so have discounted the majority of the workers employed by the transnational firms signatory to the agreements. Unless these criticisms are addressed where valid, global agreements will become irrelevant. Moreover, national unions as well as leaders of GUFs, such as the secretary-general of the IUF (Oswald 2006) have been critical of global agreements because they believe that, when not connected to broader comprehensive cross-border campaigns and stronger regulatory demands, they lean more toward CSR than toward empowering workers and strengthening global unionism.

Finding common ground requires long-term relations and collaboration. The 2005 "Labor's Platform for the Americas," agreed upon by national and regional organizations (with ICFTU and GUF participation) from the whole hemisphere, is encouraging in that respect. This is a document negotiated over time by unions accustomed to different types of industrial relations that have espoused various ideologies and, in some cases, had serious disagreements in the recent past. As a result, it could be a good model, at least in terms of its negotiation, for more vital transatlantic and global dialogues.

European unions must recognize that the trajectories of their industrial relations systems are different from those in other parts of the world. In the case of Germany, for instance, post–World War II industrial relations were the product of a cooptative strategy by the Christian Democrats, something that the reforms of the 1970s were not able to totally undo. Not only can increasingly globalizing corporations abandon their system outside Germany, but liberal reforms can also undo it within Germany (Landler 2006). To reject the need and utility of more militant tactics is to make it easier for German (or Japanese or other transnational firms) to cut the umbilical cord. On the other hand, most of the comprehensive organizing and bargaining campaigns conducted by U.S. unions engaged with the world's largest transnational corporations during the last few decades have not been long-term and global enough, or even comprehensive enough, to take on the kinds of challenges presented by these most complex, powerful, and global corporations (Banks and Russo 1999). Experience has shown that the confidence and resources necessary to carry on global campaigns take a long time to create and even longer to re-create. All unions have to decide on what kinds of permanent ties they are willing to nurture and what their goals will be. In general, however, we think that connecting campaigns to a global goal, such as global agreements, is preferable to campaigns whose goal is to enhance unionization in one or two countries, only to be disbanded once the goal is accomplished or the campaign fails. On the other hand, agreements that reject the option of campaigns are locked into a very precarious and self-limiting insider strategy.

With this context in mind we turn to specific ways in which campaigns and agreements can be fused into common strategies, taking things chronologically. Comprehensive campaigns have not so far been used to get a company to sign a global agreement. In fact some companies that have been the target of strong global campaigns still refuse to sign a global agreement or engage unions in dialogue of any kind. Yet, one can envision future instances when campaigns aiming at an agreement can be successful, particularly if unions can get companies that have already signed agreements to exert pressure on customers, investors, suppliers, or other stakeholders (on efforts that produced the Chiquita agreement see Frundt chapter 5 and Riisgaard 2004, 2005). The Turner agreement that we mentioned above is such an example. Success by the IMF in getting Mahle, "a German auto supplier to both DaimlerChrysler and Volkswagen," to sign the agreement that has been negotiated would also be a good sign (IMF 2006, 13; see also Wad chapter 2).

There is a very good chance that weak global agreements will prove to be nothing but a public relations triumph for transnational corporations. While superior to codes of conduct, global agreements could become the rationale that corporations will use to avoid more consequential arrangements in the same way that General Motors uses the Sullivan Principles developed to help deal with apartheid to avoid signing an agreement. We think that all GUFs are aware of the problem, as is evident by the BWI, IUF, and IMF reviews of the strategy.

It is here, we think, that appropriate global campaigns aimed at the signing of more profound agreements and the deepening of existing ones in the direction of the IUF's idea of "global recognition agreements" can be of great use. It is possible that nothing of consequence will result and those companies previously willing to sign agreements will reconsider their strategy. We think that discovering the limitations of the global agreement strategy sooner rather than later may be a good thing.

Campaigns may well serve to get companies to negotiate new agreements in the future as well as improve existing ones. At this juncture, however, they may be more useful in implementing agreements. In many ways, in fact, the forceful implementation of global agreements will prove how serious a company is about them (on implementation see Rüb 2006). Additionally, it can lead to improvements and patterns that deepen the agreement. Finally, implementation campaigns can help build stronger ties among unions across the company's deployment by focusing all unions around the specific challenges of an existing agreement. As we have noted, it was just this kind of implementation campaign which helped unionization of the Turkish supplier of DaimlerChrysler.

In any event, as unions have learned from major organizing and bargaining campaigns in the logistics, rubber, telecommunications, petrochemical, rubber, and apparel industries (Banks and Russo 1999; Cohen and Early 2000; Hickey 2004, Meyer 2001; Juravich and Bronfenbrenner 2003; Robertson and Plaiyoowong 2004), taking on the world's most powerful antiunion companies, whether in the United States, the United Kingdom, or Thailand depends on running a comprehensive multifaceted cross-border campaign involving diverse union and community stakeholders from around the globe and engaging the company in its key relationships on multiple levels. Forcing "good" companies to put pressure on "bad" companies or otherwise "reward" them is a strategy that has been used and should be considered. We have also seen an increasing number of campaigns where unions have joined together across borders and industries to launch long-term campaigns to organize entire industries. One such effort has been the work that PSI has done to work with unions and NGOs in the energy sector from around the world to help fight the privatization of water and energy (PSI 2006). Another is the work USW has done with the ICEM to pull together petrochemical and rubber industry unions from around the world to take on such global giants as Exxon Mobil, Bridgestone/Firestone, and Continental Tire through a combination of mutual support, comprehensive cross-border campaigns, and the establishment of lasting global organizational structures that meet regularly to build worker-to-worker exchanges, plan global solidarity actions, share strategic corporate research, and develop future strategic initiatives (USW 2006). Similarly, the IUF's ongoing global organizing campaign at Nestlé and Coca-Cola, involving numerous affiliate unions in Asia, eastern Europe, and Latin America, which so far has organized thousands of workers at both companies, demonstrates that these global initiatives are not limited to the bargaining arena (Garver et al. 2006).

Despite the importance of these initiatives, and without underestimating the difficulties of bringing any corporation to the table, we believe that getting a company such as Coca-Cola, Nestlé, or Exxon Mobil to sign a strong agreement would be a major success. We think that the chances of that occurring will be greater in the context of truly global campaigns such as those described above, which are GUF-wide, as distinguished from global campaigns limited to national unions, as so many campaigns have been to date. The ongoing involvement of GUFs in various campaigns is encouraging, but their role will remain auxiliary unless national unions are willing to provide them with the resources and authority that will allow them to be more like unions. A combination of campaigns that pool the resources of national unions and agreements that allow GUFs to play a central role would be important and reinforcing steps towards stronger global unionism.

National and global union organizations have to address pressing corporate behavior on a daily basis. To the degree that global campaigns and agreements are longer-term strategies, however, we would like to argue that corporations with strong ties to Europe are a good set of corporations to target, using national and EU-level industrial relations as platforms and sites of contestation. There are two possibilities here. One route to the globalization of this regional phenomenon would be through European transnational corporations abroad. Accordingly, there may be value to targeting European transnationals that have not signed agreements, have signed weak agreements, or are not implementing the agreements properly. If the agreement were used to unionize subsidiaries and plants of European companies where they are now not unionized, the impact would be momentous, both substantively and symbolically. It is for this reason that the Turner agreement is an important development. If the unions involved in the Renault agreement were able to bring in the Nissan unions, another major gap in participation would start closing (Markey 2005). In short, European transnational firms should be targeted not only to improve their own performance but also to deliver collateral benefits by exerting pressure on subsidiaries, suppliers, and collaborators.

The second route would be through non-European transnational corporations operating in Europe. It is noteworthy that important U.S. companies, such as Ford, GM, and GE, have been parties to agreements with EWCs and European industry federations that some consider close to collective bargaining (*European Works Councils Bulletin* 2005b). The European Metalworkers' Federation, for instance, clearly advances this strategy, while the European Company Statute may make it easier for European-level organizations to talk to corporations directly (on General Motors in Europe see chapter 7). How can this dynamic be made part of a larger global union strategy? We think that articulating global corporate campaigns around foreign companies that have signed strong agreements in Europe would be a positive development.

The direct efforts of unions should be complemented by collective efforts at improving EU-level public policies while preventing the erosion of superior national policies (Stevis 2002; Turnbull chapter 6). At this moment, for instance, there are ongoing EU-level debates over the improvement of the EWCs directive, the implications of the European Company Statute for unions, and global agreements (EESC 2006; Beirnaert 2006; Kluge and Stolit 2006; European Commission 2006). While the European Trade Union Confederation, European industry federations, and national unions may have more at stake in these changes, the impacts of these developments are felt well beyond Europe. Because Europe, like other important regions of the world political economy, is a site of global contestation, European unions should be welcoming and encouraging collaboration with global and non-European unions.

That such a route has a realistic chance for success, provided that some key companies and unions outside Europe get involved, is made evident by developments with respect to the Kyoto Protocol on Climate Change and the International Criminal Court (ICC). In both cases the United States, China, and a few other countries have refused to participate. Yet, the ICC is now in operation, while U.S. transnational firms, as well as subfederal units, are adjusting their policies to be congruent with the provisions of the Kyoto Protocol. It therefore seems likely that a strategic alliance of unions from various parts of the world could move things forward even if not all parts of the world were represented. Moreover, corporations may well decide that it is easier to adjust to the higher standard rather than have two standards worldwide. For such a scenario to work, of course, unions need to engage in a great deal of collaboration.

This is particularly pressing because a very real danger of strategies that focus on individual companies (or individual countries or regions) rather than taking a broader view is the fragmentation of unions along corporate or geographic lines. In the case of agreements, for instance, workers may end up caring more about the competitiveness of their company and less about union power. In the case of campaigns, unions may be concerned about their own problems at the expense of union problems in other parts of the world. In the case of geography, unions may remain attached to national and regional industrial relations at the same time that "their" transnationals are escaping from them. The historical trajectories of national industrial relations, despite their differences, are similar in their move from localized unions to national sectoral unions to industrial unions and union federations, all in an effort to bridge the particularism of workplace and sectoral unionism. It is for this reason that GUFs need to be strengthened and that agreements or campaigns that marginalize them will breed more particularism. Even global workers' organizations, such as world councils, that marginalize GUFs are problematic. Of course, a real commitment to stronger global unionism cannot be limited to having GUFs negotiate, sign, and even implement agreements. Without additional authority and resources granted to them by their affiliates, these global organizations will not be able to rise to the challenge. This, in short, is not simply an issue of GUFs' being cautious. Rather, the problem is national unions that do not break away from foreign policy and move in the direction of more profound global commitments.

While the involvement of GUFs and the adoption of integrated comprehensive campaigns and global agreement strategies can help prevent segmentation, it is only through the negotiation of global enabling public policies that labor will be able to unionize across countries and sectors in the same way that, under national rules, labor was allowed to unionize beyond localities and specific workplaces. Even though the current global situation is not encouraging, giving up the fight for public rules is, in our view, a bad strategy. We are hopeful that the enhanced relations between GUFs and the new international reflected in the formation of the Council of Global Unions in January 2007 will lead to a better articulation of private and public strategies. The continued coordination of national, regional, and global strategies remains central in order to take advantage of another opening like that which occurred in the late 1990s. The ICFTU did a good job of making the "social clause" a common demand in the 1990s, and while a number of criticisms can be raised with respect to the strategy and the tactics of the ICFTU, getting most unions in the world on the same page is an accomplishment comparable to that of any other period in global union politics (see Fairbrother and Hammer 2005).

Global agreements leave much to be desired, yet after decades they are still the only global instrument negotiated directly between unions and corporations.

That in itself is a positive step and something to build on. Their provisions vary, but some of them cannot be easily withdrawn—for example, recognition of world councils by corporations, agreements with European councils, and payment of costs. Finally, and particularly important, global agreements have allowed GUFs to play a more active role in global labor politics.

In addition to not being binding, global agreements are also geographically biased; they are mostly with European transnational companies and involve mostly European unions, though this is beginning to change. While unions may not be able to force unwilling corporations to the table, they can and must create arrangements that involve non-European unions more fully. If they do not do that more extensively, their efforts will be seen as an attempt by European unions to simply manage corporations in their own countries.

As a result, the role of the GUFs is an important element in ensuring that corporation-based arrangements do not work at cross-purposes. The creation of corporation-based institutions is necessary in order to enhance collaboration among unions within the same corporation, unions that are often turned against one another by corporate policies. There is evidence of a move toward such institutions. Whatever they may be, we do not think that they ought to be mere extensions of the unions from the country of origin, although these are likely to play a leading role. A significant contribution by GUFs, as well as broader national union participation in such institutions, will help ensure that they are not considered instruments of national unions.

We are not suggesting that transferring more resources and authority is the only issue that national unions and workers have to deal with. Building inclusive global union organizations that know when to fight and when to negotiate will remain an important and contested challenge. Unless some resources and authority are transferred, however, these necessary debates will never take place.

The most central debate, in our view, is about the significance of public rules that regulate capital and empower workers. We think that the greatest success of capital has been its ability to create a private space within which it can operate without democratic supervision. Anyone who chooses to contest capital by conceding the autonomy of that space has already conceded the war and may die in battle. Some unions have done very well within these parameters, as have various professional associations and unions of highly skilled workers; a global unionism that wants to globalize justice and solidarity cannot adopt such a narrow vision.

10. BEYOND WORKERS' RIGHTS

Transnational Corporations, Human Rights Abuse, and Violent Conflict in the Global South

DARRYN SNELL

The dramatic increase in foreign direct investment and the activities of transnational corporations in developing countries in the Global South have contributed to mounting concerns, locally and internationally, about the detrimental effects they are having on the societies and environments in which they operate (UNHCR 2005). The behavior of these immensely powerful and wealthy entities in nations in the Global South has not always been virtuous, nor has it always brought the sort of social and economic stability that many countries had hoped. Recent international media attention on a number of high-profile court cases implicating the likes of Exxon Mobil, Freeport-McMoran, Coca-Cola, Talisman, and other transnational corporations for their involvement in a range of human rights violations—including summary executions, torture, rape, forced relocation of indigenous peoples, and the use of forced labor—has increased public awareness about corporate irresponsibility and corporations' contributions to violence and instability in the Global South.

While the emergence of these concerns on the international scene is relatively recent, human rights NGOs, humanitarian organizations, and peace and conflict resolution practitioners have been struggling to address these problems for some time. At times unions have also sought to address these concerns either through their own initiatives or following requests for assistance from affected workers and communities or NGOs campaigning on behalf of those affected. Although many trade unions and trade union federations across the north and south have a desire to and recognize the critical need to become more involved in broader human rights struggles surrounding the activities of transnational corporations, unions are often not well prepared to respond to these requests and are typically unsure of how they can best lend assistance to resolve these ongoing and exceedingly serious problems. This chapter therefore considers two questions: What capacities do unions have at their disposal to hold transnational corporations more accountable for human rights violations and social and political instability in the Global South? How can the union movement use these capacities more effectively in cross-border and global union campaigns?

Transnational Corporations' Contributions to Violence

Developing effective responses requires some level of understanding about the nature of the problem. Over the past few years a number of initiatives have been undertaken by the United Nations, international financial agencies, governments, international nongovernmental organizations (INGOs), human rights groups, and peace and conflict resolution experts to better understand the relationship between the activities of transnational corporations and the perpetuation of human rights abuses and violent conflict in the Global South (Mary Anderson 2003; Banfield, Haufler, and Lilly 2003; International Alert 2004; Stewart and Venugopal 2005; Taylor 2003). Two interrelated but distinct concerns have emerged out of these initiatives. The first regards transnational corporations' relationship to violence and human rights abuses that take place in the vicinity of their operations, how they may have contributed to these local abuses, and what they have done to prevent them (Clapham and Jerbi 2001). The second concern is focused on more wide-ranging questions about the involvement of transnational corporations in conflict-prone countries or conflict zones and how their presence and behavior shape the broader conflict dynamics (Banfield, Haufler, and Lilly 2003). Across both of these areas of concern, three categories—direct, indirect, and inactive—are typically used to delineate the manner in which transnational corporations have contributed to violence in the Global South.

Direct Contributions

Transnational corporations are seldom considered at the forefront of violence and human rights abuses in the Global South. Governments, militaries, or armed rebel groups are typically held responsible for these abuses. Workers' rights violations and to a lesser extent environmental violations are the usual abuses associated with corporations. Direct contributions by transnational corporations to violence and human rights abuses are not unheard of, however, and can involve any number of activities ranging from the use of forced labor to a security force violently abusing and forcibly removing people from lands claimed by the corporation but where ownership rights are unclear and contested. Companies have also been accused of directly contributing to violence when they have chosen to engage in acts despite having the reasonable foresight to know their activities will intensify civil strife. In August 2005, for example, Anvil Mining, an Australian-based mining company, was accused of helping troops crush a rebel uprising in the Democratic Republic of the Congo in which more than one hundred villagers were killed. It was alleged that the company let troops use some of its vehicles in the assault despite knowing that the troops had been conducting brutal security operations in the area for days ahead of the massacre (ABC 2005b; Teh-White 2005). Similarly, Exxon Mobil has been accused of employing brutal Indonesian military troops in Ache to protect its operations despite knowing that these troops had regularly committed abuses against local villagers, including murder, rape, torture, and destruction of property (ILRF 2005).

Charges of direct complicity to violence have also occurred when transnational corporations have joined in a joint venture with a government despite having reasonable insight that the government would likely commit abuses in carrying out its part of the agreement. In Nigeria, Royal Dutch Shell, Exxon Mobil, Texaco, Chevron, Elf, and Agip have all been accused at different times of colluding with the Nigerian government and perpetuating violent acts against Niger Delta villagers who had complained about the oil industry's environmental pollution and failure to improve their impoverished situation (Adebanwi 2001).

Corporations may also directly contribute to violence through their use of racialized hiring and promotion processes. A corporation's divisive use of ethnic group rivalries to undermine union organizing or break strikes, for example, is known to exacerbate ethnic tensions in highly racialized environments to such an extent that widespread violence ensues.

At the macro level, transnational corporations may directly contribute to political and social instability within a nation by providing financial and logistical support to groups seeking to undermine or topple ruling governments. Although the charges are typically difficult to substantiate, corporations have long been suspected of supporting the actions of unscrupulous politicians and self-interested armed groups who seek to undermine governments or take control of the state machinery through political destabilization tactics or coups d'état. A corporation's support typically comes about through a mutual dislike for a ruling government that is seen as problematic or threatening to their corporate interests (Prasad and Snell 2004; Webersik 2005).

Indirect Contributions

Indirect contributions to violence are best described as any number of activities undertaken by a company that unintentionally cause harm. In some cases the problem stems from the development of poor relationships between the company and local communities. When local communities cannot see the local benefits of a corporation's activities in improving either their immediate lives or the surroundings in which they live, and the corporation fails to respond to community concerns and demands, tensions between those communities and the corporation can become strained. In conflict or postconflict settings, the failure of a corporation to respond to community interests only contributes to an already volatile climate of anger, frustration, disempowerment, and disillusionment with institutional means of resolving differences. If the communities have no institutions they can access to seek fair and equitable redress and a company simply continues to disregard their concerns, these situations can erupt into violent confrontations (Oxfam Community Aid Abroad 2004). In some cases, the corporation's facilities become the target of community anger. The taking over of the Australian-owned copper mine in Bougainville, Papua New Guinea, by local landowners in the 1980s and the sabotage of oil pipelines by angry villagers in Nigeria are some examples. In Colombia, the failure of corporations to engage constructively with local communities has contributed to a number of cases involving the kidnapping, torture, and murder of corporate executives and managers by armed groups (Zandvliet, Zornosa, and Reyes 2004).

Much of the discussion about corporations' indirect contributions to violence, however, has focused upon cases where companies have established their operations in the midst of preexisting conflicts. In these situations, corporations become inextricably part of the conflict setting and "inadvertently become embroiled in the intergroup struggles that underlie and propel the conflict" (Anderson and Zandvliet 2001, 1). By operating in a country where the government is perpetrating gross human rights abuses, some argue, corporations aid and abet these abuses through their provision of financial and other material support to the government. Revenues generated from corporate activities enable governments, militaries, and others to purchase weapons and ammunition needed to pursue their ambitions (OECD 2002). In the late 1990s, "blood diamonds" and "conflict diamonds" became popular phrases used to describe diamonds from war-torn areas that were used to fund military activity by their traders (Lwanda 2003). The involvement of corporations in the purchasing and selling of these diamonds was identified by advocacy groups and human rights NGOs as a major part of the problem.

Inaction

The failure of a company to act while witnessing human rights violations is another way that international corporations have been seen as contributing to violence. This position is based on the moral argument that he who is present at a wrongdoing and does not lift a hand to prevent it is as guilty as the wrong-doers. Transnational corporations have been criticized on a number of oc-casions for failing to intervene to prevent or to report cases of violence and human rights abuses that have occurred in or near their operations. Serving as silent witnesses while doing nothing to help bring the perpetrators of vio-lence to justice contributes to an environment in which the perpetrators feel they can escape persecution for their crimes and enables the warring parties to continue fighting.

Inactive contributions to violence and human rights abuses rarely receive a legal hearing. Companies typically maintain that they are not obligated to intervene or to report these incidents and that to do so would be seen by war-ring parties as taking sides in a conflict and would draw unnecessary attention to their operations and potentially put their employees and assets at risk. The corporate responsibility movement, nonetheless, has pursued cases of inac-tion by corporations through various advocacy campaigns.

Response Strategies and Trade Union Capacities

As the previous discussion indicates, a corporation's contribution to violence is often difficult to assess and may occur in a variety of ways and at a range of levels. Addressing specific cases of corporate complicity in human rights viola-tions and violent conflict in the Global South has required advocacy groups to ask two interrelated questions: What is the nature of the relationship between corporations and violent conflict and/or human rights abuses taking place in a particular setting? What are the most appropriate and effective ways to allevi-ate these problems in this given context? Answering these sorts of questions has required advocacy organizations to conduct strategic research on the con-flict situations and on the corporations themselves.

In recent years, a handful of INGOs have taken the initiative to investi-gate cases where corporations have been implicated in human rights abuses or violent conflict. Typically these investigations occur after some major in-cident or ongoing complaints about a corporation's activities. Although the methods adopted to carry out these investigations vary, they consistently in-volve some form of on-site investigation of the locality in which the incident took place. The cases investigated by these organizations generally reflect the organization's interests or the interests of the individuals or groups whom they claim to represent. Survival International, for example, investigates cases where corporations have been implicated in abuses against indigenous peoples (Survival International 2005). Global Witness, an organization con-cerned with human rights abuses in the natural resource sector, investigates the activities of international mining companies. With the exception of cases involving some form of workers' rights abuses, where trade unions have sporadically conducted their own inquiries or fact-finding missions, trade unions have generally come to rely upon INGOs for information and analysis about other forms of corporate abuses in the Global South. The area in which trade unions have proved to be far superior to INGOs is in the area of strategic corporate research. Trade unions tend to have greater access to information about company activities (for example, locations of company operations, workforce characteristics, profit centers, supply chains, and sources of revenue); the companies' private owners, investors, or shareholders; and their relationships with international institutions and national governments (see chapter 1). This information helps in identifying leverage points and company vulnerabilities and who the likely allies and enemies will be in a given campaign. Through the combination of both types of research, trade unions, humanitarian NGOs, and other civil society organizations have developed a number of intervention and response strategies. The following discussion highlights the diversity of these response strategies and identifies some of the capacities trade unions have drawn upon. The discussion is organized around types of responses. The first involves cases where a corporation has been identified as contributing to violence or human rights abuses and there is a desire on the part of the victims and trade unions and NGOs advocating on their behalf to seek some form of justice for the victims and/or immediate rectification of the problem. The second category of responses focuses on prevention.

Holding Corporations Accountable

In situations where workers and communities have been on the receiving end of violence, the options for these victims to receive some level of recourse or reparation are often limited. Government and police authorities often deny the situation took place, and the legal avenues open to the affected parties to seek redress in their national courts are often inadequate because of weaknesses in judicial institutions and judicial laws covering these matters or the financial burdens associated with legal challenges. In countries where individuals have the ability to openly protest, local unions, NGOs, and religious and humanitarian groups have sought to draw attention to the situation through various forms of direct action such as organized boycotts, rallies, strikes, and public vigils for the victims. In situations where such public displays are illegal or viewed with contempt by authorities, affected workers and communities have often appealed to and solicited the support of northern unions, INGOs, foreign governments, and various international organizations, such as the United Nations or the Organization for Economic Co-operation and Development (OECD), for assistance.

PROSECUTION

Prosecuting corporations for human rights abuses in the Global South has proven extremely challenging. The victims are unlikely to get a fair trial in their home countries, and international human rights law is very weak in binding companies to any legal obligations. Confronted with this situation, northern trade unions and INGOs have turned to national laws in their own countries to bring legal cases against corporations. The International Peace Academy and Fafo Institute for Applied International Studies, a think tank funded and founded by the Norwegian Confederation of Trade Unions, has played a leading role in working to identify existing national laws in northern countries that could be used to take corporations to court for negligent activities in the Global South (Taylor 2003).

Trade unions and advocacy groups across Europe, the United Kingdom, North America, and Australia are just beginning to explore how local legislation can be used to prosecute northern-based corporations for their criminal activities abroad. In Australia, for example, Transparency International is considering using a little-used federal law making bribery of foreign officials a criminal offense to bring about a legal case against Australian Wheat Board managers who were identified by the UN as paying kickbacks to Saddam Hussein's former regime during the UN's sponsored Oil-for-Food Program (Bolt 2005). Money contributed by the Australian Wheat Board and other companies through bribery and corruption during this period is said to have helped the Hussein government to remain in power and continue its brutal campaigns of torture, murder, and intimidation on the Iraqi population.

In the United States, several companies have been sued in U.S. courts under the Alien Tort Claims Act (ATCA) for their alleged involvement in human rights abuses abroad. ATCA allows noncitizens to file civil action cases in U.S. courts for violations of international law that occurred outside U.S. borders. In 1996, in one of the first ATCA cases to come before the U.S. courts, Burmese villagers sued Unocal in federal court in California for human rights violations arising out of the company's involvement in a gas pipeline project in Burma. The plaintiffs in the Unocal case were Burmese villagers who claimed that they had been subjected to forced labor, murder, rape, and torture during the construction of the gas pipeline through their country (Eviatar 2005). In November 2001, Talisman, Canada's largest energy company, was sued in federal court in New York City for alleged human rights violations in Sudan (Dow Jones Newswires 2005). The plaintiffs were Sudanese villagers who alleged that Talisman, which was engaged in Sudan's oil industry, had aided the Sudan government's ethnic cleansing campaign against black and non-Muslim minorities by supplying financial and logistical support to the government (Bennett 2002). In August 2005, Nigerians represented by the human rights group Earth Rights International filed legal challenges against Chevron that accused the company of being complicit in military attacks on their villages in the oil-rich Niger Delta (ILRF 2005).

Trade unions have also sought to use ATCA to bring cases against transnational corporations for workers' rights abuses in the Global South. The Washington, D.C.–based International Labor Rights Fund (ILRF), established in the 1980s by a coalition of trade unionists, human rights activists, academics, and religious leaders, has been at the forefront of many ATCA cases. The ILRF has worked in close collaboration with affected communities, trade unions, and other human rights NGOs in the Global South who have found it difficult to obtain justice for victims in their national settings. One of the most high-profile cases has involved SINALTRAINAL, Colombia's largest Coca-Cola union, represented by the United Steelworkers of America and other lawyers, who filed a lawsuit accusing Coca-Cola management of using paramilitaries to crush Coca-Cola unions. The union claims that at least eight of its leaders have been murdered and workers have been arbitrarily detained, tortured, and sacked for their involvement with the union (SINALTRAINAL 2005).

Convincing northern courts to consider legal cases against corporations for abuses they may have committed in the Global South is not proving easy. The legislation governing the conduct of corporations abroad is typically weak in northern countries; the courts are normally prepared to consider only those cases in which direct evidence of corporate complicity in violent acts can be demonstrated, and the financial and legal resources of corporations to fight these cases far outstrip what unions and INGOs have available to them. To date no one has won an ATCA case in the United States, and few cases have been won elsewhere. This does not mean they have been entirely unsuccessful. In a few cases corporations have agreed to out-of-court settlements that have compensated victims for their losses. Additionally, these high-profile court cases have worked to draw media attention to these problems and create enormous financial and public relations costs for corporations. How this translates into rectifying the problems and contributing to greater corporate responsibility in the Global South remains open to question.

SHAREHOLDER CAMPAIGNS

In recent years, shareholder campaigns have proven to be an important means for unions to get publicly traded companies to take notice of their concerns. As more trade union members have become shareholders through investment and pension schemes, unions have started to exercise their muscle as shareholders by introducing resolutions at corporate annual meetings. These resolutions have focused on concerns ranging from traditional workers' rights matters to proposed company layoffs to CEO executive packages. The May 2000 shareholder campaign directed against Rio Tinto, the world's largest mining company, represents one of the most important of these campaigns. This campaign was not only one of the first international shareholder campaigns but one of the first major attempts by unions to use shareholder campaigns to raise concerns about corporate violations of human rights. The campaign, spearheaded by the United Kingdom's Trade Union Congress (TUC) and the ICEM, involved the American Federation of Labor and Congress of Industrial Organizations (AFL-CIO), the Australian Council of Trade Unions (ACTU), and the Australian Construction, Forestry, Mining and Energy Union (CFMEU). These unions and trade union bodies worked to build a network that included representatives from trade unions in Indonesia, Namibia, South Africa, and Europe and involved human rights groups, environmental organizations, and indigenous peoples (Workers Online 2000). Through this network the unions involved were able to compile invaluable information about the company's operations, profit sources, assets, working conditions, and union coverage in its operations worldwide, as well as information about its ties to violence and human rights abuses and its environmental record. The ICEM launched a website focused on Rio Tinto's "tainted history" that made much of this information publicly available. This information enabled unions to respond strategically and build not only international trade union solidarity but solidarity with INGOs and affected communities in the Global South. In Australia, trade unions helped bring representatives of the affected communities of Rio Tinto's Indonesian Kelian Gold Mine to Brisbane, providing them the opportunity to ask company executives at their annual general meeting (AGM) about the company's involvement in local environmental destruction and violent attacks on their community by the local police force (Mineral Policy Institute 2000). Striking miners, trade union officials, environmentalists, and concerned shareholders and political leaders were provided similar opportunities to ask questions during the company's AGMs in London and Perth. This barrage of questioning set the stage for the submission of two resolutions at the London, Brisbane, and Perth general meetings. The first resolution aimed to influence corporate governance by calling upon the appointment of an independent deputy chairman. The second resolution called for the company to uphold international human rights obligations and implement a code of labor standards consistent with International Labor Organization (ILO) and UN conventions.

Considerable international media attention was generated by the campaign, and although the resolutions were ultimately defeated, around 20 percent of shareholders' votes supported them (ABC 2005a). Additionally, political figures in both the United Kingdom and Australia began to ask highly critical questions about the company's overseas operations. Soon after the meetings, Rio Tinto agreed to recognize and negotiate with trade unions and hold discussions with human rights groups (Workers Online 2000). While concerns continue to be raised about Rio Tinto's contributions to violence and human rights violations, particularly with regard to the company's Indonesian operations (Asia-Pacific Human Rights Network 2001; Global Witness 2005), the 2000 shareholder campaign demonstrated to many trade unions and human rights groups that worker-shareholder activism, when run effectively and as part of a global campaign, can make important contributions toward improving company practices and providing a voice to affected communities and victims in the Global South.

BOYCOTTS AND DIVESTMENT CAMPAIGNS

Boycotts and divestment campaigns have been a long-standing strategy used by INGOs and the trade union movement to get corporations to take direct or indirect responsibility for violence occurring in the Global South. Those on the list of current corporate targets include Caterpillar for selling bulldozers to Israel despite knowing they will be used to destroy Palestinian homes and infrastructure in the Occupied Palestinian Territories; DeBeers for their supposed complicity in efforts by the Botswanan government to forcibly remove indigenous peoples from their ancestral lands; and Coca-Cola for its relationships with paramilitary groups and repression of trade unions in Colombia. While there is often considerable media and scholarly attention drawn to these campaigns, the success of such tactics is often debatable. Unions and NGOs have frequently become divided over the use of boycotts, with considerable disagreement occurring about their results and when and when not to introduce them. Unions, in particular, have real concerns about the implications of boycotts for the workers employed in the targeted companies and their unions. Maintaining solidarity within the union movement is often challenging, and divisions between unions often emerge. The Coca-Cola boycott, for example, which is supported by SINALTRAINAL and a number of INGOs, has not received support from one of the most important potential allies in this campaign, the International Union of Food, Agricultural, Hotel, Restaurant, Catering, Tobacco and Allied Workers' Associations (IUF). The IUF, a global union federation (GUF) headquartered in Switzerland, which represents the highest proportion of Coca-Cola workers worldwide, has publicly condemned the call for a global Coca-Cola boycott. It views the boycott as potentially damaging to years of efforts spent working with the Teamsters, the United Steelworkers of America, Jobs with Justice, and other unions to get Coca-Cola to negotiate and sign a global workers' rights agreement with its unions whereby the IUF would cover all of Coca-Cola's employees, including bottlers (IUF 2003). These sorts of divisions, which can have detrimental effects for these campaigns, illustrate the difficulties international boycotts present for unions. Unions that already represent significant numbers of workers in the targeted companies and/or have made a significant philosophical and resource commitment to a global organizing strategy at the same company may find themselves pitted against those who see the boycott as a moral and strategic response in a broader social justice and human rights struggle. Often those on both sides of these disputes are individuals and organizations who normally are close allies and good friends. These disagreements, for which there are no easy answers, also plague divestment campaigns.

Divestment campaigns almost exclusively center on cases where corporations have set up their operations in conflict zones or settings where human rights abuses are widespread. As in the case of boycotts, there is little consensus within the NGO community or among unions as to when companies should not invest or should not be present in a particular country (Zandvliet 2005). Advocates of divestment campaigns argue that corporations located in conflict zones provide additional means for the warring parties to prolong their brutal campaigns. Critics, however, maintain that divestment has the potential for contributing to a worsening situation. It may allow a less scrupulous company to become involved in the country, or it may create a larger pool of disillusioned and desperate individuals from whom warring parties can recruit as job loss and economic hardship set in (Bennett 2002). The success of divestment campaigns also often depends on strong cross-border alliances among trade unions and other advocacy organizations. These are not always easy to secure and maintain. In the 1980s, the Congress of South African Trade Unions, as part of its antiapartheid struggle, called upon northern trade unions to support a selective divestment campaign aimed at forcing oil companies out of South Africa. The oil companies were singled out for the role they played in providing oil and petroleum to the police and military. American unions, while supportive of the antiapartheid struggle, became divided over the divestment campaign for fear it would result in layoffs of U.S. workers.

As a consequence of these divisions, the international union movement has been very hesitant to adopt this tactic or lend assistance to NGOs, advocacy organizations, or religious groups involved in divestment campaigns. According to the International Confederation of Free Trade Unions (ICFTU 2005, 1), "Burma is the only country in the world for which the international trade union movement calls for disinvestment." The decision by ICFTU to take such a strong stand, according to the ICFTU, has been informed by the documentation of widespread violations against workers' rights, including the use of forced labor, and ICFTU's own investigations, which have demonstrated that it is next to impossible for a foreign company to do business in Burma without aiding and abetting the military dictators responsible for so much oppression. The ICFTU has received strong support for its divestment campaign from global unions, the European Trade Union Congress (ETUC), and other national union bodies as well as other INGOs and humanitarian organizations that have campaigned for over a decade to get the international community,

including governments and businesses, to do more to apply pressure on the
Burmese military government to improve its appalling human rights record
(ICFTU 2005).

As part of the ICFTU's campaign it has maintained a comprehensive list of
companies with business links to Burma, which it distributes widely; written
letters to hundreds of companies concerning their operations in Burma and
asked them to withdraw from the country; and called upon pension funds to
reconsider their relationship with companies associated with Burma. Global
union federations and the ICFTU have also used their influence within the
ILO to get the organization to take a stronger role in matters concerning human rights abuses in Burma, particularly the practice of forced labor (ICF-
TU-ETUC 2005). This has been an extremely important development, and
it illustrates how the trade union movement is able to make use of its unique
position within the ILO to activate procedures to investigate serious violations of ILO standards by member states (International Council on Human
Rights Policy 2002). While it remains to be seen if these actions will lead to
an improved human rights record in Burma, the negative publicity generated
against companies investing in Burma has contributed to company and pension decisions to divest from Burma and has kept others from considering the
country as an investment option (OECD 2002).

Prevention Strategies

Boycotts, divestment and shareholder campaigns, and attempts to prosecute
corporations have proved challenging for unions because of competing demands, financial costs, and differences over how best to respond to an immediate situation, but they have proved to be useful ways to hold corporations
accountable and draw attention to cases where corporations have directly or
indirectly contributed to violent conflict and/or human rights abuses. With
growing awareness about the relationship between corporate activity and violent conflict in the Global South a stronger focus on prevention has emerged.
Trade unions, although rarely recognized for their efforts, have become significant players alongside INGOs and international governance institutions
in prevention efforts. Unlike most response strategies, prevention has been
carried out less in the public domain and more through careful negotiation
with transnational corporations, international governance institutions, and national governments. Two dominant strategies have emerged. The first attempts
to regulate corporate behavior through legally binding obligations. The second seeks to get corporations to voluntarily agree to behave in a particularly
responsible manner that is unlikely to contribute to violence or ongoing social
unrest. The following discusses the role and capacities of unions in these two
areas.

STRENGTHENING LEGAL OBLIGATIONS

Unions and INGOs agree there is a lot of work to be done to develop "enforceable, transparent and binding extra-territorial controls" (Oxfam Community Aid Abroad 2004, 1) that would require corporations to adhere to universal human rights standards. As the situation currently stands, international law does not hold transnational corporations to the same set of human rights standards and obligations that it applies to nation-states. The creation of a global regulatory framework over corporate behavior, while it is far more likely to change the behavior of transnational corporations than any other development (Compa and Diamond 1996), is proving extremely difficult. Corporations are openly hostile to any such suggestions, and the political will of governments to increase regulatory powers over private-sector activities is largely nonexistent. The trend among most governments in the current neoliberal environment is to wind back any remaining legislation that constrains corporate activities. During the Unocal case in the United States, for example, the Bush administration filed an unsuccessful brief that sought to destroy the legal basis of the Burmese villagers' suit. Subsequently, the Bush government has embarked on a wholesale attack on ATCA and has received strong backing from the Blair government in the United Kingdom and the Howard government in Australia (Hermer and Day 2004). The dismantling by conservative governments around the world of legislation that governs corporate behavior has meant trade unions and NGOs have had to dedicate most of their time to trying to protect what little remains rather than advance new regulatory mechanisms at the national or international level.

IMPROVING CORPORATE CODES OF CONDUCT

The one area where corporations and governments are prepared to hold negotiations with unions, INGOs, and international agencies has been that regarding voluntary measures to promote responsible business behavior. This activity has resulted in a number of international policies that express a desire for corporations to uphold human rights obligations. These include the OECD Declaration on International Investment, the ILO Tripartite Declaration of the Principles Concerning Multinational Enterprises and Social Policy, the ILO Declaration on Fundamental Principles and Rights at Work, the ILO Convention on Indigenous and Tribal Peoples, the UN Declaration on Human Rights, and the UN Convention on the Elimination of Racial Discrimination. There have also emerged a handful of internationally recognized business guidelines developed by various international bodies that express the need for corporations to uphold human rights obligations. These include the UN's Norms of Responsibility of Transnational Corporations and Other Business Enterprises with Regard to Human Rights, which stipulates that companies are "obligated to respect" human rights in both peace and conflict situations; the OECD's

Guidelines for Multinational Enterprises, whose recommendations cover ten areas of business ethics including human rights, labor rights, information disclosure, and taxation; and the UN's Business Guide for Conflict Impact Assessment and Risk Management, which specifically applies to corporations operating in conflict settings. The UN Global Compact, launched by the secretary general in 2000, is another important international initiative that invites companies to voluntarily commit themselves to a set of nine principles relating to labor rights and other human rights and the protection of the environment.

In most cases, these initiatives have emerged in response to concerns raised by trade unions and/or INGOs and active lobbying on their behalf by international organizations. At times unions and INGOs have carried out these activities jointly; the Voluntary Principles on Security and Human Rights is one example. The Voluntary Principles—developed out of discussions among the ICEM, a handful of human rights NGOs, and companies involved in the extractive industries—deal with a range of issues, including the management of security operations by businesses in conflict settings and how to incorporate human rights concerns in risk assessment (OECD 2002). The U.S. and U.K. governments have subsequently endorsed the principles, contributing to greater international and industry recognition.

One of the limitations of the principles—and of so many other initiatives, including the global compact—is that they are not legally binding and are not accompanied by monitoring and oversight mechanisms, which makes enforcement extremely difficult (International Council on Human Rights Policy 2002). This unfortunate development has meant that the intent of these initiatives has not been fully realized, as many companies agree to sign on to the initiatives but do little to abide by their contents. Unions and INGOs continue to lobby corporations and international agencies about the need to strengthen monitoring and compliance arrangements within the respective agreements but have had little success. Unions and INGOs need to identify alternative ways to overcome the shortcomings of these voluntary initiatives. One of the ways unions could begin to strengthen the intent of some of these voluntary initiatives is to include them as part of international framework agreements. The ICEM, for example, could request that mining companies sign on to global framework agreements that include the Voluntary Principles on Security and Human Rights with added monitoring and compliance provisions. The additional challenges this would present for global unions while negotiating such agreements are unknown, but if the effort were successful, it could overcome some major flaws in what are significant yet largely ineffectual international initiatives.

It would be inaccurate to suggest that all the recent major prevention initiatives have taken place in the UN's Geneva offices or corporate boardrooms in the north as a consequence of campaigns run by Global unions or INGOs.

Unions and NGOs in the Global South are drawing upon their own unique capacities to influence corporate behavior within their borders. Campaigns forrevenue-sharing agreements (RSA) are one example. RSAs aim to "allocate and distribute the benefits of private-sector activity among national and regional governments and local communities more equitably" (International Peace Academy 2002, 2) so that the risks of violence are reduced. RSAs typically seek to ensure that affected local communities are properly compensated for their losses and that they receive some benefits from ongoing company operations. RSAs, unfortunately, often suffer from the typical problems of not being legally binding and not having adequate independent monitoring mechanisms. In Chad and Cameroon, however, a very effective, albeit not entirely successful, cross-border campaign for an RSA over a proposed oil and pipeline project sought to overcome these problems. The campaign was run by local human rights groups, development NGOs, and trade unions in Chad and Cameroon concerned about the detrimental effects of the project on local communities and on the volatile social and political situation in the two countries, where innumerable human rights violations, including extrajudicial killings, were taking place.

The Chad/Cameroon oil exploitation and pipeline project involved the extraction of oil from three fields in southern Chad and the construction of a 1,070-kilometer pipeline from the oil fields to Kribi on the Atlantic coast of Cameroon. An oil consortium made up of Exxon Mobil, Chevron, and Petronas was to carry out the work (Friends of the Earth International 2003). Soon after the initial reports of the proposed project emerged in the local media, a civil society advocacy network was formed by local NGOs, community organizations, and trade unions. Their timely response was extremely critical given that the RSA they desired needed to be settled before any deals were struck between the oil companies and respective governments. Following failed attempts to get a hearing from the governments or the corporations, the advocacy network explored other avenues to bring about change. After conducting further research into the project, the World Bank was identified as a potential leverage point over the governments and oil companies. The oil companies, as the advocacy network had learned, were prepared to undertake the project only if it received the support of the World Bank. The network, working at this point with INGOs such as Amnesty International and Environmental Defense, actively pursued the World Bank and requested that it not finance the project until the group's concerns were addressed. While not all the issues raised by the advocacy network were addressed, the World Bank agreed to back the project only if the Chadian government adopted a law on the management and sharing of oil revenue that included a local oversight committee made up of civil society representatives (Djiraibe 2003). This was an important victory because it meant that the RSA was enacted into law and became legally binding for the

corporations and the government. In 2000, following the government's introduction of required legislative changes, the World Bank approved the project.
In 2001, an international advisory group was established by the World Bank to
monitor the project, which continued to be plagued with workers' rights abuses
and corruption allegations. By 2003, the project had been completed and some
two hundred thousand barrels per day were traveling along the pipeline. By
this time the Chadian government was showing little interest in honoring the
mandated RSAs. In 2005, the government amended the revenue management
law to bypass the joint government-civil society revenue oversight committee
and reallocated a larger percentage of the oil revenue to the government and
security forces. In January 2006, the World Bank, following mounting local
and international pressure, withdrew its support to Chad for breaching the
loan agreement (World Bank 2006). The Exxon Mobil consortium, meanwhile,
continues to operate largely unaffected. In another context, however, the World
Bank's influence may be able to prevent corporate projects from fostering corruption and human rights violations and destabilizing vulnerable societies.

The activity of transnational corporations in the Global South is certain to
expand significantly over the coming years. This predicted expansion of corporate investment in the Global South and within conflict zones only adds to the
urgency of ameliorating the negative social consequences of their activity. Trade
unions will increasingly be looked to for help in solving these serious matters. If
northern unions are serious about challenging corporate abuse, they cannot ignore requests for assistance from affected communities in the Global South. It is
no longer acceptable for union leaders and union members to take the line that
these matters are beyond the scope of trade union concerns and capabilities.
Moving beyond workers' rights and embracing broader human rights struggles,
as the previous discussion has highlighted, presents challenges for trade unions,
but they are not insurmountable. Trade unions have demonstrated a number
of capacities upon which they can draw to hold corporations accountable for
past human rights abuses and complicity in acts of violence and to prevent
future harms. Whether engaging in strategic research on the corporations in
question, aiding in the prosecution of offending companies, carrying out shareholder or divestment campaigns, or working with INGOs, corporations, and
international bodies to develop codes of practice that encourage corporations
to uphold human rights obligations, trade unions can play a significant role in
local and international efforts, and it is crucial that they continue to do so. The
challenge for unions is to build upon their unique capacities and achievements
through some of their other activities. Strengthening voluntary codes of practice through global framework agreements may be one such option.

One thing that is becoming patently obvious is that much of this work
needs to be carried out through cross-border or global campaigns in coalition

with NGOs and other advocacy organizations. Undoubtedly there will be differences in views between trade unions and NGOs when it comes to dealing with these matters. This is to be expected. However, labor unions and NGOs have more in common with each other than they do with corporations involved in perpetuating violence (Compa 2005). Both share the desire to halt abusive behavior by companies and make them more accountable to international human rights obligations. It is important for unions and NGOs to learn from each other, come to appreciate each other's views, capacities, and constraints, and discover constructive ways to work together so that close allies do not become enemies and campaigns do not become mired down in disputes. Partnerships with NGOs and other advocacy organizations are no longer optional—they are a necessity for protecting human rights and the lives of workers across the north and south (Gallin 2000).

CONCLUSION

KATE BRONFENBRENNER

The goal of this book was to provide a body of original scholarly research that captured global union efforts to take on and win against the world's largest transnational firms. More specifically, the book aimed to focus on comprehensive cross-border organizing and bargaining campaigns that took place, for the most part, outside the United States. Many might think it would have been a difficult goal to achieve, since the generally held presumption is that cross-border campaigns are primarily a U.S. invention. Yet, as the Global Unions Conference in February 2006 clearly demonstrated, union cross-border strategies can be found wherever there are workers, unions, and large, foreign-owned transnational companies, which today includes nearly every country in the world.

In fact, for most workers and unions in the Global North, the challenge of organizing and bargaining with transnational firms, particularly foreign-owned transnational firms, is really a phenomenon of the last few decades. As several of the chapters in this book point out, it is also one that has been differentially experienced by unions in some countries in western Europe, which have only just begun to wrestle with global restructuring of employment, joint efforts by governments following neoliberal strategies and major transnational firms to shift public policy toward employer interests, and aggressive efforts to eliminate unions where they already exist and keep unions out where they have yet to emerge.

For workers in the Global South, however, the concept of transnational capital goes back as far as European colonization in the 1600s. Like Sukthankar and Kolben in chapter 3 of this book, Geoffrey Jones in his book *Multinationals and Globalization* describes the East India Tea Company as a protomulti-national enterprise functioning as a vertically integrated firm that undertook a full range of activities from the procurement of commodities in Asia to their wholesaling in Europe (2005, 17). As time progressed, the full range of these activities included not only tea and spices but silk-spinning factories in India and led eventually to responsibility for governing in India, starting with revenue collection in Bengal.

While East India Tea may seem to be on entirely different scale than a company with the kind of scope, power, and global influence of Wal-Mart, it was, in many ways, the Wal-Mart of its day. Its primary goods—tea, silks, and spices—were produced in Asia but sold to a world market and therefore required a vast fleet of ships and a land-based warehouse, packaging, and distribution system. And, like Wal-Mart, its profits depended on keeping the wages as low as possible among its producers and it could only do so thanks to the full support of the state (the Crown), even to the point of using slave labor long after it had been banned in all other colonies of the British Empire (Jones 2005; Sukthankar and Kolben chapter 3).

East India Tea, of course, was just the beginning. Workers throughout the Global South, whether producing gold from South Africa, oil in the East Indies, tin in Malaya, coffee in Brazil, or bananas in Latin America, were employed by large foreign- owned transnational firms a century before most U.S. and European workers were(Jones 2005).

Certainly European and U.S.-owned companies sold to foreign markets. But it was not until the late 1970s and early 1980s that workers in United States and Europe began to more routinely confront the challenge of foreign ownership of their companies. In contrast, unions in the Global South have never operated in a world where they were not dealing with powerful foreign-owned transnational firms, closely supported by the military, trade, tax, employment, labor, and investment policies not just of their own governments but of the governments of parent companies as well. Jobs might move from one country in the Global South to another, and firms from one country in the Global North might buy out firms owned by another firm in the Global North, but without question, if any union in Asia, Latin America, or Africa wanted to challenge the owners of capital, it would have to exert pressure not just on local managers. In fact, employers were so closely tied to the state that in many countries the national and the foreign government would work hand in hand to send in police or soldiers to intimidate, threaten, or, in some cases, simply make labor leaders disappear. It is therefore not surprising that labor issues then and now have been at the core of so many independence movements.

We can also assume that key to all these struggles were the principals of grassroots coalition building and leveraging power. After all, how could workers in the Philippines, South Africa, or Guatemala even hope to take on transnational firms or neofascist dictatorships without leverage of some kind? Equally important, given the linkages between imperialist and colonial governments and transnational firms, even without unions, how could they effectively challenge either the state or the foreign-owned companies for whom they toiled without recognizing those linkages and effectively challenging both economic and political power?

As Tom Juravich explains in chapter 1, many unions in the Global North are just beginning to figure this out. Most spent the last two decades thinking that it was the other countries that were stealing their companies and their jobs, not the seemingly stateless entities that own these firms. And as they reached out for help from unions in the Global South to aid them in their battles while simultaneously blaming them for stealing their jobs, it never occurred to many of them that the unions in those countries had faced the world's most powerful corporate giants from the earliest days of their own unionization and might be able to teach them a thing or two about taking these companies on. Most scholars writing about the development of cross-border campaigns in the Global North treat them as a northern invention, ignoring the rich tradition of global solidarity in sectors such as mining or maritime, or the historic cross-border campaigns such as the decades-long organizing struggle against United Fruit still being played out today (Frundt chapter 5).

This has not been just a historical problem, however. Even today the literature on global union strategies has been overwhelmingly U.S.-centric or Eurocentric, and in its narrowness of focus a great deal has been lost. As the research and analysis captured in this book tell us, workers are building global unions to take on global companies through a diversity of strategies around the globe. There are several key lessons we can learn from these campaigns. In particular these lessons have to do with the role of the state, membership and leadership education and engagement, strategic research, and the nature of the campaigns themselves.

Role of the State

First, the state plays a very different role across countries and industries. In several cases unions relied on legal campaigns that were doomed to failure absent linkages with a comprehensive leverage strategy focused on both capital and the state because the laws were virtually unenforceable or at best simply not enforced. This was clearly the case in the Euromedical campaign in Malaysia, where, as Peter Wad explains in chapter 2, over a period of thirty years the union fought and won its case in every labor industrial relations and judicial forum, all the way to the highest court in the nation, only to be ignored by the company at every turn. It was only through pressure on key decision makers in the parent company outside Malaysia that Euromedical was forced to concede.

As Valeria Pulignano explains in chapter 7, for the European unions, moving toward comprehensive cross-border campaigns has meant breaking away from nationally based vertical structures that are rooted in the labor legislation of each country. Specifically, in many European countries this requires shifting from company-based works councils toward company-wide and European-wide structures. This is indeed a difficult challenge because it involves breaking down not only cultural and language barriers but also long-standing practices that have developed as an outgrowth of the different labor laws, policies, and societal norms in each country. It also requires withstanding conscious efforts by the employer to pit workers against one another by region, country, or production line in order to obtain greater concessions. A further unacknowledged dimension is that many corporations are no longer regionally concentrated firms but truly global transnational companies, spread across every continent. Such developments further limit the effectiveness of national or regionally focused legislation (such as that promulgated by the European Union) in regulating transnational labor and employment law violations.

Similarly, Peter Turnbull (chapter 6) describes how when the European Parliament issued its first ports package in February 2001, severely threatening the job security of dockers throughout Europe, some European transport unions thought that they could simply use the legislative lobbying process to make minor amendments to the directives to protect their jobs. However, the International Transport Workers Federation (ITF) understood that without the development of what Turnbull calls a new unconventional repertoire of collective action, including coordinated strikes at international ports across Europe and mass demonstrations at the European Parliament, neither the state nor the shipping industry employers would change their position.

In many cases the laws on the books are merely for show, and the state has no capacity for or inclination toward enforcement. This was the case in Sri Lanka, where the union circumvented this sham process—by building networks of nongovernmental organizations (NGOs) and unions, locally, nationally, and internationally; engaging in escalating actions in the workplace and the community; and bringing in the European Union (EU), the World Trade Organization (WTO), and the Fair Labor Association (FLA) to investigate trade violations by employers in export processing zones (EPZs) (chapter 4).

In other cases unions and labor NGOs have also learned to use the state and state labor bodies for their own purposes. As Darryn Snell describes (chapter 10), several NGOs and unions took on those transnational firms with the worst human rights records in the Global South by filing court cases in U.S. courts for violations under the Alien Tort Claims Act (ATCA), the most high-profile case being the suit against Coca-Cola for its use of the paramilitary to crush the union at its facilities in Colombia. Others, such as the union at Euromedi-cal in Malaysia, have used an Organization for Economic Co-operation and Development (OECD) contact point as an additional relationship to pressure a parent company to get involved in settling a dispute (Wad chapter 2).

Thus the cases in this book show the state in two very different lights. The first is as the arm of the large transnational enterprise, either as one more institution over which capital has controlling interest or as a tool over which capital has the means to exert enormous influence. But these chapters also tell another story, of the state as a key stakeholder or decision maker, which the union is able to successfully leverage as part of a multifaceted comprehensive campaign for union recognition or collective bargaining.

This points to the ultimate weakness in so many of these campaigns. They are by nature piecemeal and mostly defensive. They are only rarely strategic, tackling entire industries, companies, and sectors with a long-term offensive plan. Certainly any long-term strategy would have to include breaking the hold that the world's largest transnational firms have over not only global trade and investment policy and national, state, and local government but also over supra-state institutions such as the EU or the North American Free Trade Agreement (NAFTA). Treating the state as just one more leverage point is not enough.

What is missing is a strategy that actually separates the state from capital it-self. There certainly have been some notable moves in that direction, most sig-nificantly the leading role that independent unions have played in helping to oust neoliberal governments from power in Latin American (Lujan 2006). Yet still the majority of unions and union federations remain closely allied with their political parties and unwilling or afraid to take on global capital directly. The global union federations (GUFs) and the national union federations were not leading the demonstrations in the streets in Seattle, Quebec, Milan, or Miami. And while independent unions in Latin American have led the way in pushing out neoliberal governments in several key countries in that part of the world, each of those movements is still a work in progress, and unions in the rest of the world do not seem eager to follow suit. Until unions actu-ally do more to break the linkage between the state and capital, some of the largest, most profitable companies in the world—Exxon Mobil, Coca-Cola, and Wal-Mart—will also continue to be some of the most serious violators of fundamental labor and human rights (Snell chapter 10; Brenner, Eidlin, and Candaele 2006).

Membership and Leadership Education and Engagement

Another important lesson raised by the cases in this book is the critical role played by membership and leadership education in cross-border campaigns.

Pulignano's chapter (7) is a story just as much about the challenges of cross-border campaigns as about the potential for cross-border strategies in Europe. Many of the local unions responded to the employer's appeal to put their own interests first, rather than uniting with works councils in other GM subsidiaries and countries to save jobs across Europe. Extensive workplace education about the issues and worker-to-worker exchanges between plants and countries would have been essential to build the links and find the common ground to develop the kind of solidarity necessary to pull off a cross-Europe campaign. In fact, that slow building of worker-to-worker networks and membership education formed the foundation in both the docker and EPZ textile workers campaigns (Turnbull chapter 6; Gunawardana chapter 4). Similar problems emerged in the First Student campaign, where the lack of a full exchange of ideas, goals, and interests, upon which long-term cross-border alliances depend, contributed to some of the tensions around respect and mutual interest between the Service Employees International Union (SEIU) staff on one hand and the rank-and-file leadership from the U.K. union on the other. Yet in the follow-up to the initial campaign, education and active engagement between the two organizations have also played a role in building on the earlier effort to make the process more mutual and effective for the future (Tattersall chapter 8).

As Stevis and Boswell's chapter (9) on international framework agreements (IFAs) makes clear, the leaders of national unions, national union federations, and GUFs also have a great deal of learning to do if cross-border campaigns are going to succeed. One of the most significant limitations of IFAs is that they tend to be concentrated in European-based firms in industries where western European-based unions and GUFS have the most influence, such as autos and transportation. Moreover, most GUFS have not made a priority of expanding IFAs to include the full range of the firm's operations outside Europe. Yet as Stevis and Boswell explain, for IFAs to be an effective tool they need to be linked with comprehensive campaigns in order to make them enforceable, and they need to be expanded to include the full range of the company's operations, outside Europe to North America and the Global South as well. The other danger of IFAs, codes of social responsibility (CSRs), and other global agreements is that national and supranational union bodies tend to look to them as substitutes for the building of a global labor movement. If the campaigns discussed in this book have taught us anything, it is that any authority—whether it be a judicial decree, an IFA, an OECD finding, or a recognition agreement—is only as good as the power of the multilevel grassroots networks of workers and their allies in labor organizations and NGOs to enforce those agreements, through local, national, and international actions in the workplace and the community. And as Turnbull and Gunawardana most aptly showed, it is education that is most central to building those networks at each level.

Perhaps one of the most important lessons from these cases is that for cross-border campaigns to succeed, unions and NGOs from the north and south need to learn a great deal not only about the global economy but about each other. Service-sector unions have much to learn from industrial unions that have been taking on large transnational firms for a much longer time than they have, yet industrial unions have a lot to learn from service-sector unions about community coalitions and community-based campaigns. The greatest waste of all is for each organization, out of pride, arrogance, or simple lack of awareness of others' efforts, to single-handedly reinvent the wheel rather than share scarce resources, skills, and knowledge. The most effective way for them to learn about each other is through the worker and leader exchanges and networks that form the building blocks of the campaign at each level of the organization, locally, nationally, and globally.

Research

As each of the campaigns in this book shows, it is also vital that workers, unions, and NGOs at all levels of their organizations gain a better understanding of both how the corporate ownership structure of the world's largest transnational firms is changing and how power and profits flow through these firms. As we can see from each of these cases, in many ways the companies these workers face act remarkably similarly at the ground level. There is a common thread of working longer and harder for less, multitasking, work restructuring, de-skilling, downsizing, playing workers against each other, cutting wages and benefits, de-unionizing where unions exists, fiercely opposing unions where they have yet to arrive, and ultimately shifting work around the world in search of lower production costs, greater flexibility, and fewer regulations.

Yet while the human resource officers for these firms may all be reading from the same instruction manual, and their decisions may wreak similar havoc on workers' lives, there remain enormous variations in how firms are structured and how power flows within each firm. If workers, unions, and their allies do not understand these differences, then they do not stand a chance of interfering with the key power relationships within the corporation. As we have seen from the cases in this book, there is a great deal of difference in how the union runs a campaign when the ultimate parent is a Danish shipping firm (APM-Maersk; see Wad chapter 2), a U.S.-owned banana producer (Frundt chapter 5), or an apparel firm in a Sri Lankan EPZ (Gunawardana chapter 4).

But in the model we are talking about, it is not enough that the union conduct a critique of the company and identify the company's profit centers, growth strategies, and decision makers, and the key relationships among all of these. In a global, comprehensive campaign, this information then needs to be shared with all stakeholders at every level, whether they are other unions, environmental groups, community action groups, union-company councils, national union federations, or GUFs. These stakeholders need to share, update, synthesize, and continue to monitor these firms as their structures and strategies change, sometimes in direct response to the union campaign.

Ideally, of course, this process should occur before campaigns start and continue after they end so that workers, unions, and their local, national, and international allies remain in a constant state of awareness of the firm's changing strategies and vulnerabilities. But even if the information sharing does not start until the campaign begins, what is key is that it never stop and that the structures to make that possible remain intact even after the crisis of the campaign is over. Each campaign also depends on being able to identify the key relationships among the profit centers, growth strategies, and key decision makers so the union can interfere with those relationships in developing a campaign.

Wal-Mart provides a perfect example of why this new, more strategic and more global framework for understanding corporate structure and the flow of corporate power is so critical. For the last decade there has been an ongoing effort to organize Wal-Mart in the United States and Canada. The company has made clear its determination to remain, in its words, union free—even distributing a manual with that title to all its managers (Wal-Mart Stores Inc. 1997) and shutting down (Demetrakakes 2003; Miller 2004; Zellner and Bernstein 2000; Struck 2005) or threatening to shut down (Heinzl and Strauss 1997) every retail unit that tries to organize. It has also shown blatant disregard for nearly every labor and employment law in existence, committing unfair labor practices during organizing campaigns; discriminating based on race, gender, and disability; and violating wage and hour, child labor, health and safety, and immigration laws (Miller 2004; Laska 2006; Russell 2004; Buckley and Daniel 2003; Drogin 2003). The union response has been to organize a consumer campaign against Wal-Mart, portraying it as a bad corporate citizen that forces down wages and living standards and causes taxes to be raised wherever it moves. Yet the customers keep coming, and Wal-Mart just continues on the same path.

However, prior to the global conference we conducted an in-depth strategic research report on Wal-Mart. Our findings were clear. While the face of Wal-Mart might be its retail stores, our research found that its strategic vulnerability is its distribution network, through which everything supplied to Wal-Mart and sold out of Wal-Mart must travel. But the unions in North America who have been organizing Wal-Mart held firm, believing the campaign focused on the retail consumer was the only way to go.

Then on July 30, 2006, just before the World Cup quarter-final match between England and Portugal, when Wal-Mart's ASDA subsidiary in the United

Kingdom expected to serve twenty-four customers a second during the buildup to the game, thousands of workers at ASDA's distribution center threatened to go out on strike for union recognition. Wal-Mart immediately gave in, agreeing to a joint committee to oversee a recognition procedure (with neutrality) at twenty warehouses and giving the General Municipal, Boilermakers and Allied Trade Union full access to the depots (Clement 2006). Since then workers have voted overwhelmingly for recognition at two previously unorganized ASDA distribution depots in Chepstow and Erith (*Morning Star* 2006).

Any campaign to organize Wal-Mart must connect workers in distribution to suppliers and then finally to workers in retail. Retail workers may be the last and most difficult to organize; thus if Wal-Mart is ever going to become a unionized firm, organizing may have to be centered on workers in supply and distribution, particularly in countries in Asia, where so many of the producers and the distribution hubs are concentrated. Yet, given that it is the world's largest employer and that nearly every single product—apparel, food, appliances, sporting goods, books, auto parts, electronics, household goods, pharmaceuticals, toys, and financial services—is now sold there, Wal-Mart has the power to drive down wage and working standards for every other product and service. Not organizing Wal-Mart is not a choice for the global labor movement.

However, perhaps more than that of any other transnational firm, the case of Wal-Mart illustrates the importance of ongoing strategic corporate research that will allow the global labor movement to find the leverage points to interfere with the company's key relationships around the world. Equally important, Wal-Mart is an example of a company where long before a campaign is mounted, it will be essential to establish structures to link workers in retail, distribution, and supply—from NGOs concerned with environmental, anti-sweatshop, child labor, civil, and labor rights to customer and concerned citizen groups at the local, national, and international levels. It will also be crucial to share information across these groups about the structure of the company, its power, its key relationships, and its vulnerabilities to help prepare for the kind of global campaign it will take to organize Wal-Mart in the future.

Strengthening Global Unions through Cross-Border Campaigns

Finally, there are several key lessons that the global labor movement can learn from the cases in this book about strengthening global unions through cross-border campaigns. The core purpose of the global conference and of this book was not simply to strengthen union capacity to take on the world's largest transnational corporations but also to shift the balance of power between capital and labor so that unions could be a more effective voice in fighting for social and economic justice for all workers.

This is a much more complex proposition than it may seem because the global labor movement is truly divided within and across countries, sectors, industries, regions, and hemispheres. Yet, as these cases show, victory against the world's most powerful transnational firms depends not only on global solidarity among unions but also on solidarity between unions and NGOs at multiple levels. This means that relationship building at every level of the labor movement is paramount to the future of global unions. What is required is not just coalition building for the sake of one campaign but the kind of slow, one-on-one network building that Gunawardana writes about in her chapter on the women workers in the EPZs in Sri Lanka (see chapter 3). These relationships also cannot be parachuted into place from on high. Neither a GUF nor a national union federation can establish a relationship between unions and workers in two different countries. Instead, those relationships are best built through exchanges and joint actions between the unions and workers themselves. The same is true of relationships between unions and NGOs and other stakeholders. But most important of all, as Tattersall so aptly points out in the model of community unionism she presents in chapter 8, at every level the relationships that unions develop with other unions and with their allies cannot be unidirectional. They must involve mutual interests and shared values and be a priority for the long haul.

Nowhere does this become more important than in the relationship between unions in different regions of the world and sectors of the economy. The IFAs that fail to incorporate their subsidiaries in the Global South under the same terms as those in the Global North should be considered out of compliance, and no such IFAs should be considered in effect. More to the point, GUFs and their affiliates should mount aggressive global campaigns against those companies until they are willing to stop the double standard and bring subsidiaries of the company, whether in the Global South, eastern Europe, or North America, into compliance with the agreement.

The weakness of IFAs is just one problem that GUFs need to address. They need to work on becoming truly global federations, focusing on building global union power and assisting with industry- and company-wide comprehensive cross-border organizing and bargaining campaigns. They must work to strengthen union power in every sector in every part of the world, not just those sectors where a history of codetermination and high union density has made IFAs more attainable. GUFs should open rather than close the door to debate about different union strategies for challenging global capital and should help provide open forums to encourage and facilitate that debate. Most important of all, the GUFs and national trade unions in each country need to see cross-border campaigns as more than a two-way street, recognizing that in fact the strength of the global labor movement depends on the efforts of unions in the Global North to assist in developing strong and independent trade unions in the Global South that can take on global capital at the production and distribution level. This includes providing financial resources, global solidarity actions, assistance with NGOs, and pressure on the parent company at headquarters and branches in the countries in the Global North where the GUFs are based. At the same time, unions in the Global South are uniquely situated to use their position in the global supply chain to support unions that are engaged in contract and organizing struggles in Europe, Australia, New Zealand, and North America. As we have learned only too well in the last five years, a weakened U.S. labor movement can have devastating economic, political, and environmental consequences for workers and unions in every country because it simply emboldens supranational bodies such as the World Bank, the WTO, and International Monetary Fund (IMF), over which U.S.-based transnationals have so much control.

Another key lesson that comes out of the campaigns highlighted in this book is that they can take on a life of their own. With so many different allies and constituency groups involved, it is important to remember the original focus of the comprehensive campaign. It is not about leverage for leverage's sake. It is not about finding dirt on the boss or destroying the company. For the workers involved in these campaigns, no matter what terrible deeds this employer may have done, at the end of the day it is still their employer, the one that pays their bills, keeps food on the table, and keeps the community alive. They do not want that company destroyed or run out of town. Nor do they want it to destroy their community, its land, air, or water supply, their health, or their ability to have children.

Thus unions and their allies must strike a balance when launching these campaigns. From the beginning, they must make the members or rank-and-file workers being organized not just the public face of the campaign (although that is important) but also full participants in each stage of the process, from strategic research to developing the critique of the company to designing and implementing the campaign. As part of this process they must learn how and when to work with their members to determine victory and de-escalate the campaign. But in doing so they have to remember that their allies in group actions may not have obtained their goals in the fight. Thus, if part of the campaign was an investigation into health and safety or environmental violations industry-wide, then the union cannot settle those as part of their recognition or contract settlement. Otherwise they will never be able to build a coalition again. This is all the more important when these coalitions are across borders and the company starts asking the union in the Global North to end its support for the organizing drive in the Global South as part of the settlement. These, then, are the ultimate tests of global unions. If a campaign cannot withstand these pressures to break ranks, then transnational capital has already won because global solidarity has been thwarted. But if the unions can hold together even in settlement, then they have proven that they have built a lasting coalition that will move on to the next struggle.

It is also important to remember that these kinds of union victories are at this point relatively few and far between. If global capital were to feel any real threat that unions were beginning to take back power on a significant scale, they would adjust their strategies accordingly, and unions around the world would face a much more formidable foe. Therefore, global unions cannot become attached to any individual strategy or model but must remain one step ahead of the employer by constantly adapting and readapting union strategies and tactics.

What the cases in this book show is that the world's unions have a greater potential than most realize to take on the most powerful corporations and win. These cases also show how difficult that can be. It requires enormous effort, creativity, and a willingness to take risks and reach across differences. But going from individual cases to something bigger requires something else as well. As difficult as times are for workers in the Global North, and as much as the wealth accumulated by global capital comes mostly from taking enormous profits at the expense of all workers, part of the reason that capital is able to do what it does is that hundreds of years of colonialism and imperialism have restrained workers' power, wages, and labor costs. This not only has made many a CEO and corporate shareholder very rich but has helped make a middle-class lifestyle affordable for millions and millions of workers in the Global North that would not have been possible otherwise.

The first step in global wealth redistribution is stopping the race to the bottom by putting the resources from the unions in the Global North into doing everything possible to assist workers and unions in the Global South in building strong and independent unions to organize and bargain on their behalf with the transnational firms that are robbing them of their wealth. The second step is to join with unions from the Global South in mounting targeted global campaigns against the world's largest transnational firms. Finally, the third step is to emulate the unions of Latin America, which do not limit their efforts to the organizing and bargaining arena. They understand that for there to be real change, unions must also seek to change the political context and challenge the neoliberal paradigm by electing officials who are willing to work with the global labor movement to redefine a more just form of globalization—one that does not accept that the IMF, World Bank, and WTO should be setting trade and investment policy, and in turn wage and living standards, for workers around the world.

However, even the most effective global organizing, bargaining, and political campaigns cannot assume that unions can raise the living standards of those in the Global South without sacrificing some of what they have in the Global North. Years of colonialism, imperialism, and environmental degradation come with a price. Labor's greatest chance of building a strong and vital global labor movement is sharing its power and wealth, because unions and workers in the Global North need the solidarity and power of unions and workers in the Global South just as much as those in the Global South need them. Workers and unions in every country need constant vigilance by labor academics to monitor and track the changing nature of the corporate leviathans with whom they struggle each day. At the same time, the labor academics need the institutional support of the unions if they are to continue to do the kind of high-quality strategic research that is so critical to understanding the changing nature of global corporate power.

The challenge faced by workers and unions as they confront transnational firms is one that may have begun hundreds of years ago, but it is now coming to the fore. Without question, a united global labor movement is the single greatest force for global social change and the single greatest hedge against the global race to the bottom when the unions reach across borders to realize that potential. Global unions are the future.

REFERENCES

ABC. 2005a. "Change of Plans for Unions." *Inside Business.* http://www.abc.net.au/insidebusiness/contents/2005/s1410757.htm.

——. 2005b. "The Kilwa Incident." *Four Corners.* http://www.abc.net.au/4corners/content/2005/s1384238.htm.

Ackers, Joan. 2004. "Gender, Capitalism and Globalisation." *Critical Sociology* 30 (1): 17–41.

Action Aid. 2005. "Tea Break: A Crisis Brewing in India." http://www.actionaid.org/wps/content_document.asp?doc_id=381.

Adebanwi, Wale. 2001. "Nigeria: A Shell of a State." *Dollars and Sense* 226: 19–37.

AIF (The Labour Movement's International Forum). 2003. *Faglige rettigheder kræver handling globalt—en konkret sag* (*Trade union rights demands global action—a concrete case*). Copenhagen: AIF.

——. 2006. "AIF Organization and Structure." http://www.aif.dk/?id=14.

Alston, Philip. 2005. "'Core Labour Standards' and the Transformation of the International Labour Rights Regime." In *Social Issues, Globalisation and International Institutions: Labour Rights and the EU, ILO, OECD and WTO*, edited by Virginia A. Leary and Daniel Warner, 1–87. Leiden, Neth.: Martinus Nijhoff.

Amicus. 2006. *International Framework Agreements.* December 5. http://www.amicustheunion.org/Default.aspx?page=4867.

AMRC (Asia Monitor Resource Center). 2006. "Editorial: AMRC's Asian Transnational Corporation Project and the Network." http://www.amrc.org.hk/5702.htm.

Anderson, Mary. 2003. "An Overview of Findings to Date: Five Observations." Cambridge, MA: Collaborative for Development Action. http://www.cdainc.com.

Anderson, Mary, and Luc Zandvliet. 2001. "Corporate Options for Breaking Cycles of Conflict." http://www.cdainc.com.

Anderson, Michael. 1993. "Work Construed: Ideological Origins of Labour Law in British India to 1918." In *Dalit Movements and the Meanings of Labour in India*, edited by P. Robb, 87–120. Delhi: Oxford University Press.

Anner, Mark, Ian Greer, Marco Hauptmeier, Nathan Lillie, and Nik Winchester. 2006. "The Industrial Determinants of Transnational Solidarity: Global Inter-Union Politics in Three Sectors." *European Journal of Industrial Relations* 12 (1): 7–27.

Argueta, Mario. 1992. *Historia de los Sin Historia*. Tegucigalpa, Hond.: Edi. Guaymuras.

Arrigo, Linda Gail. 1980. "The Industrial Workforce of Young Women in Taiwan." *Bulletin of Concerned Asian Scholars* 12 (2): 25—30.

Asia-Pacific Human Rights Network. 2001. "Associating with the Wrong Company." http://www.corpwatch.org.

Ayadurai, Dunston. 1992. *Industrial Relations in Malaysia: Law and Practice*. Kuala Lumpur: Butterworths Asia.

Bais, Karolien. 2005. *Corporate Social Responsibility: Perspectives from the South*. Amsterdam: SOMO-Centre for Research on Multinational Corporations.

Banaji, Jairus. 1996. "Globalization and Restructuring in the Indian Food Industry." In *Agrarian Questions*, edited by H. Bernstein and T. Brass, 191–210. London: Frank Cass.

Banana Link / War on Want. 2003. "What is Solidarismo? Costa Rica Style Union-Busting." London: Banana Link.

Banfield, Jessica, Virginia Haufler, and Damian Lilly. 2003. *Transnational Corporations in Conflict Prone Zones: Public Policy and a Framework for Action*. London: International Alert.

Banks, Andrew, and John Russo. 1999. "The Development of International Campaign-Based Network Structures: A Case Study of the IBT and ITF World Council of UPS Unions." *Comparative Labor Law & Policy Journal* 20 (4): 543–68.

Bartmann, Martin. 2005. "Employment Security in the Automobile Industry: Differing Strategies of Unions and Works Councils in Sweden and Germany." GERPISA seminar, Paris.

Barton, Harry, and Peter Turnbull. 1999. *End of Award Report: Labour Regulation and Economic Performance in the European Port Transport Industry*. ESRC Award R000235425. Boston Spa: Economic and Social Research Council.

——. 2002. "Labour Regulation and Competitive Performance in the Port Transport Industry: The Changing Fortunes of Three Major European Seaports." *European Journal of Industrial Relations* 8 (2): 133–56.

Baskin, Jeremy. 1991. *Striking Back: A History of Cosatu*. New York: Verso.

Bastian, Hope. 2006. "Keeping Fair Trade Fair in Mexico." *NACLA Report on the Americas* 39 (6): 6–9.

Beirnaert, Jeroen. 2006. *Case Study in Best Practices in EWC Functioning*. Brussels: Social Development Agency.

Bennett, Juliette. 2002. "Multinational Corporations, Social Responsibility and Conflict." *Journal of International Affairs* 55 (2): 393–413.

Benson, Peter Suppli, Bjørn Lambek, and Stig ørskov. 2004. *Mærsk: Manden og magten* (*Maersk: The Man and the Power*). Copenhagen: Politiken Books.

Bergstrom, Rupini, James Mackintosh, and Richard Milne. 2005. "Blow for Saab as GM Picks Germany Mid-Sized Car." *Financial Times*, March 5.

Biyanwila, Janaka. 2006. "Women Workers Organizing in Free Trade Zones: Steering Alliances and Movement Politics." In *21st Century Work—High Road or Low Road?* Proceedings of the 6th AIRAANZ Conference, 1:73–83.

BOI (Board of Investments). 2003a. "Katunayake Free Trade Zone Handbook of Work Stoppages." http://www.boi.lk.

——. 2003b. "A Profile of the Zones." http://www.boi.lk.

——. 2004. "Labor Standards and Employment Relations Manual." http://www.boi.lk.

——. 2006. "Workers Councils Guidelines." http://www.boi.lk.

Bolt, Cathy. "AWB Staff Could Face 10 Years Jail." 2005. *The Age*, November 22..

Börzel, Tanja A. 2002. "Pace-Setting, Foot-Dragging, and Fence-Sitting: Member State Responses to Europeanization." *Journal of Common Market Studies* 40 (2): 193–214.

Boswell, Terry, and Dimitris Stevis. 1997. "Globalization and International Labor Organizing." *Work and Occupations* 24 (3): 288–308.

Bourque, Reynald. 2005. "Les Accords-Cadres Internationaux (ACI) et la Negociacion Collective Internationale a l'ere de la Mondialisation." In *Programme education et dialogue*, 37. Geneva: Institut international d'etudes sociales.

Brecher, Jeremy, and Tim Costello. 1990. *Building Bridges: The Emerging Grassroots Coalition of Labor and Community*. New York: Monthly Review Press.

Brecher, Jeremy, Tim Costello, and Brendan Smith. 2006. "International Labor Solidarity: The New Frontier." *New Labor Forum* 15 (1): 9–18.

Brenner, Aaron, Barry Eidlin, and Kerry Candaele. 2006. "Wal-Mart Stores, Inc.: Strategic Corporate Research Report." Monograph prepared for distribution at "Global Companies–Global Unions–Global Research–Global Campaigns" conference, New York, February. Ithaca: ILR Office of Labor Education Research.

Brewer, James. 2004. "Strikes Threaten to Burst Shipping Profits' Balloon." *Lloyd's List*, October 4.

Brisbin, Richard, Jr. 2002. *A Strike Like No Other Strike: Law and Resistance during the Pittston Coal Strike of 1989—1990*. Baltimore: Johns Hopkins University Press.

Bronfenbrenner, Kate, and Tom Juravich. 2001. "The Evolution of Strategic and Coordinated Bargaining Campaigns of the 1990s: The Steelworkers Experience." In *Rekindling the Movement: Labor's Quest for Relevance in the 21st Century*, edited by Lowell Turner, Harry C. Katz, and Richard W. Hurd, 211–37. Ithaca: Cornell University Press.

Bronfenbrenner, Kate, and Stephanie Luce. 2004. "The Changing Nature of Corporate Global Restructuring: The Impact of Production Shifts on Jobs in the U.S., China, and around the Globe." Report submitted to the U.S.-China Economic and Security Review Commission, October 14.

Buckley, Neil, and Caroline Daniel. 2003. "Wal-Mart vs. the Workers: Labour Grievances Are Stacking Up at the World's Biggest Company." *Financial Times*, November 20.

Carlier, Manual. 1998. "Position of the European Shipowners on the Green Paper." Paper presented at the conference on the *Green Paper on Sea Ports and Maritime Infrastructure*, Future Prospectives for European Sea Ports, Barcelona, May 7–8.

Carossino, A. 1982. "Report Drawn Up on Behalf of the Committee of Transport on the Role of Ports in the Common Transport Policy." Document 1-844/82, European Parliament Working Documents.

Caspersz, Donella. 1998. "Organising Export Processing Zone Workers: Some Considerations for Trade Unions." Paper presented at the Association of Industrial Relations Academics of Australia and New Zealand Conference, Wellington, New Zealand.

Castree, Noel, Neil Coe, Kevin Ward, and Mike Samers. 2004. *Spaces of Work: Global Capitalism and the Geographies of Labor*. London: Sage.

CAW (Committee for Asian Women). 1998. *A Resource Book for Training and Organization among Asian Women Workers*. Hong Kong: Committee for Asian Women.

——. 2003. *Asian Women Workers' Newsletter* 22.

CEC (Commission of the European Communities). 1992. *The Future Development of the Common Transport Policy: A Global Approach to the Construction of a Community Framework for Sustainable Mobility*. COM(92) 494 final. Brussels: Commission of the European Communities.

——. 1997. *Green Paper on Sea Ports and Maritime Infrastructure*. COM(97) 678 final. Brussels: Commission of the European Communities.

——. 2001. *Proposal for a Directive of the European Parliament and of the Council on Market Access to Port Services*. COM(2001) 35 final. Brussels: Commission of the European Communities.

——. 2003. *The Sectoral Social Dialogue in Europe*. Directorate-General for Employment and Social Affairs. Luxembourg: Commission of the European Communities.

——. 2004. *Proposal for a Directive of the European Parliament and of the Council on Market Access to Port Services*. COM(2004) 0654 final. Brussels: Commission of the European Communities.

Centre for Education and Communication. 2005a. *Globalisation and Its Effect on Tea Plantation Workers*. New Delhi: Centre for Education and Communication.

——. 2005b. "International Tea Day flyer." http://www.cec-india.org/leftlinks/02/folder.2005–12–06.2965235999/index_html.

——. 2006. "December 15: International Tea Day." http://www.cec-india.org/leftlinks/02/folder.2005–12–06.2965235999/Tea_day.

Chambron, Anne-Claire. 2005. "Can Voluntary Standards Provide Solutions?" In *International Banana Conference II Preparatory Papers*, 57–85. Brussels.

Chang, Hsu-chung. 2006. Speech at the "Global Companies–Global Unions–Global Research–Global Campaigns" conference, New York, February. http://www.ilr.cornell.edu/globalunionsconference/multimedia/.

Chaulia, Sreeram. 2002. "Social Clause in WTO: Cases for and Against." *Economic and Political Weekly*, February 16. http://www.epw.org.in/showArticles.php?root=2002&leaf=02&filename=4110&filetype=html.

Chhachhi, Amrita, and Renée Pittin, eds.. 1996. *Confronting State, Capital and Patriarchy: Women Organizing in the Process of Industrialization*. New York: St. Martin's.

Clapham, Andrew, and Scott Jerbi. 2001. "Categories of Corporate Complicity in Human Rights Abuses." Background paper for the Global Compact dialogue on the role of the private sector in zones of conflict, New York.

Clean Clothes Campaign. 2002. "CCC Gucci Action in Amsterdam." http://www.cleanclothes.org/companies/gucci-02–10–31.htm.

Clement, Barrie. 2006. "Unions Call Off ASDA Strike after Last-Minute Peace Deal." *The Independent* (London), June 30.

Cohen, Larry, and Steve Early. 2000. "Globalization and De-Unionization in Telecommunications: Three Case Studies in Resistance." In *Transnational Cooperation among Labor Unions*, edited by M. Gordon and L. Turner, 202–22. Ithaca: Cornell University Press.

Collectif de l'ethique sur l'etiquette. 2005. Les accords-cadres internationaux. Document de Travail, October 2005. http://www.ethique-sur-etiquette.org/docs/Doc_de_travail_sur_les_ACI_0511.pdf.

Coller, Xavier. 1996. "Managing Flexibility in the Food Industry: A Cross-National Comparative Case Study in European Multinational Companies." *European Journal of Industrial Relations* 2 (2): 153–72.

COLSIBA/TransFair USA. 2005. "Summary of the Memorandum of Understanding between COLSIBA and TransFair USA." June.

Compa, Lance. 2005. "Labor Unions, NGOs and Corporate Codes of Conduct." In *Development NGOs and Labor Unions*, edited by D. Eade and A. Leather, 241–48. Bloomfield, CT: Kumarian Press.

——. 2006. *NGO Labor Tensions on the Ground*. Carnegie Council on Ethics and International Affairs. http://www.cceia.org/viewMedia.php/prmID/895.

Compa, Lance, and Stephen Diamond. 1996. *Human Rights, Labor Rights and International Trade*. Philadelphia: University of Pennsylvania Press.

Connor, Tim, and Kelly Dent. 2006. "Offside! Labor Rights and Sportswear Production in Asia." Report for Oxfam International. http://www.oxfam.org.uk/what_we_do/issues/trade/offside_sportswear.htm.

Cooke, William. 2005. "Exercising Power in a Prisoner's Dilemma: Transnational Collective Bargaining in an Era of Corporate Globalization?" *Industrial Relations Journal* 36 (4): 283–302.

CoR (Committee of the Regions). 2005. "Opinion of the Committee of the Regions on the *Proposal for a Directive of the European Parliament and of the Council on Market Access to Port Services*." Brussels: Committee of the Regions.

CTW (Change to Win). 2006. "Change to Win: Strategic Organizing Center." http://www.changetowin.org/organizing.html.

Deloitte. 2005. *Impact Assessment Port Services Directive: The Netherlands*. Utrecht, Neth.: Deloitte Consultancy B.V.

della Porta, Donatella, and Hanspeter Kriesi. 1999. "Social Movements in a Globalizing World: An Introduction." In *Social Movements in a Globalizing World*, edited by D. della Porta, H. Kriesi, and D. Rucht, 3–22. Houndmills, U.K.: Macmillan.

Demetrakakes, Pan. 2003. "Is Wal-Mart Wrapped in Union Phobia?" *Food & Packaging*, August 21.

Dent, Kelly. 2000. "Harassment of Workers in Sri Lanka: Still an Invisible Issue." http://www.tieasia.org.au.

de Palacio, Loyola. 2004. "European Sea Ports in a Dynamic Market—Ports and the EU Agenda." Paper presented at European Sea Ports Conference, Rotterdam, June 17.

Department of Transport. 2005. *EC Directive on Market Access to Port Services: Briefing for UK Members of the European Parliament Economic and Social Committee of the Regions*. London: Department of Transport.

Devraj, Ranjit. 2003. "A Depressing Flavor." *India Together*. http://www.indiatogether.org/2003/nov/eco-teawoes.htm.

Deyo, Frederic C. 1989. *Beneath the Miracle: Labor Subordination in the New Asian Industrialism*. Berkeley: University of California Press.

Djiraibe, Delphine. 2003. *The Chad/Cameroon Pipeline Project*. N'Djamena, Chad: Chadian Association for the Promotion and Defense of Human Rights.

Dosal, Paul. 1993. *Doing Business with the Dictators: A Political History of United Fruit in Guatemala, 1899–1944*. Wilmington, DE: Scholarly Resources.

Dow Jones Newswires. 2005. "US Judge Allows Talisman Energy Sudan Genocide Lawsuit." August 31.

Dreiling, Michael. 1998. "From Margin to Center: Environmental Justice and Social Unionism as Sites for Intermovement Solidarity." *Race, Gender & Class* 6 (1): 51–69.

Drewes, Elke. 2005. "Wie Fair Sind Bio-Bananen?" *DW-World.DE/Deutschewelle*, September 23.

Drogin, Richard. 2003. "Statistical Analysis of Gender Patterns in Wal-Mart Workforce." Report. Berkeley, CA: Drogin, Kakigi & Associates.

Eade, Deborah. 2004. "International NGOs and Unions in the South: Worlds Apart or Allies in the Struggle?" *Development in Practice* 14 (1–2): 71–84.

ECSA (European Community Shipowners' Association). 2005. "European Parliament Working Document on Market Access to Port Services." Brussels: European Community Shipowners' Association.

EESC (European Economic and Social Committee). 2005. "Opinion of the European Economic and Social Committee on the *Proposal for a Directive of the European Parliament and of the Council on Market Access to Port Services."* Paper presented to European Economic and Social Committee, Brussels.

———. 2006. "Opinion of the European Economic and Social Committee on European Works Councils: A New Role in Promoting European Integration." http://eescopinions.eesc.europa.eu/EESCopinionDocument.aspx?identifier=ces–2006_ac.doc&language=EN.

EIRO (European Industrial Relations Observatory). 2001. "Uncertainty If Opel Restructures." http://www.eiro.eurofound.eu.int/2001/09/feature/be0109301f.html.

Elias, Juanita. 2004. *Fashioning Inequality: The Multinational Company and Gendered Employment in a Globalizing World.* Aldershot, U.K.: Ashgate.

———. 2005. "Stitching Up the Labor Market. Recruitment, Gender and Ethnicity in the Multinational Firm." *International Feminist Journal of Politics* 7 (1): 90—111.

Ellem, Bradon. 2003. "New Unionism in the Old Economy: Community and Collectivism in the Pilbara's Mining Towns." *Journal of Industrial Relations* 45 (4): 423–41.

———. 2005. "Dialectics of Scale: Global Capital and Local Unions in Australia's Iron Ore Industry." *Economic and Industrial Democracy* 26 (3): 335–58.

Ellem, Bradon, and John Shields. 2004. "Beyond the Will to Unity: Theorizing Peak Union Formation, Organization and Agency." In *Peak Unions in Australia: Origins, Purpose, Power and Agency,* edited by B. Ellem, R. Markey, J. Shields, 32–53. Annandale, Aus.: Federation Press.

Ellemose, Søren. 2004. *Århundredes Stjerne: A.P. Møller-Mærsk Gruppen 1904–2004 (The Star of the Century: The A.P. Moller-Maersk Group 1904–2004).* Copenhagen: CBS Publishing.

Elson, Diane, and Pearson, Ruth. 1981. "Nimble Fingers Make Cheap Workers: An Analysis of Women's Employment in Third World Exports Manufacturing." *Feminist Review* 7 (Spring): 87–107.

ESPO (European Sea Ports Organisation). 1996. *Report of an Enquiry into the Current Situation in the Major Community Sea-Ports. The Fact Finding Report.* Brussels: European Sea Ports Organisation.

———. 1998. *Response to the "Green Paper on Sea Ports and Maritime Infrastructure."* Brussels: European Sea Ports Organisation.

———. 2004. *Directive Proposal on Market Access to Port Services—Initial Response of ESPO.* Brussels: European Sea Ports Organisation.

———. 2005a. *Market Access to Port Services: European Parliament—TRAN Committee—Public Hearing 14 June.* Statement by Giuliano Gallanti, chairman of ESPO.

———. 2005b. *Market Access to Port Services: Paper Adopted by ESPO General Assembly.* Brussels: European Sea Ports Organisation.

Euraque, Dario. 1996. *Reinterpreting the Banana Republic: Region and State in Honduras, 1870–1972.* Chapel Hill: University of North Carolina Press.

EUROBAN, COLSIBA, IUF, WINFA, US/LEAP. 2005. "Toward a Multi-Stakeholder Forum on Bananas." White paper available from eurban@telez.fr.

European Commission, General Directorate, Employment, Social Affairs and Equal Opportunities. 2006. "Working Document: Transnational Texts Negotiated at Corporate Level: Facts and Figures." Prepared for the study seminar "Transnational Agreements," May 17. http://ec.europa.eu/employment_social/labour_law/docs/transnational_agreements_facts_en.pdf.

European Foundation for the Improvement of Living and Working Conditions. 2003. *EWC Case Studies: The DaimlerChrysler Group.* Dublin: European Foundation for the Improvement of Living and Working Conditions.

European Industrial Relations Review. 2001. "EWCs Taking On a Bargaining Role?" 332 (September): 24–27.

——. 2002. "European Company Statute Adopted," 336 (January): 21–25.

——. 2005a. "Accord on Workforce Reductions at Opel," January, 26–28.

——. 2005b. "Global Agreements—State of Play," 381 (October): 14–18.

European Metalworkers' Federation. 2000. "The Role of the Trade Union Coordinators in Existing EWCs." EMF resolution, Brussels.

——. 2001. "Collective Bargaining with the European." Resolution Adopted at the 3rd EMF Collective Bargaining Conference, Frankfurt.

——. 2004a. "Copenhagen Declaration by Trade Union Leaders from IGMetall, Svenska Metall, SIF, CF and European Metalworkers' Federation in Respect of GM Europe Restructuring." EMF press release, Brussels.

——. 2004b. "European Metalworkers' Federation Newsletter." Brussels.

——. 2005a. "The European Metalworkers' Federation's Approach to GM Restructuring." EMF information letter, Brussels.

——. 2005b. "European Metalworkers' Federation Policy Approach towards Socially Responsible Company Restructuring." Policy paper, Luxembourg, June 7–8.

——. 2005c. "GME Restructuring and Framework Agreements: An Example of EMF European Company Policy." EMF resolution, Brussels.

European Trade Union Confederation. 2006. "European Works Councils (EWCs)." http://www.etuc.org/a/125.

European Works Councils Bulletin. 2004a. "Global Agreements—State of Play, Part One," 52:5–10.

——. 2004b. "Global Agreements—State of Play, Part Two," 53:10–16.

——. 2005a. "GM, Ford and GE Cases Highlight EWC's Bargaining Role," 56:7–13.

——. 2005b. "International CSR Consultative Committee Set Up at EDF," 57:11–15.

——. 2006. "EMF Adopts Restructuring Guidelines." March/April, 12.

Eviatar, Daphne. 2005. "A Big Win for Human Rights." *Nation,* May 9.

ExpressTextile. 2004. "Hindustan Lever to Exit from Hybrid Cotton Seeds Venture." http://www.expresstextile.com/20040429/corporateupdate03.shtml.

Fairbrother, Peter, and Nikolaus Hammer. 2005. "Global Unions: Past Efforts and Future Prospects." *Relations Industrielles/Industrial Relations* 60 (3): 405–31.

FAST (Food and Allied Service Trades), AFL-CIO (Research Associates of America). 2006. *Manual of Corporate Investigation.* http://www.fastaflcio.org/.

FEPORT (Federation of European Private Port Operators). 1998. "Position of FEPORT on the Commission's *Green Paper on Sea Ports and Maritime Infrastructure.*" Paper presented to the Federation of European Private Port Operators, Brussels.

——. 2005. "Position Paper on the Proposed Directive *On Market Access to Port Services.*" Paper presented for the Federation of European Private Port Operators, Brussels.

Fine, Julie and Michael Howard. 1995. "Women in the Export Processing Zones of Sri Lanka." *Dollars and Sense* 202: 26–27, 39—40.

FLA (Fair Labor Association). 2004. "Fair Labor Association Year Two Annual Public Report." http://www.fairlabor.org/2004report.

Flores, Juan Jose. 1993. *El Solidarismo desde Adentro.* San José, Costa Rica: Aceprola.

FNV Company Monitor. 2003. FNV Mondial, September.

Frank, Dana. 1998. *Buy American: The Untold Story of Economic Nationalism.* Boston: Beacon.

——. 2005. *Bananeras: Women Transforming the Banana Unions of Latin America.* Boston: South End Press.

Franklin, Stephen. 2002. *Three Strikes*. New York: Guilford Press.

Franz, Klaus. 2002. "We Need to Become More International." Interview in *Mitbestimmung*, International Edition (electronic version). Hans Böckler Stiftung. http://www.boeckler. de/cps/rde/xchg/SID-3D0AB75D-473D7DB5/hbs/hs.xsl/164_28982.html.

Frege, Carola, Edmund Heery, and Lowell Turner. 2004. "The New Solidarity? Trade Union Coalition-Building in Five Countries." In *Varieties of Unionism: Strategies for Union Revitalisation in a Globalizing Economy*, edited by C. Frege and J. Kelly. Oxford: Oxford University Press.

Frege, Carola, and John Kelly. 2003. "Union Revitalization Strategies in Comparative Perspective." *European Journal of Industrial Relations* 9 (1): 7–24.

———. 2004. *Varieties of Unionism: Strategies for Union Revitalisation in a Globalizing Economy*. Oxford: Oxford University Press.

FreshPlaza. 2007. "Nicaraguan Banana Growers Solidarity with Ecuadorian WTO Complaint." http://www.freshplaza.com.

Friends of the Earth International. 2003. "Banks Celebrate Pipeline while NGOs Mourn." Media release, October 9.

Frundt, Henry. 1995. "The Rise and Fall of AIFLD in Guatemala." *Social and Economic Studies*, June.

———. 2004a. "Ending Central American Quotas: How Global Firms and Local Unions Respond." Paper presented at the Latin American Studies Association conference, Las Vegas.

———. 2004b. "Unions Wrestle with Corporate Codes of Conduct." *Working USA* 7 (4): 36–69.

———. 2005. "Hegemonic Resolution in the Banana Trade." *International Political Science Review* 26 (2): 215–37.

Frundt, Henry, and Norma Chinchilla. 1987. "Trade Unions in Guatemala." In *Latin American Labor Organizations*, edited by G. M. Greenfield and S. Marman, 395–432. New York: Greenfield Press.

FST (Federation of Transport Workers' Unions in the European Union). 1993. FST Minutes, October 15.

Fussell, Elizabeth. 2000. "Making Labor Flexible: The Recomposition of Tijuana's Maquiladora Female Labour Force." *Feminist Economics* 6 (3): 59—79.

Gallin, Dan. 2000. *Trade Unions and NGOs: A Necessary Partnership for Social Development*. Geneva: UNRISD.

———. 2002. "Labor as a Global Social Force: Past Divisions and New Tasks." In *Global Unions? Theory and Strategies of Organized Labor in the Global Political Economy*, edited by J. Harrod and R. O'Brien, 235–50. London: Routledge.

Gallin, Rita S. 1990. "Women and the Export Sector in Taiwan: The Muting of Class Consciousness." In *Women Workers and Global Restructuring*, edited by K. Ward, 172—92. Ithaca: ILR Press.

Garcia, Marco. 2005. Commentary. North American Preparatory Seminar for the Second International Banana Conference, Washington, D.C., February.

Garver, Paul, Kirill Buketov, Hyewon Chong, and Beatriz Sosa Martinez. 2006. "The IUF's Global Labor Organizing Strategy." Paper presented at the "Global Companies–Global Unions–Global Research–Global Campaigns" conference, New York, February. http:// www.ilr.cornell.edu/globalunionsconference/research/papers/garver.pdf.

Garwood, Shae. 2002. "Working to Death: Gender, Labour and Violence in Ciudad Juarez, Mexico." http://www.peacestudiesjournal.org.uk/docs/working2.pdf.

———. 2005. "Politics at Work: Transnational Advocacy Networks and the Global Garment Industry." *Gender and Development* 13 (3): 21–33.

Gearhart, J. 2005. Commentary. North American Preparatory Seminar for the Second International Banana Conference, Washington, D.C., February.

George, Nicholas and James Mackintosh. 2004. "Closure Fears at GM plant." *Financial Times*, September 3.

Gereffi, Gary. 1994. "The Organization of Buyer-Driven Global Commodity Chains: How U.S. Retailers Shape Overseas Production Networks." In *Commodity Chains and Global Capitalism*, edited by G. Gereffi and M. Korzeniewicz, 95–122. Westport, CT: Greenwood Press.

Ghosh, Jayati. 2001. "Globalization, Export-Oriented Employment for Women and Social Policy: A Case Study of India." Paper prepared for UNRISD Project on Globalization, Export-Oriented Employment for Women and Social Policy, Geneva.

Gibb, Euan. 2005. "International Framework Agreements: Increasing the Effectiveness of Core Labour Standards." Master's thesis, Global Labour University, University of Kassel and Berlin School of Economics.

Global Reporting Initiative. 2006. Reports database. http://www.globalreporting.org/Home.

Global Witness. 2005. *Paying for Protection: The Freeport Mine and the Indonesian Security Forces*. London: Global Witness.

Goodwin, Karin. 2006. "Child Labour Used in Brazilian Mines That Supply ICI." *Independent* (London), March 7.

Gordon, Michael E. 2000. "Export Processing Zones." In *Transnational Cooperation among Labor Unions*, edited by L. Turner and M. E. Gordon. Ithaca: Cornell University Press.

Gordon, Michael, and Lowell Turner. 2000. *Transnational Cooperation among Labor Unions*. Ithaca: Cornell University Press.

Goss, Richard, 1990. "Economic Policies and Seaports: 1. The Economic Functions of Seaports." *Maritime Policy & Management* 17 (3): 207–19.

Grahl, John, and Paul Teague. 2003. "The Eurozone and Financial Integration: The Employment Relations Issues." *Industrial Relations Journal* 34 (5): 396–410.

Greven, Thomas, and John Russo. 2003. "Transnational 'Corporate Campaigns': A Tool for Labour Unions in the Global Economy?" *International Journal of Comparative Labour Law and Industrial Relations* 19 (4): 495–513.

Grossman, Lawrence. 1998. *The Political Ecology of Bananas*. Chapel Hill: University of North Carolina Press.

Gunatilaka, Ramini. 1999. "Labour Legislation and Female Employment in Sri Lanka's Manufacturing Sector." In *Research Studies: Labour Economics Series* no. 14. Colombo, Sri Lanka: Institute of Policy Studies.

Gupta, Partha. 2002. *Imperialism and the British Labour Movement 1914–1964*. New Delhi: Sage.

Hammer, Nikolaus. 2005. "International Framework Agreements: Global Industrial Relations between Rights and Bargaining." *Transfer: European Review of Labour and Research* 11 (4): 511–30.

Hancké, Bob. 2000. "European Works Councils and Industrial Restructuring in the European Motor Industry." *European Journal of Industrial Relations* 6 (1): 35–59.

Harari, Raúl. 2005. "The Working and Living Conditions of Banana Workers in Latin America." In *International Banana Conference II Preparatory Papers*, 57–85. Brussels.

Harrod, Jeffrey, and Robert O'Brien. 2002. "Organized Labour and the Global Political Economy." In *Global Unions? Theory and Strategies of Organized Labour in the Global Political Economy*, edited by J. Harrod and R. O'Brien, 3–28. London: Routledge.

Haworth, Nigel, and Steve Hughes. 2002. "Internationalization, Industrial Relations Theory and International Relations." In *Global Unions? Theory and Strategies of Organized Labour in the Global Political Economy*, edited by J. Harrod and R. O'Brien, 64–79. London: Routledge.

Hazards Magazine. 2006. "Global Framework Agreements." *http://www.hazards.org/unioneffect/agreements.htm.*

Heinzl, John, and Marina Strauss. 1997. "Wal-Mart's Cheer Fades GIMME A W!/The Retailer's Image of a Big, Happy Team Is Going Sour as Workers Bicker over the Arrival of the First Union." *Globe and Mail* (Toronto), February 15.

Hengeveld, Richard, and Jaap Rodenburg, eds. 1995. *Embargo: Apartheid's Oil Secrets Revealed.* Amsterdam: Amsterdam University Press.

Hermanson, Jeff. 2004. "Global Corporations, Global Campaigns—The Struggle for Justice at Kukjdong International in Mexico." Washington, D.C.: American Center for International Labor Solidarity/AFL-CIO.

Hermer, Richard, and Martyn Day. 2004. "Helping Bush Bushwhack Justice." *Guardian*, April 27.

Herod, Andrew. 1997. "From a Geography of Labor to a Labor Geography: Labor's Spatial Fix and the Geography of Capitalism." *Antipode* 29 (1): 1–31.

———. 2001. "Labor Internationalism and the Contradictions of Globalization: Or, Why the Local Is Sometimes Still Important in a Global Economy." *Antipode* 33 (3): 407–26.

Hewamanne, Sandya. 2003. "Performing 'Dis-respectability': New Tastes, Cultural Practices and Identity Performances by Sri Lanka's Export Processing Zone Garment-Factory Workers." *Cultural Dynamics* 15 (1): 71–101.

Heyzer, Noleen, ed. 1986. *Working Women in South-East Asia: Development, Subordination and Emancipation.* Philadelphia: Open University Press.

Hickey, Robert. 2004. "Preserving the Pattern: Membership Mobilization and Union Revitalization at PACE Local 4–227." *Labor Studies Journal* 29 (1): 1–20.

Hindustan Lever Employees Union. 2005. Newsletter of the Unilever World Wide Trade Union Network, January, 5.

Hix, Simon, Tapio Raunio, and Roger Scully. 2003. "Fifty Years On; Research on the European Parliament." *Journal of Common Market Studies* 41 (2): 191–202.

Hoerr, John. 1988. *And the Wolf Finally Came: The Decline of the American Steel Industry.* Pittsburgh: University of Pittsburgh Press.

Human Rights Watch. 2002. *Tainted Harvest.* New York: Human Rights Watch.

Hyman, Richard. 1975. *Industrial Relations: A Marxist Introduction.* London: Macmillan.

———. 1999. "Imagined Solidarities: Can Trade Unions Resist Globalization?" In *Globalization and Labour Relations*, edited by P. Leisink, 94–115. London: Edward Elgar.

———. 2004 "The Future of Trade Unions." In *Unions in the 21st Century. An International Perspective*, edited by A. Verma and T. Kochan, 17–29. London: Palgrave.

———. 2005. "Trade Unions and the Politics of the European Social Model." *Economic & Industrial Democracy* 26 (1): 9–40.

ICEM (International Federation of Chemical, Energy, Mine and General Workers' Unions). 2006. "Eni's Global Agreement Called into Play Over Nigerian Security Concerns." http://www.icem.org.

ICFTU (International Confederation of Free Trade Unions). 1997. "The ICFTU/ITS Basic Code of Labour Practice." http://www.icftu.org/www/english/tncs/tncscode98.html.

———. 2005. "Burma and Multinational Companies: Who Profits and How It Works." http://www.icftu.org.

ICFTU-ETUC (International Confederation of Free Trade Unions-European Trade Union Confederation). 2005. "Burma: ICFTU-ETUC letter to EU regarding 'Common Position.'" http://www.icftu.org.

IDC News. 2004. November 3.

IFBWW (International Federation of Building and Wood Workers). 2004. "IFBWW Experiences with Global Company Agreement." http://www.ifbww.org/files/global-agreements. pdf.

ILO (International Labor Organization). 1996. "Economic Reforms and Labour Policies in India." South Asia Multidisciplinary Team, New Delhi.

——. 1998. "Export Processing Zones Growing Steadily Providing a Major Source of Job Creation. Labor/Productivity Problems Continue to Mount. ILO to Hold Tripartite Meeting of Experts." http://www.ilo.org/public/english/bureau/inf/pr/1998/34.htm.

——. 2003. "Information Note on Corporate Social Responsibility and Labour Standards." ILO Multinational Enterprises and Social Policy. http://www.ilo.org/public/english/ employment/multi/publ/index.htm.

——. 2004. "Export Processing Zones." http://www.ilo.org/public/english/dialogue/sector/ themes/epz.htm.

ILOLEX. 2006. Database of International Labor Standards (Conventions and Recommendations of the International Labor Organization). http://www.ilo.org/ilolex/english/ convdisp1.htm.

ILRF (International Labor Rights Fund). 2005. Summary of ATCA Cases Involving Multinational Corporations. http://www.laborrights.org.

IMF (International Metalworkers' Federation). 2005. "Report of the Secretariat: 31st IMF World Congress, Vienna, Austria, May 22–26." http://www.imfmetal.org/main/files/ congress2005_secrrep_english.pdf.

——. 2006. "Background to International Framework Agreements in the IMF." http://www. imfmetal.org/main/index.cfm?n=47&l=2&c=14431.

Industrial Relations Department. 2003a. "Biyagama Free Trade Zone Work Stoppages." Work stoppage registry, Board of Investments, Biyagama Free Trade Zone.

——. 2003b. "Katunayake Free Trade Zone Work Stoppages." Work stoppage registry, Board of Investments, Katunayake Free Trade Zone.

International Alert. 2004. "Promoting a Conflict Prevention Approach to OECD Companies and Partnering with Local Business." London: International Alert.

International Brotherhood of Teamsters. 2006. Stronger together at Quebecor. http://www. teamster.org/divisions/gciu/quebecor.asp.

International Council on Human Rights Policy. 2002. "Beyond Voluntarism: Human Rights and the Developing International Legal Obligations of Companies." Versoix, Switz.: International Council on Human Rights.

International Peace Academy. 2002. Options for Promoting Corporate Responsibility in Conflict Zones: Perspectives from the Private Sector. New York: International Peace Academy.

IOE (International Organization of Employers). 2003. Annual report. http://www.ioe-emp. org/fileadmin/user_upload/documents_pdf/annualreports_doc/english/1e_ar2003_ eng_txt.pdf.

——. 2005. International Framework Agreements: An Employers' Guide. Geneva: IOE.

ITF (International Transport Workers' Federation). 2002. Minutes of the Dockers' section meeting, ITF Congress, 2002, Vancouver.

ITF/ETF (International Transport Workers' Federation/European Transport Workers' Federation). 2004. Joint statement, London, November 22.

IUF (International Union of Food, Agriculture, Hotel, Restaurant, Catering, Tobacco and Allied Workers' Associations). 1995. "IUF Draft Code of Conduct for the Tea Sector." http://www.ilo.org/public/english/dialogue/actrav/genact/child/part2_a/agric.htm.

———. 2003. "IUF Coca-Cola Affiliates Reject Call for a Global Coca-Cola Boycott." http://www.iuf.org.uk.

———. 2006. "Item 5: Confronting and Negotiating with Transnational Companies (b) Development of International Framework Agreements (IFA's)." IUF Executive Commission document. In author's possession.

Janelle, Donald, and Michel Beuthe. 1997. "Globalization and Research Issues in Transport." *Journal of Transport Geography* 5 (3): 199–206.

Jayakody, Soma, and Goonatilake, Hema. 1988. "Industrial Action by Women Workers in Sri Lanka: The Polytex Garment Workers." In *Daughters in Industry: Work, Skills, and Consciousness of Women Workers in Asia*, edited by N. Heyzer, 292–307. Kuala Lumpur: Asian and Pacific Development Centre.

Jenkins, Rob. 2000. *Democratic Politics and Economic Reform in India*. Cambridge: Cambridge University Press.

Johnston, Paul. 1994. *Success While Others Fail: Social Movement Unionism and the Public Workplace*. Ithaca: ILR Press.

Joint Apparel Association. 2006. http://www.jaafsl.com.

Joint United States-European Union Release. 2001. "U.S. Government and European Commission Reach Agreement to Resolve Long-Standing Banana Dispute." April 11.

Jonasdottir, Anna G. 1988. "On the Concepts of Interest, Women's Interests and the Limitations of Theory." In *The Political Interests of Gender*, edited by K. Jones and A. G. Jonasdottir. London: Sage.

Jones, Geoffrey. 2005. *Multinationals and Global Capitalism: From the Nineteenth to the Twenty-First Century*. New York: Oxford University Press.

Josling, Tim, and Tim Taylor. eds. 2003. *Banana Wars: The Anatomy of a Trade Dispute*. Cambridge, MA: CABI Publishing.

Juravich, Tom, and Kate Bronfenbrenner. 1999. *Ravenswood: The Steelworkers' Victory and the Revival of American Labor*. Ithaca: Cornell University Press.

———. 2003. "Out of the Ashes: The Steelworkers' Global Campaign at Bridgestone/Firestone." In *Multinational Companies and Global Human Resource Strategies*, edited by W. Cooke, 249–68. Westport, CT: Quorum Books.

Juravich, Tom, William F. Hartford, and James Green. 1996. *Commonwealth of Toil: Chapters in the History of Massachusetts Workers and Their Unions*. Amherst: University of Massachusetts Press.

Juriansz, Pelham. 2003. "CPA Mediates in Jaqakana Crisis." *Sunday Observer*, online edition. http://www.sundayobserver.lk/2003/10/12/bus03.html.

Just Tea. 2005. http://www.justtea.org.

Justice, Dwight. 2001. "The International Trade Union Movement and the New Codes of Conduct." http://www.icftu.org/displaydocument.asp?Index=991215157&Language=EN

Kaarsholm, Lotte F., Charlotte Aagaard, and Osama Al-Habahbeh. 2005. "Uncle Sams gode ven" ("The Good Friend of Uncle Sam"). *Information*, December 3–4.

Karamitsos, Fotis. 2005. Maritime Director, European Commission, quoted in "Brussels Stands Firm on Self-Handling" by Justin Stares, *Lloyd's List*, April 29.

Kasturisinghe, Channa. 2003. "Top Garment Manufacturer Denies Ill-Treatment of Workers." *Daily News* (online edition). http://www.dailynews.lk/2003/09/24/bus02.html.

Katz, Harry. 1985. *Shifting Gears*. Cambridge, MA: MIT Press.

Kaufman, Bruce E. 1992. *The Origins and Evolution of Industrial Relations in the United States*. Ithaca: ILR Press.

Kepner, Charles. 1936. *Social Aspects of the Banana Empire*. New York: Columbia University Press.

Kluge, Norbert, and Michael Stolit. 2006. *The European Company—Prospects for Worker Board-Level Participation in the Enlarged EU*. Brussels: Social Development Agency (SDA) and European Trade Union Institute for Research, Education and Health and Safety (ETUI-REHS).

Knight, Richard. 2001. "Oil Embargo Against Apartheid South Africa." http://richardknight. homestead.com/files/oilembargo.htm.

Knoke, David. 1990. *Organizing for Collective Action: The Political Economies of Associations*. Hawthorne, NY: A. de Gruyter.

Kochan, Thomas, Harry Katz, and Robert McKersie. 1986. *The Transformation of American Industrial Relations*. New York: Basic Books.

Kontaktpunkt. 2005. *Årsrapport til CIME 2005 (Annual Report to CIME 2005)*. http://www. bm.dk/kontaktpunkt/aarsberetning_2005.asp.

Krut, Riva, and Harris Gleckman. 1998. *ISO 14001: A Missed Opportunity for Sustainable Development*. London: Earthscan.

Kuruvilla, Sarosh, and Christopher L. Erickson. 2002. "Change and Transformation in Asian Industrial Relations." *Industrial Relations* 41 (2): 171–227.

Labor Research Review. 1993. "No More Business As Usual: Labor's Corporate Campaign." 12 (2): 6–104.

Lamb, Harriet, and Steve Percy. 1987. "Union Levers." *New Internationalist*, June. http:// www.newint.org/.

Lambek, Bjørn. 2002. "Sympatikonflikt truer A.P.Møller" ("Sympathy Conflict Threatens A.P. Moller"), *Politiken*, October 6.

Landler, Mark. 2006. "Uneasy Days for Chiefs in Germany." 2006. *New York Times*, November 14, national edition, sec. C1.

Langille, Brian. 2005. "Core Labour Rights—the Real Story." In *Social Issues, Globalisation and International Institutions: Labour Rights and the EU, ILO, OECD and WTO*, edited by Virginia A. Leary and Daniel Warner, 89–124. Leiden, Neth.: Martinus Nijhoff.

Langley, Lester, and Thomas Schoonover. 1995. *The Banana Men: American Mercenaries and Entrepreneurs in Central America, 1880–1930*. Lexington: Kentucky University Press.

Lanka Business Online. 2006. "Guilt Trip." http://www.lankabusinessonline.com/fullstory. php?newsID=1625076867

Laska, Lewis L. 2006. "99 Verdicts Against Wal-Mart." http://www.wal-martlitigation.com/ 99verdic.htm (accessed December 1)..

Lee Ching Kwan. 1998. *Gender and the South China Miracle: Two Worlds of Factory Women*. Berkeley: University of California Press.

Levinson, Charles. 1972. *International Trade Unionism*. London: Allen & Unwin.

LHMU (Liquor Hospitality and Miscellaneous Workers Union). 2006. "Clean Start: Fair Deal for Cleaners." http://lhmu.org.au/lhmu/campaigns/Clean_Start/.

Lichtenstein, Nelson. 1995. *The Most Dangerous Man in Detroit: Walter Reuther and the Fate of American Labor*. New York: Basic Books.

Lillie, Nathan. 2004. "Global Collective Bargaining on Flag of Convenience Shipping." *British Journal of Industrial Relations* 42 (1): 47–67.

Lillie, Nathan, and Miguel Martinez-Lucio. 2004. "International Trade Union Revitalization: The role of National Union Approaches." In *Varieties of Unionism: Strategies for Union Revitalization in a Globalizing Economy*, edited by C. Frege and J. Kelly, 159–80. Oxford: Oxford University Press.

Lloyd's List. 2005. "Everyone Hates It." January 25.

Longlen, Sue. 2005. Commentary. North American Preparatory Seminar for the Second International Banana Conference, Washington, D.C., February.

Lujan, Berta. 2006. Speech at the "Global Companies–Global Unions–Global Research–Global Campaigns" conference, New York, February. http://www.ilr.cornell.edu/global unionsconference/multimedia/.

Lwanda, George. 2003. *Conflict Diamonds and the African "Resource Curse."* Umhlanga Rocks, S. Africa: African Centre for Constructive Resolution of Disputes.

Maersk. 2005. "A.P. Moller—Maersk Group. Facts." http://www.maersk.com.

Mair, Andrew. 1997. "Strategic Localization: The Myth of the Postnational Enterprise." In *Spaces of Globalization: Reasserting the Power of the Local*, edited by K. R. Cox, 64–88. New York: Guilford.

Malik, Ehsan. 2003. "Making an Elephant Fly: The Inside Story of Re-making Unilever Ceylon." *Lanka Business Report—Lanka Business Online CEO Forum*, April 24. http://www.lankabusinessonline.com.

Mantzaris, Evangelos. 1995. *Labour Struggles in South Africa: the Forgotten Pages 1903–21.* Durban: Collective Resources Publications.

Marginson, Paul, and Keith Sisson. 2002a. "European Dimensions to Collective Bargaining: New Symmetries within Asymmetric Processes?" *Industrial Relations Journal* 33 (4): 332–50.

——. 2002b. "European Integration and Industrial Relations: A Case of Convergence *and* Divergence?" *Journal of Common Market Studies* 40 (4): 671–92.

Markey, Raymond. 2005. "Globalisation and Participation: The Global Reach of European Works Councils." Paper presented at the 13th Annual Conference of the International Employment Relations Association, Aarborg, Denmark, July.

Marks, Gary, and Doug McAdam. 1999. "On the Relationship of Political Opportunities to the Form of Collective Action: The Case of the European Union." In *Social Movements in a Globalizing World*, edited by D. della Porta, H. Kriesi, and D. Rucht, 97–111. London: Macmillan.

Martin, Andrew, and George Ross. 2000. "European Integration and the Europeanization of Labor." In *Transnational Cooperation among Labor Unions*, edited by M. E. Gordon and L. Turner, 120–49. Ithaca: ILR Press.

Martinez-Lucio, Miguel, and Syd Weston. 1995. "Trade Unions and Networking in the Context of Change: Evaluating the Outcomes of Decentralization in Industrial Relations." *Economic and Industrial Democracy* 16 (2): 233–51.

Mathew, Babu. 2003. "A Brief Note on Labour Legislation in India." *Asia Labour Update*, January–March.

McAdam, Doug, Sidney Tarrow, and Charles Tilly. 2001. *Dynamics of Contention.* New York: Cambridge University Press.

McCahill, Tim. 2006. "French Activist Detained at JFK Airport." http://www.phillyburbs.com/pb-dyn/news/1–02092006–610461.htm.

McKay, Steve. 2005. "The Squeaky Wheel's Dilemma: New Forms of Labor Organizing in the Philippines." *Labor Studies Journal* 30 (4): 41–63.

Metzgar, Jack. 1985. "Running the Plant Backwards in UAW Region 5." *Labor Research Review* 5 (1): 35–44.

Meyer, Douglas. 2001. "Building Union Power in the Global Economy: A Case Study of the Coordinated Bargaining Committee of General Electric Unions (CBC)." *Labor Studies Journal* 26 (1): 60–75.

Miller, Rep. George. 2004. "Everyday Low Wages: The Hidden Price We All Pay for Wal-Mart." Washington, D.C.: Democratic Staff of the Committee on Education and the Workforce, U.S. House of Representatives.

Mineral Policy Institute. 2000. "Rio Tinto's Shame File." http://www.mpi.org.au.

Ministry of Employment and Labor. 2003. *Sri Lanka Labor Gazette: National Journal of Labor Affairs* 54 (2).

Misra, S.M. 2002. *Labour and Industrial Laws*. 19th ed. Allahabad, India: Central Law Publications.

Moberg, Mark. 2005. "Fair Trade and Eastern Caribbean Banana Farmers: Rhetoric and Reality in the Anti-Globalization Movement." *Human Organization* 64 (1): 4–15.

Mohanty, Chandra Talpade. 2004. *Feminism without Borders: Decolonizing Theory, Practicing Solidarity*. Durham, NC: Duke University Press.

Mohapatra, Prabhu P. 2006. "The Politics of Representation in the Indian Labour Diaspora: West Indies 1880–1920." Archives of Indian Labour, http://www.indialabourarchives.org/publications/prabhu2.htm

Morning Star (U.K.). 2006. "Britain—Asda Workers Welcome Union." November 21.

Moody, Kim. 1997. *Workers in a Lean World*. London: Verso.

Müller, Torsten, Hans-Wolfgang Platzer, and Stefan Rüb. 2005. "Global Trade Union Responses in Global Companies: Global Union Networks, World Works Councils and International Framework Agreements—Status Quo and Prospects." Unpublished ms.

Multinational Monitor. 1986. "Working against Apartheid: Trade Unions in South Africa. An Interview with Nomonde Ngubo." April 15.

Munck, Ronald, ed. 2004. *Labor and Globalization: Results and Prospects*. Liverpool: Liverpool University Press.

Myers, Gordon. 2004. *Banana Wars: The Price of Free Trade*. London: Zed Books.

Nash, June, and María Patricia Fernández-Kelly. 1983. *Women, Men, and the International Division of Labor*. Albany: SUNY Press.

Nissen, Bruce. 1999. "Living Wage Campaigns from a 'Social Movement' Perspective: The Miami Case." *Labor Studies Journal* 25 (3): 29–50

Noorani, Abdul Gafoor Abdul Majeed. 2005. *Indian Political Trials: 1775–1947*. New Delhi: Oxford University Press.

Northrup, Herbert, and Richard Rowan. 1979. *Multinational Collective Bargaining Attempts*. Philadelphia: University of Pennsylvania, Center for Human Resources.

NUECMRP (National Union of Employees in Companies Manufacturing Rubber Products). 2001. "Euromedical Industries Sdn.Bhd.—A Struggle for Trade Union Representation." Photocopy.

——. 2002. "Issues." Photocopy.

——. 2003. "After 28 Years a Union at Last." Press statement, October 29.

Obach, Brian. 2004. *Labor and the Environmental Movement: The Quest for Common Ground*. Cambridge, MA: MIT Press.

Obeyesekere, Gananath. 1984. *The Cult of the Goddess Pattini*. Chicago: University of Chicago Press.

OECD (Organization for Economic Co-operation and Development). 2000. *Codes of Corporate Conduct: An Expanded Review of Their Contents*. Paris: OECD.

——. 2002. "Multinational Enterprises in Situations of Violent Conflict and Widespread Human Rights Abuse." Working Paper 1, International Investment.

Ong, Aihwa. 1987. *Spirits of Resistance and Capitalist Discipline: Factory Women in Malaysia*. Albany: SUNY Press.

Ørskov, Stig, and Bjørn Lambek. 2003. "Globalt fagforbund lægger pres på A. P. Møller" ("Global Union Federation Put Pressure on A. P. Moller"). *Politiken*, November 13.

Oswald, Ron. 2006. Closing plenary address at the "Global Companies–Global Unions–Global Research–Global Campaigns" conference, New York, February. http://www.ilr.cornell.edu/globalunionsconference/multimedia/.

Oxfam Community Aid Abroad. 2004. "Mining Ombudsman Case Report: Vatukoula Gold Mine." Melbourne: Oxfam.

Pacific and Asian Women's Network Newsletter. 1993. Volume 2.

Parker, L. 2005. Commentary. North American Preparatory Seminar for the Second International Banana Conference, Washington, D.C..

Pauly, David, and John Walcott. 1978. "Unions: Labor's New Muscle." *Newsweek*, April 3.

Pearson, Ruth. 1995. "Male Bias and Women's Work in Mexico's Border Industries." In *Male Bias in the Development Process*, edited by D. Elson, 133—63. Manchester, U.K.: Manchester University Press.

Perillo, Robert. 2000. "The Current Crisis in the Latin American Banana Industry." In *A Strategic Analysis of the Central American Banana Industry: An Industry in Crisis*, edited by R. Perillo and M. Trejos, 11–20. Chicago: US/LEAP for COLSIBA/AFL-CIO/ACILS.

Perillo, Robert, and Maria Trejos, eds. 2000. *A Strategic Analysis of the Central American Banana Industry: An Industry in Crisis*. Chicago: US/LEAP for COLSIBA/AFL-CIO/ACILS.

Piven, Frances Fox, and Richard A. Cloward. 2000. "Power Repertoires and Globalization." *Politics and Society* 28 (3): 413—30.

Polanyi, Karl. 1957. *The Great Transformation*. Boston: Beacon Press.

Prasad, Satendra, and Darryn Snell. 2004. "Fiji: Enabling Civic Capacities for Conflict Prevention and Peacebuilding." In *Searching for Peace in the Asia Pacific: An Overview of Conflict Prevention and Peacebuilding Activities*, edited by A. Heijmans, N. Simmonds and H. Veen, 543–63. Boulder, CO: Lynne Rienner.

PSI. 2006. http://www.world-psi.org/.

Pulignano, Valeria. 2005. "EWCs and Cross-National Employee Representative Coordination. A Case of Trade Union Cooperation?" *Economic and Industrial Democracy* 26 (3): 383–412.

Quan, Katie. 2006. "Women Crossing Borders to Organize." Paper presented at the "Global Companies–Global Unions–Global Research–Global Campaigns" conference, New York, February. http://www.ilr.cornell.edu/globalunionsconference/research/.

Rajabali, Anjum. 1987. "Contracting Out." *New Internationalist*, June, 18–22. http://www.newint.org/issue172/contracting.htm.

Rajapaksa, Mahinda. 2004. Comments at launching of the book *Twentieth Century Tea Research in Sri Lanka* (Tea Research Institute). http://www.primeminister.gov.lk/view Speech.php?id=28.

Ramsay, Harvie. 1997. "Solidarity at Last? International Trade Unionism Approaching the Millennium." *Economic and Industrial Democracy* 18 (4): 503–37.

——. 1999. "In Search of International Union Theory." In *Globalization and Patterns of Labour Resistance*, edited by J. Waddington, 192–220. New York: Mansell.

Rasmussen, Peter. 2006. "Solidaritetsarbejde ændrer form" ("Solidarity Work Is Changing"). *Fagbladet 3F*. http://forsiden.3f.dk/apps/pbsc.dll/forside.

Ratnayake, Dennis. 1984. "Sri Lanka: The Katunayake Export Promotion Zone." In *Export Processing Zones and Industrial Employment in Asia: Paper and Proceedings of a Technical Workshop*, edited by E. Lee. Bangkok: International Labor Organization Asian Employment Programme.

Raynolds, Laura. 2003. "The Global Banana Trade." In *Banana Wars: Power, Production, and History in the Americas. (American Encounters/Global Interactions)*, edited by S. Striffler and M. Moberg, 23–47. Durham, NC: Duke University Press.

RENGO. 2006. "Action Policy 6: Enhancement of International Activities for Fairer Globalization." http://www.jtuc-rengo.org/about/actionpolicy/a_policy06.html

Reynolds, David. 1999. "Coalition Politics: Insurgent Union Political Action Builds Ties between Labor and the Community." *Labor Studies Journal* 24 (3): 54–75.

——. 2004. *Partnering for Change: Unions and Community Groups Build Coalitions for Economic Justice.* Armonk, NY: M.E. Sharpe.

Rieger, Elmar, and Stephan Leibfried. 2003. *Limits to Globalization: Welfare States and the World Economy.* Cambridge: Polity Press.

Rigby, Mike, and Teresa Lawlor. 1994. "Spanish Trade Unions 1986–1994: Life after National Agreements." *Industrial Relations Journal* 25 (4): 258–71.

Riisgaard, Lone. 2004. "The IUF/COLSIBA Framework Agreement: A Case Study." Working Paper 94, International Labour Office at Geneva.

——. 2005. "International Framework Agreements: A New Model for Securing Workers Rights?" *Industrial Relations* 44 (4): 707–37.

Robertson, Phillip S., Jr., and Somsak Plaiyoowang. 2004. "The Struggle of the Gina Workers in Thailand: Inside a Successful International Labour Solidarity Campaign." Southeast Asia Research Centre Working Paper Series no. 75, City University of Hong Kong.

Rosa, Kumudhini. 1994. "The Conditions and Organizational Activities of Women in Free Trade Zones: Malaysia, Philippines, and Sri Lanka 1970–1990." In *Dignity and Daily Bread: New Forms of Economic Organising among Poor Women in the Third World and the First,* edited by S. Rowbotham and S. Mitter. London: Routledge.

Rose, Fred. 2000. *Coalitions across the Cultural Divide.* Ithaca: Cornell University Press.

Rowbotham, Sheila, and Swasti Mitter. 1994. *Dignity and Daily Bread.* London: Routledge.

Royal Labour Commission. 1929. Report.

Rüb, Stephan. 2004. *Social Minimum Standards in Multinational Groups: Arguments and Practical Help to Initiate, Negotiate, and Implement an International Framework Agreement.* Frankfurt: IG-Metall Vorstand.

——. 2006. *Implementing and Monitoring an International Framework Agreement.* Frankfurt: IG-Metall, International/Europe Department.

Rudikoff, Lisa. 2005. "International Framework Agreements: A Collaborative Paradigm for Labor Relations." Global Law Working Paper 01/05 for symposium Transnational Corporations and Human Rights, New York University School of Law.

Russell, Marta. 2004. "A Brief History of Wal-Mart and Disability Discrimination" *ZNet.* February 15.

Sadler, David, and Bob Fagan. 2004. "Australian Trade Unions and the Politics of Scale: Reconstructing the Spatiality of Industrial Relations." *Economic Geography* 80 (1): 23–43.

Safa, Helen. 1981. "Runaway Shops and Female Employment: The Search for Cheap Labor." *Signs* 7 (2): 418–33.

Salaff, Janet. 1981. *Working Daughters in Hong Kong.* Cambridge: Cambridge University Press.

Samarasinghe, Gameela, and Chandrika Ismail. 2000. *A Psychological Study of Blue Collar Female Workers.* Colombo, Sri Lanka: Women's Education and Research Centre.

Samath, Feizal. 2003. "Trade Unions Chalk Up Two Key Victories." InterPress Service, August 28.

Sassoon, Victor. 1929. "The Assam Tea Industry." In the Report of the Royal Labour Commission.

Saundry, Richard, and Peter Turnbull. 1999. "Contractual (In)Security, Labour Regulation and Competitive Performance in the Port Transport Industry: A Contextualised Comparison of Britain and Spain." *British Journal of Industrial Relations* 37 (2): 273–96.

Savage, Lydia. 1998. "Geographies of Organizing: Justice for Janitors in Los Angeles." In *Organizing the Landscape: Geographical Perspectives on Labor Unionism,* edited by A. Herod, 225–54. Minneapolis: University of Minnesota Press.

Scharpf, Fritz W. 1999. *Governing in Europe: Effective and Democratic?* Oxford: Oxford University Press.

———. 2002. "The European Social Model: Coping with the Challenges of Diversity." *Journal of Common Market Studies* 40 (4): 645–70.

Schilstra, Keimpe and Evert Smit. 1994. "Union or Commonwealth? The Balance of Power and the Organisational Structure Debate in the Dutch Federation of Trade Unions." *Industrial Relations Journal* 25 (4): 272–80.

Schroeder, Wolfgang, and Rainer Weinert. 2004. "Designing Institutions in European Industrial Relations: A Strong Commission versus Weak Trade Unions?" *European Journal of Industrial Relations* 10 (2): 199–217.

Schultz, Jim. 2005. "The Politics of Water in Bolivia." *The Nation*, January 28.

SEIU (Service Employees International Union). 2004a. "Building a New Circle of Strength for Working Families." *SEIU 2004 Annual Report*. http://www.seiu.org/who/2004_report/circleofstrength.cfm.

———. 2004b. "Global Strength." SEIU convention resolution.

———. 2004c. "Uniting Our Strength to Win Big." *SEIU 2004 Annual Report*. http://www.seiu.org/who/2004%5Freport/.

———. 2005. *Making Globalization Work: How the SEIU Is Building Partnerships to Unite Workers Across Borders*, SEIU international leaflet.

———. 2006. "What Is SEIU?" http://www.seiu.org/faqs/faq_whatisseiu.cfm.

Sherlock, Stephen. 2001. "Labour and the Remaking of Bombay." In *Organizing Labour in Globalizing Asia*, edited by J. Hutchison and A. Brown, 147–67. London: Routledge.

Silver, Beverly J. 2003. *Forces of Labor: Workers' Movements and Globalization since 1870*. Cambridge: Cambridge University Press.

SINALTRAINAL. 2005. "Columbia: Students on Coca-Cola Protest Kidnapped—SINALTRAINAL Statement." http://www.labournet.org.

Smit, Evert. 1992. "Theoretische Reflecties bij de Arbeidssociologische Studies over de Rotterdamse Haven." *Tidschrift voor Arbeidsvraagstukken* 8 (2): 100–12.

Social Observatory. 2006. http://www.observatoriosocial.org.br/portal.

Soonok, Chun. 2003. *They Are Not Machines: Korean Women Workers: Their Fight for Democratic Trade Unionism in the 1970s*. London: Ashgate.

Standing, Guy. 1999. "Global Feminisation through Flexible Labour." *World Development* 27 (3): 583–602.

Stares, Justin. 2005. "Saga of Ports Directive Descends into Farce: ESPO Changes Tack after Confusion." *Lloyd's List*, November 23.

Steger, Manfred. 2005. *Globalism: Market Ideology Meets Terrorism*. Lanham, MD: Rowman and Littlefield.

Steiert, Robert. 2001. "European Works Councils. World Works Councils and the Liaison Role of the Trade Unions: A Test of International Union Policy." *Transfer: European Review of Labour and Research* 1:1–18.

Steinbeck, John. 1939. *The Grapes of Wrath*. New York: Modern Library.

Stevis, Dimitris. 1998. "International Labor Organizations, 1864–1997: The Weight of History and the Challenges of the Present." *Journal of World-Systems Research* 4:52–75.

———. 2002. "Unions, Capitals and States: Competing (Inter)Nationals in North American and European Integration." In *Global Unions? Theory and Strategies of Organized Labour in the Global Political Economy*, edited by J. Harrod and R. O'Brien, 131–50. London: Routledge.

Stevis, Dimitris, and Terry Boswell. 2001. "Labor Politics and Policy in International Integration: Comparing NAFTA and the European Union." In *The Politics of Social Inequality*, Research in Political Sociology 9, edited by B. Dobratz, L. Waldner, and T. Buzzell, 335–64. Amsterdam: Elsevier.

Stewart, Frances, and Rajesh Venugopal. 2005. "Violent Conflict in Developing Countries: Group Inequalities and MNC Involvement." *Oxford Development Studies* 33 (1): 1–5.

Stirling, John, and Barbara Tully. 2004. "Power, Process, and Practice: Communications in European Works Councils." *European Journal of Industrial Relations* 10 (1): 73–89.

Streeck, Wolfgang. 1998. "The Internationalization of Industrial Relations in Europe: Prospects and Problems." *Politics & Society* 26 (4): 429–59.

Striffler, Steve and Mark Moberg. 2003. *Banana Wars*. Durham, NC: Duke University Press.

Struck, Doug. 2005. "Wal-Mart Leaves Bitter Chill." *Washington Post*, April 14.

Survival International. 2005. *Bushmen Aren't Forever*. London: Survival International.

Sutton, Paul. 1997. "The Banana Regime of the European Union, the Caribbean and Latin America." *Journal of Interamerican Studies and World Affairs* 39 (2): 5–36.

Swinney, Dan. 1982. "UE Local 227 Strike at Morse Cutting Tool." *Labor Research Review* 1 (1): 4–17.

T&G (Transport and General Workers Union). 2006a. "Justice for Cleaners: Fighting for a Fair Wage and Respect in the Workplace!" http://www.tgwu.org.uk.

——. 2006b. "T&G: About Us." http://www.tgwu.org.uk.

——. 2006c. "T&G Organising." http://www.tgwu.org.uk.

Tarrow, Sidney. 1999. "International Institutions and Contentious Politics: Does Internationalization Make Agents Freer—or Weaker?" Paper presented to the American Sociological Association, Chicago.

——. 2005. *The New Transnational Activism*. Cambridge: Cambridge University Press.

Tattersall, Amanda. 2005. "There Is Power in Coalition: A Framework for Assessing How and When Union-Community Coalitions Are Effective and Enhance Union Power." *Labor and Industry* 16 (3): 97.

——. 2006. "Bringing the Community In: Possibilities for Public Sector Union Success Through Community Unionism." *International Journal of Human Resource Development and Management* 6 (2/3/4): 186.

Taylor, J. Gary, and Patricia J. Scharlin. 2004. *Smart Alliance*. New Haven: Yale University Press.

Taylor, Mark. 2003. "Corporate Fallout Detectors and Fifth Amendment Capitalists: Corporate Complicity in Human Rights Abuses." Keynote address, UN Global Compact Learning Forum, Berlin, December.

Teh-White, Katherine. 2005. "A Tale of Two Mines—and How It Was a Far, Far Better Thing That BHP Did." *The Age*, July 14.

Thompson, Ginger, and Nazila Fathi. 2005. "Asia's Deadly Waves: Earlier Disasters; For Honduras and Iran, World's Aid Evaporated." *New York Times*, January 11.

TIE-Asia. 2003. "Victory for FTZWU Workers at Jaqalanka Ltd, Sri Lanka." http://tieasia.org.

——. 2005. "Victory for FTC Workers at Jaqalanka Ltd." http://www.tieasia.org.

Todd, Patricia, Russell Lansbury, and Ed Davis. 2004. "Industrial Relations in Malaysia: Some Proposals for Reform." Paper presented at the IIRA 2004 conference, Seoul, June 23–26.. http://www.kli.re.kr/iira2004/intro/intro01.htm.

Tørres, Liv, and Stein Gunnes. 2003. *Global Framework Agreements: A New Tool for International Labour*. Oslo: FAFO.

Touma, Guillermo. 2005. Commentary. North American Preparatory Seminar for the Second International Banana Conference, Washington, D.C., February.

Trumka, Richard. 2006. Speech at the "Global Companies–Global Unions–Global Research–Global Campaigns" conference, New York, February. http://www.aflcio.org/mediacenter/prsptm/sp02092006.cfm *and* http://www.ilr.cornell.edu/globalunionsconference/multimedia/.

Tuffs, Steven. 1998. "Community Unionism in Canada and Labor's (Re)organisation of Space." *Antipode* 30 (3): 227–50.

Turnbull, Peter. 2000. "Contesting Globalization on the Waterfront." *Politics & Society* 28 (3): 273–97.

———. 2006. "The War on Europe's Waterfront—Repertoires of Power in the Port Transport Industry." *British Journal of Industrial Relations* 44 (2): 305–26.

Turnbull, Peter, and David Sapsford. 2001. "Hitting the Bricks: An International Comparative Study of Conflict on the Waterfront." *Industrial Relations* 40 (2): 231–57.

Turnbull, Peter, and Victoria Wass. 1995. *Reform and Structural Adjustment in the World's Ports: The Future for Labour and the Unions.* London: International Transport Workers' Federation.

———. 1997. "Dockers and Deregulation in the International Port Transport Industry." In *Transport Regulation Matters,* edited by J. McConville, 126–53. London: Cassell.

———. 2007. "Defending Dock Workers—Globalization and Labor Relations in the World's Ports." *Industrial Relations* 46 (3): 582–612.

Turnbull, Peter, and Syd Weston. 1992. "Employment Regulation, State Intervention and the Economic Performance of European Ports." *Cambridge Journal of Economics* 16 (4): 385–404.

Turnbull, Peter, Charles Woolfson, and John Kelly. 1992. *Dock Strike: Conflict and Restructuring in Britain's Ports.* Aldershot, U.K.: Avebury.

Ulman, Lloyd. 1975. "Multinational Unionism: Incentives, Barriers, and Alternatives." *Industrial Relations* 14 (1): 1–31.

UNCTAD (United Nations Conference on Trade and Development). 1987. *Measuring and Evaluating Port Performance and Productivity.* UNCTAD Monographs on Port Management, no.6. Geneva: United Nations.

UNHCR (United Nations High Commission for Refugees). 2005. "Report of the United Nations High Commissioner on Human Rights on the Responsibilities of Transnational Corporations and Related Business Enterprises with Regard to Human Rights." Paper presented at the United Nations High Commission for Refugees, Geneva.

United Steelworkers (USW). 2006. "United Steelworkers White Paper: IMF World Conference on International Framework Agreements." September 26–27. Unpublished ms.

Unomedical. 2005. *Årsrapport 2004 (Annual Report 2004).* http://www.unomedical.com.

US/LEAP. 2000. "Del Monte Workers Return to Work But Victory Is Bittersweet," 3:1, 6.

———. 2002. "Banana Workers Fight Ends for Now; New Campaign Begins," 3:1, 3.

———. 2005. "DOLE: One Conflict Resolved; New One Erupts," 3:1.

———. 2006. "Shifting Sands in the Banana Sector," 1:1–8.

Van Hooydonk, Eric. 2005. "The European Port Services Directive: The Good or the Last Try?" *Journal of International Maritime Law* 11 (3): 188–220.

van Roozendaal, Gerda. 2002. *Trade Unions and Global Governance: The Debate on the Social Clause.* London, NY: Continuum.

Von Holdt, Karl. 2002. "Social Movement Unionism: the Case of South Africa." *Work, Employment and Society* 16 (2): 283–304.

Wad, Peter. 1997. "Enterprise Unions and Structural Change in Malaysia." Working Paper 13, Institute of Malaysian and International Studies, October.

———. 2004. "Transforming Industrial Relations in the Malaysian Auto Industry." In *Labour in Southeast Asia: Labour Processes in a Globalised World,* edited by R. Elmhirst, and R. Saptari, 235–64. London: Routledge Curzon.

Waddington, Jeremy. 2005. "Trade Unions and the Defence of the European Social Model." *Industrial Relations Journal* 36 (6): 518–40.

Waldinger, Roger, Chris Erickson, Ruth Milkman, Daniel J. B. Mitchell, Abel Valenzuela, Kent Wong, and Maurice Zeitlin. 1998. "Helots No More: A Case Study of the Justice for Janitors Campaign in Los Angeles." In *Organizing to Win: New Research on Organizing Strategies*, edited by K. Bronfenbrenner, S. Friedman, R. W. Hurd, R. A. Oswald, and R. L. Seeber, 102–20. Ithaca: Cornell University Press.

Walker, Matthew. 1986. "The Cost of Doing Business in South Africa: Anti-Apartheid Coalition Boycotts Shell." *Multinational Monitor,* April 15.

Wal-Mart Stores Inc. 1997. "A Manager's Toolbox to Remaining Union Free." Bentonville, Ark.: Wal-Mart Stores, Inc., 1–50.

Walsh, Jess. 2000. "Organizing the Scale of Labor Regulation in the United States: Service-Sector Activism in the City." *Environment and Planning A* 32 (9): 1593–610.

War on Want. 2006. *The Global Workplace: Challenging the Race to the Bottom, A Manual for Trade Union Activists.* London: War on Want.

Ward, Kathy. 1990. *Women Workers and Global Restructuring.* Ithaca: ILR Press.

Waterman, Peter. 1990. *International Communication and International Solidarity: The Experience of the Coordinadora of Spanish Dockworkers.* The Hague: Institute of Social Studies.

Watson, Bruce. 2005. *Bread and Roses: Mills, Migrants, and the Struggle for the American Dream.* New York: Viking.

Webersik, Christian. 2005. "Fighting for Plenty: The Banana Trade in Southern Somalia." *Oxford Development Studies* 33 (1): 81–97.

Weeraratne, Bilesha. 2005. "Labour Standards and International Trade: The Case of EU GSP Concessions to Sri Lanka." Working paper no. 8. Institute of Policy Studies, Sri Lanka.

Weiler, Anni. 2004. *European Works Councils in Practice.* Dublin: European Foundation for the Improvement of Living and Working Conditions.

Wick, Ingeborg. 2005. *Workers' Tool or PR Ploy?* 4th rev. ed. Bonn: Friedrich-Ebert-Stiftung.

Wills, Jane. 2002. *Union Future: Building Networked Trade Unionism in the UK.* Glasgow: Bell & Bain.

WINFA. 2005a. Press release on conversion of banana industry, August 2.

———. 2005b. "St. Joseph's Declaration." Joint statement issued by WINFA affiliates. December 4.

Witt, Matt, and Rand Wilson. 1998. "Part-Time America Won't Work: The Teamsters Fight for Good Jobs at UPS." In *Not Your Father's Union Movement*, edited by J. Mort, 179–88. London: Verso.

Workers Online. 2000. "Rio Tinto Appeals for Industrial Peace." http://workers.labor.net.au/55/news7_rio.html.

World Bank. 2006. "Bank Freezes Pipeline Fund to Chad." http://www.worldbank.org.

WTO (World Trade Organization). 1999. "Recourse to Article 22.6 Arbitration Report for Dispute Settlement DS27." Report. April 9.

Wright, Erik Olin. 2000. "Working-Class Power, Capitalist-Class Interests, and Class Compromise." *American Journal of Sociology* 105 (4): 957–1002.

WWW (Women Working Worldwide). 2002. "Women Working and Codes of Conduct." http://www.poptel.org.uk/women-ww.

Yap Mun Ching. 2002. "Eurmodical Denies Objecting to Union Bid, Merely Its Choice." *Malaysiakini,* April 4. http://www.malaysiakini.com/news/2000204100015220.php.

Yussuff, Hassan. 2006. Speech at the "Global Companies–Global Unions–Global Research–Global Campaigns" conference, New York, February. http://www.ilr.cornell.edu/globalunionsconference/multimedia.

Zandvliet, Luc. 2005. "Opportunities for Synergy: Conflict Transformation and the Corporate Agenda." In *The Berghof Handbook for Conflict Transformation,* edited by D. Bloomfiels, M. Fisher, and B. Schmelzle, 1–17. Berlin: Berghof Research Center for Constructive Conflict Management.

Zandvliet, L., Yezid Campos Zornosa, and David Reyes. 2004. "Efforts to Operate Constructively in a Context of Conflict: Best Corporate Practices in Columbia." Cambridge, MA: Collaborative for Development Action. http://www.cdainc.com.

Zieger, Robert. 1995. *The CIO: 1935–1955.* Chapel Hill: University of North Carolina Press.

Zellner, Wendy, and Aaron Bernstein. 2000. "Up Against the Wal-Mart." *BusinessWeek,* March 13.

Zepeda, German. 2005. Commentary. North American Preparatory Seminar for the Second International Banana Conference, Washington, D.C., February.

Zinn, Kenneth S. 2000. "Solidarity Across Borders: The UMWA's Corporate Campaign against Peabody and Hanson PLC." In *Transnational Cooperation among Labor Unions,* edited by M. E. Gordon and L. Turner, 223–37. Ithaca: Cornell University Press.

CONTRIBUTORS

Terry Boswell (1955–2006) was a professor of sociology at Emory University for twenty-two years. He left behind an influential body of work in the areas of stratification and labor markets, global labor politics, revolutions, and the political economy of the world system. His publications include *The Spiral of Capitalism and Socialism: Toward Global Democracy* (with Christopher Chase-Dunn), the 2001 winner of the Outstanding Book Award from the Political Economy of the World-System Section of the American Sociological Association. His book (with Dimitris Stevis) titled *Globalization and Labor: Democratizing Global Governance* was published in 2007.

Kate Bronfenbrenner is the director of labor education research at Cornell University's School of Industrial and Labor Relations. She is a leading authority on union organizing and bargaining strategies in the global economy; the impact of global trade investment policy on employment, wages, and unionization; and race and gender in the U.S. labor movement since the 1980s. She worked for many years as an organizer and union representative with the United Woodcutters Association in Mississippi and Service Employees International Union in Boston. She is the coauthor and editor of several books on union strategies including *Union Organizing in the Public Sector: An Analysis of State and Local Elections*, *Organizing to Win: New Research on Union Strategies*, and *Ravenswood: The Steelworkers' Victory and the Revival of American Labor*.

Henry Frundt is a union activist and scholar who has researched trade and labor issues for more than thirty-five years. A former local union president, he co-convenes the Social Issues faculty at Ramapo College and serves as a delegate to the American Federation of Teachers' State Council of N.J. State College Locals. He is a board member of the U.S. Labor Education in the Americas Project and has served as a U.N. NGO Commissioner for Disarmament and Peace Education, and as secretary of the Labor Studies section of the Latin American Studies Association. He has received awards from the Organization of American States, the Fulbright Association, and the Society for the Psychological Study of Social Issues. His publications include the award-winning *Trade Conditions and Labor Rights: U.S. Initiatives, Dominican and Central American Responses, Refreshing Pauses: Coca-Cola and Human Rights in Guatemala, An Agribusiness Manual*, and numerous articles in professional journals.

Samanthi Gunawardana is a PhD candidate at the University of Melbourne (Australia) and is a new faculty member of the Department of Labor Studies at Penn State University. Since 2001 she has been researching the employment system of Sri Lankan Export Processing Zones and the experiences of women workers.

Tom Juravich is a professor and the director of the Labor Relations and Research Center at the University of Massachusetts, Amherst, where he teaches courses in labor research, contemporary labor issues, and advanced corporate research. He has written extensively on union bargaining and organizing strategies, new workplace systems, worker culture, and the nature and history of work.

Kevin Kolben is an assistant professor at Rutgers Business School. A lawyer specializing in international labor rights and international economic regulation, he has worked extensively in South and Southeast Asia. He was a senior associate with Human Rights First in its Workers Rights Department and has also worked as a union organizer for several U.S. unions.

Valeria Pulignano is a professor of sociology of labor at the Katholieke Universiteit of Leuven (Belgium). She is associate fellow at the Industrial Relations and Organizational Behavior Group and at the Industrial Relations Research Unit at the University of Warwick (United Kingdom). Her research interests include comparative European industrial relations, trade union organization, industrial restructuring and work organization, multinational companies, systems of employee representation at both the local level and in the European Union, globalization and international labor. Currently she is involved in a project at the European Trade Union Institute in Brussels, Trade Unions Anticipating Restructuring in Europe, founded under Article Six of the European Social Fund.

Darryn Snell is a lecturer in sociology at Monash University (Australia). He is a founding member of the Research Unit for Work and Communications Futures at Monash University. He has worked extensively on labor and development questions, particularly as they apply to small island states in the South Pacific, and on issues related to conflict and peace-building in the Global South. His current research explores the relationship between multinational corporations, human rights abuses, and conflict in the Global South.

Dimitris Stevis is a professor of international politics at Colorado State University, where he is also a member of the American Association of University Professors. His general research focuses on the environmental and labor regulation of global and regional integration. He has been researching international labor politics since the early 1990s, paying particular attention to the history and current status of global and regional union organizations. Most of his work on global labor has been with Terry Boswell, with whom he has a book titled *Globalization and Labor: Democratizing Global Governance*, published in 2007.

Ashwini Sukthankar, a human and labor rights lawyer in New York City, is the coordinator of the International Commission for Labor Rights. Previously she was the director of research and monitoring for the Worker Rights Consortium. Sukthankar earned her JD at Harvard Law School in 2002.

Amanda Tattersall is completing a PhD on community unionism at the University of Sydney (Australia) and is currently based at Cornell University's School of Industrial and Labor Relations, completing field work on U.S. and Canadian campaigns. She works for Unions NSW, the central labor council in Sydney, as a union organizer primarily responsible for community outreach work.

Peter Turnbull is a professor of Human Resources Management and Labor Relations at the Cardiff Business School, Cardiff University (Wales). His published work includes *The Dynamics of Employee Relations* and *Social Dialogue in the Process of Structural Adjustment and Private Sector Participation in Ports*. He has been involved in research reports for international and national organizations in the United Kingdom, including the ILO, the EU and the U.K. government. His areas of research span theories of employment relations and human resources management, labor market economics, work reorganization, ports and dock workers, trade unions and comparative employment relations.

Peter Wad is an associate professor in the Department of Intercultural Communication and Management at Copenhagen Business School (Denmark). Educated as a cultural sociologist at Copenhagen University, he has undertaken trade union research in Malaysia since the mid-1980s and more recently in South Korea and Japan. His work has appeared in journals such as *Asian Labor Update* and anthologies, including Roger Southall's *Trade Unions and the New Industrialization of the Third World*, Rebecca Elmhirt and Ratna Saptari's *Labor in Southeast Asia: Local Processes in a Globalized World*, and Chang Dae-oup and Ed Shepherd's *Automobile Workers and Industry in Globalizing Asia*.

INDEX